"Mixed Race" Identities in Asia and the Pacific

"Mixed race" is becoming an important area for research, and there is a growing body of work in the North American and British contexts. However, understandings and experiences of "mixed race" across different countries and regions are not often explored in significant depth. New Zealand and Singapore provide important contexts for investigation, as two multicultural, yet structurally divergent, societies. Within these two countries, "mixed race" describes a particularly interesting label for individuals of mixed Chinese and European parentage.

This book explores the concept of "mixed race" for people of mixed Chinese and European descent, looking at how being Chinese and/or European can mean many different things in different contexts. By looking at different communities in Singapore and New Zealand, it investigates how individuals of mixed heritage fit into or are excluded from these communities. Increasingly, individuals of mixed ancestry are opting to identify outside of traditionally defined racial categories, posing a challenge to systems of racial classification and to sociological understandings of "race". As case studies, Singapore and New Zealand provide key examples of the complex relationship between state categorization and individual identities. The book explores the divergences between identity and classification, and the ways in which identity labels affect experiences of "mixed race" in everyday life. Personal stories reveal the creative and flexible ways in which people cross boundaries, and the everyday negotiations between classification, heritage, experience, and nation in defining identity. The study is based on qualitative research, including in-depth interviews with people of mixed heritage in both countries.

Filling an important gap in the literature by using an Asia/Pacific dimension, this study of race and ethnicity will appeal to students and scholars of mixed race studies, ethnicity, Chinese diaspora and cultural anthropology.

Zarine L. Rocha is the Managing Editor of *Current Sociology* and the *Asian Journal of Social Science*. She has worked at the United Nations Research Institute for Social Development, the United Nations Environment Programme and the World Economic Forum.

Chinese Worlds

Chinese Worlds publishes high-quality scholarship, research monographs, and source collections on Chinese history and society. "Worlds" signals the diversity of China, the cycles of unity and division through which China's modern history has passed, and recent research trends toward regional studies and local issues. It also signals that Chineseness is not contained within borders – ethnic migrant communities overseas are also "Chinese worlds".

The series editors are Gregor Benton, Flemming Christiansen, Delia Davin, Terence Gomez and Hong Liu.

1 **The Literary Fields of Twentieth-Century China**
Edited by Michel Hockx

2 **Chinese Business in Malaysia**
Accumulation, ascendance, accommodation
Edmund Terence Gomez

3 **Internal and International Migration**
Chinese perspectives
Edited by Frank N. Pieke and Hein Mallee

4 **Village Inc.**
Chinese rural society in the 1990s
Edited by Flemming Christiansen and Zhang Junzuo

5 **Chen Duxiu's Last Articles and Letters, 1937–1942**
Edited and translated by Gregor Benton

6 **Encyclopedia of the Chinese Overseas**
Edited by Lynn Pan

7 **New Fourth Army**
Communist resistance along the Yangtze and the Huai, 1938–1941
Gregor Benton

8 **A Road Is Made**
Communism in Shanghai 1920–1927
Steve Smith

9 **The Bolsheviks and the Chinese Revolution 1919–1927**
Alexander Pantsov

10 **Chinas Unlimited**
Gregory Lee

11 **Friend of China – The Myth of Rewi Alley**
Anne-Marie Brady

12 **Birth Control in China 1949–2000**
Population policy and demographic development
Thomas Scharping

13 **Chinatown, Europe: An Exploration of Overseas Chinese Identity in the 1990s**
Flemming Christiansen

14 **Financing China's Rural Enterprises**
Jun Li

15 **Confucian Capitalism**
Souchou Yao

16 **Chinese Business in the Making of a Malay State, 1882–1941**
Kedah and Penang
Wu Xiao An

17 **Chinese Enterprise, Transnationalism and Identity**
Edited by Edmund Terence Gomez and Hsin-Huang Michael Hsiao

18 **Diasporic Chinese Ventures**
The life and work of Wang Gungwu
Gregor Benton and Hong Liu

19 **Intellectuals in Revolutionary China, 1921–1949**
Leaders, heroes and sophisticates
Hung-yok Ip

20 **Migration, Ethnic Relations and Chinese Business**
Kwok Bun Chan

21 **Chinese Identities, Ethnicity and Cosmopolitanism**
Kwok Bun Chan

22 **Chinese Ethnic Business**
Global and local perspectives
Edited by Eric Fong and Chiu Luk

23 **Chinese Transnational Networks**
Edited by Tan Chee-Beng

24 **Chinese Migrants and Internationalism**
Forgotten histories, 1917–1945
Gregor Benton

25 **Chinese in Eastern Europe and Russia**
A middleman minority in a transnational era
Nyíri Pál

26 **Chinese Entrepreneurship in a Global Era**
Raymond Sin-Kwok Wong

27 **The Politics of Rural Reform in China**
State policy and village predicament in the early 2000s
Christian Göbel

28 **The Politics of Community Building in Urban China**
Thomas Heberer and Christian Göbel

29 **Overseas Chinese in the People's Republic of China**
Glen Peterson

30 **Foreigners and Foreign Institutions in Republican China**
Edited by Anne-Marie Brady and Douglas Brown

31 **Consumers and Individuals in China**
Standing out, fitting in
Michael B. Griffiths

32 **Documentary, World History, and National Power in the PRC**
Global rise in Chinese eyes
Gotelind Müller

33 **Ethnic Chinese Entrepreneurship in Malaysia**
On contextualisation in international business studies
Michael Jakobsen

34 **Chinese Student Migration and Selective Citizenship**
Mobility, community and identity between China and the United States
Lisong Liu

35 **"Mixed Race" Identities in Asia and the Pacific**
Experiences from Singapore and New Zealand
Zarine L. Rocha

"Mixed Race" Identities in Asia and the Pacific

Experiences from Singapore and New Zealand

Zarine L. Rocha

LONDON AND NEW YORK

First published 2016
by Routledge
2 Park Square, Milton Park, Abingdon, Oxon OX14 4RN

and by Routledge
711 Third Avenue, New York, NY 10017

First issued in paperback 2017

*Routledge is an imprint of the Taylor & Francis Group,
an Informa business*

© 2016 Zarine L. Rocha

The right of Zarine L. Rocha to be identified as author of this work has been asserted by her in accordance with sections 77 and 78 of the Copyright, Designs and Patents Act 1988.

All rights reserved. No part of this book may be reprinted or reproduced or utilised in any form or by any electronic, mechanical, or other means, now known or hereafter invented, including photocopying and recording, or in any information storage or retrieval system, without permission in writing from the publishers.

Trademark notice: Product or corporate names may be trademarks or registered trademarks, and are used only for identification and explanation without intent to infringe.

British Library Cataloguing in Publication Data
A catalogue record for this book is available from the British Library

Library of Congress Cataloging-in-Publication Data
A catalog record for this book has been requested.

ISBN 13: 978-1-138-49463-3 (pbk)
ISBN 13: 978-1-138-93393-4 (hbk)

Typeset in Times New Roman
by Apex CoVantage, LLC

For my family

Contents

	Acknowledgements	x
1	Finding the "mixed" in "mixed race"	1
2	Histories of "mixed race" in New Zealand and Singapore	16
3	The personal in the political	46
4	Being and belonging	79
5	Roots, routes and coming home	124
6	Conclusion	155
	Bibliography	169
	Index	185

Acknowledgements

This book grew from personal curiosity and empathy into an entirely more academic endeavour. I am grateful to the many people who have inspired and guided me through research, doctoral study and publication. Daniel P. S. Goh gave me the space to carry out my project and the guidance to finish it. The National University of Singapore funded my studies, and staff in the Department of Sociology provided academic and administrative support. Many others, all around the world, were generous with their time, listening to my ideas and giving me valuable advice. Thank you particularly to Terence Gomez, for suggesting a PhD many years ago, and for being pleasantly surprised by the first chapter of this book. This book is also influenced by the excellent work of many researchers before me, whose words I have had the privilege to draw on as I write.

Thank you also to my family, for wholeheartedly embracing difference and mixedness of all kinds. From Kenya to Brazil, across the United States, Switzerland, India, Australia, Singapore and New Zealand, we are a diverse group, with many different heritages and habits. It has made me who I am today. My parents and my sister inspired this area of research in the first place, as we happily combine chappatis and Marmite. And of course, to Gabe and Leonard – this is for you.

Most of all, I am indebted to the participants I interviewed for this book: the talented and unique group of people who shared their stories with me, talking about their lives and their experiences. Your stories showed such courage, and I hope they will be valuable for you and others.

1 Finding the "mixed" in "mixed race"

What does it mean to be "mixed race"? "Mixed race" identities have been the subject of growing interest over the past two decades, particularly in North America and Britain. In multicultural societies, increasing numbers of people of mixed ancestry are identifying themselves outside of traditional racial categories, challenging systems of racial classification and sociological understandings of "race"[1]. Over the past century, "mixed race" has been reviled and stigmatized, and more recently, celebrated as a transcendence of boundaries. Yet, whether seen as transgressive or progressive, crossing racial boundaries is often seen as different, even threatening to established social structures. As a result, attempts to recognize or assert mixed identities have frequently been met with resistance and resentment.

"Mixed race" is not easy to define, encompassing aspects of ancestry, identity, culture and classification. Highlighting the fluidity of identities, feelings of mixedness do not always fit neatly with heritage: an individual of mixed parentage may not identify as mixed, privately or publicly. Neither can "mixed race" be seen as a clearly defined ethnic or racial group, as the commonality of mixedness is based on difference and dislocation, rather than sameness and positioning (Song 2012). Nevertheless, the changing meanings of "mixed race" across time provide a window into shifting aspects of racial and ethnic belonging. Mixedness both challenges and reinforces assumptions of biology and blood. It draws out the intertwining between the social, political, historical and biological, stressing the simultaneous fluidity and fixity of both mixed and "singular" racial identities. Within increasingly multicultural and mixed populations, identities which cross boundaries reveal the weak points of classification structures, and the blurred edges of ethnic and racial groups in the face of constant social change (Parker and Song 2001).

Against a background of such dynamic change and emerging research, there remain important gaps in the literature. While there is a growing body of work emerging in the North American and British contexts, understandings and experiences of "mixed race" across different contexts are not often explored in significant depth (see Edwards et al. 2012). Exploring what "mixed race" means in other, less obvious contexts can highlight both the strengths and weaknesses of our current understandings. Much previous work has explored the fluid nature of identity and the diversity of ways to be mixed. Such findings are enriched when held up against structurally very different societies.

New Zealand and Singapore provide important contexts for exploration, as two multicultural, yet structurally divergent, societies. Both countries have a history of British colonialism with markedly different impacts: each with a legacy of racial categorization, but with a rigid understanding of race and mixedness in Singapore, and a more fluid and voluntary approach in New Zealand. Within these two countries, "mixed race" describes a particularly interesting label for individuals of mixed Chinese and European parentage. Studying this particular ethnic "combination" raises key issues around race, gender, post-colonial hierarchies and minority/majority relations.

The Chinese in New Zealand and the Europeans in Singapore are successful, economically mobile minority groups, with intermarriage occurring despite perceived social distance, but with divergent histories and experiences of acceptance and integration. How does mixedness differ in a Chinese majority/European minority population, as in Singapore, as compared to a European majority/Chinese minority population, as in New Zealand? Individuals of mixed Chinese and European heritage present a population (rather than a cohesive group) in both countries, with diverse experiences reflecting power dynamics and sociohistorical implications within either society[2]. New Zealand and Singapore provide important contrast cases, both in relation to each other, and as compared to the histories of race and the contemporary realities of mixed identities in other societies around the world.

Most certainly, "mixed race" is a socially constructed category, drawing on the equally constructed category of race. It is, however, a category that has real and lasting effects and meanings for the lives of individuals and the trajectories of societies. To better understand these meanings across both levels, the manifestations of (mixed) race can be placed at the centre of analysis, using a novel application of racial formation theory (Omi and Winant 1986, 1994) through a narrative lens. Such an approach looks at "mixedness" from a fresh angle, moving away from the classification of forms of mixed identity, towards a new characterization of mixed narratives (drawing on Somers 1994).

The characterization of narratives approaches identity as complex, variable and fluid, rather than static, staying still to be classified. By tracing threads of racial formation, it is possible to juxtapose state-level narratives of racial formation with individual narratives of identity creation, development and maintenance. There are two key processes to explore: *how* individuals of mixed heritage negotiate and narrate their racial identities within a racially structured social framework; and *why* – the ways in which the institutionalization and classification of race have affected this negotiation and narration over time and across contexts (see also Siddique 1990:107). This under-theorized connection between structure and agency is key to developing a richer understanding of "mixed race" identity as a valid social phenomenon and strategic identity choice, rather than a psychological feature. It provides further insight into the complexity of identity within social structure, and the inherently fluid and multifaceted nature of all identities.

"Mixed race" is understood and experienced differently in the multicultural contexts of Singapore and New Zealand. Each country illustrates opposite ends of the spectrum in how "mixed race" has been addressed in the past: New Zealand's emphasis on voluntary and fluid ethnic identity and Singapore's fixed four-race framework provide key points of comparison to other national contexts. In both cases, race is significant and managed by the state, but in different ways. Despite contemporary overarching narratives of diversity and multiplicity, individual mixed identities have been simultaneously acknowledged and ignored – recognized officially through categorization or acknowledgement of intermarriage, but practically subsumed under the broader categories which structure institutional and everyday interactions.

In Singapore, race is a collective identity, as an enforced form of group identity, positioned within a narrative of a nation's development and survival. Against a racially structured background, where all individuals are classified as Chinese, Malay, Indian or Other, being "mixed race" positions individuals as out of place. Such identities are symbolically recognized through the recent inclusion of double-barrelled races in the classification structure, but do not meaningfully disrupt the categories. The multiracial framework in Singapore both reinforces race and discourages racially based identity claims – with claims at the group level in particular seen as disrupting the communitarian system of group equality (Chua 1998:36). In this context, it is the denial of race that politicizes identity at the individual level, rather than an assertion of mixedness.

In New Zealand, racial/ethnic identity is promoted as individualistic and voluntary (to a certain extent), located within a bicultural, post-colonial story of nationhood. Race has largely been replaced by ethnicity in state discourse, and is officially fluid and multiple for individuals. However, previous understandings of race and racialized groupings linger. In this context, laying a personal claim to a race/ethnicity (or multiples) politicizes identity, as although multiple and fluid identities are ostensibly widely accepted, being singularly raced is the norm. Mixed identities are positioned precariously against the bicultural/multicultural tension within New Zealand society, as mixedness is officially recognized, but socially questioned.

"Mixed race" is then out of the ordinary in both contexts. Individual narratives of mixedness can result in dissonance between the individual and the state framework, with mixed identities disrupting, maintaining or even reinforcing the status quo. "Mixed race" highlights the tension between macro categorization of identities and the lived experiences of individuals, illustrating how the narrativization of the self reflects and absorbs the narratives of the nation (Hall 1996:4). An exploration of mixedness across these two contexts highlights the connections between public and private narratives. By looking at "mixed race" across macro, meso and micro levels, we look at the relationship between these differing narratives and their positionings across histories of race.

Race and "mixed race"

Research on "mixed race" fundamentally relates to the understanding of race itself. In contemporary social science research, race is commonly understood as a socially and politically constructed concept, a form of social organization that erroneously links phenotype and ancestry to assessments of personal and social qualities and intrinsic worth. Historically, European racial theory placed significant value on purity and blood descent, reflecting the importance of ancestry and descent as a means to stratify society and disempower certain groups (see Perkins 2005; Wetherell and Potter 1992). Although the biological basis for racial categorization was widely discredited in the second half of the twentieth century, the assumptions behind and reasons for these biological understandings of race lingered. Moving forward, it became the practices and symbols of hierarchy and difference in relation to different human bodies, rather than the biology of race itself, which reinforced the significance of race in everyday life (Omi and Winant 1994; Parker and Song 2001).

"Mixed race" highlights the balance between recognizing the constructed nature of race and its continued social importance, and perpetuating its social construction through reification of the idea that pure races can mix (Rockquemore et al. 2009). Explorations of "mixed race" illuminate race as a biologically meaningless yet socially powerful form of categorization and identity, providing a unique way to view and analyze existing concepts of race and racial boundaries. The concept of "racial mixing"[3] continues to have significant power, revealing anxieties over and overlaps between popular notions of race, gender, nation and morality.

In contemporary research, conceptions of race, culture, ethnicity and ancestry are often interchanged and conflated, frequently reinforcing historically racialized categories under different names. Moving away from discussions of race and "mixed race", and its associated assumptions of biology and hierarchy, some researchers and policy makers have rejected the use of race in describing and analyzing social life. The concept of "ethnicity" is used instead, aiming to describe the positive aspects of a subscribed form of group identity, rather than negative aspects of an ascribed category for belonging. Race is relegated to discussions of history, blood, skin colour and ancestry, while ethnicity is ideally based around belief in common descent and cultural commonalities and customs. However, these categories are not easily separated, nor should they be. Although analytical distinctions can promote the positive, shifting and socially constructed aspects of ethnicity as a group identity, the distinctions between race and ethnicity are blurred and shifting (Gunew 2004:21). Both categories are essentially socially constructed, and each relies on a combination of external and internal identification for membership.

While race remains a useful category for analysis in recognizing the continued power of phenotype, the contemporary interest in "mixed race" highlights key contradictions in sociological thought. Race is widely acknowledged as socially constructed, with important social and political consequences. Yet "mixed race" has become the new frontier in ethnic and racial studies, leaving researchers struggling to make sense of what it means to be "mixed", without reifying the idea that separate races exist *to be* mixed. Thus, research on "mixed race" is often fragmented and contradictory, resting shakily both on contextual histories of racialized oppression and on the inconsistencies of contemporary theories of race (see Rockquemore et al. 2009). Similar to research on the concept of race, research on "mixed race" increasingly emphasizes fluidity and multiplicity as way to circumvent essentialist understandings of "mixed race" as "mixed blood". However, as in the case of race, theory does not always match individual and social understandings (Song 2010b), leading to dissonance between theoretical frameworks, popular social understandings and individual experiences.

Terminology is equally fraught with contradictions in discussions of "mixed race". There are a number of contextual terms used, and given the diversity of the "mixed" population, there is no consensus on which term is most appropriate (Aspinall 2009; Ifekwunigwe 2004). Terms such as "mixed race", "multiracial" and "biracial" are frequently used in the North American context, while in the UK "mixed ethnicity" or "mixed heritage" are more common in academic circles. Colloquial and often derogatory terms are plentiful in both contexts, ranging from "half caste" to "mulatto", "mixed blood" to "mongrel" (Aspinall 2003:273–274). Each of these terms carries with it historical and theoretical assumptions, reinforcing ideas of binary racialization and the purity of race, imputing identities solely to heritage, or focusing on the concept of "mixed" as confused or less than whole (Tizard and Phoenix 2002). Out of this definitional confusion, "mixed race" remains the most common choice in popular and academic discussions, despite the danger of reinscribing race as biological. For the purposes of this book, "mixed race" or "mixed" will be used, with the scare quotes drawing attention to mixedness as defined by popular conceptions of race and difference.

Placing these concepts and questions in context, a specialized area of "mixed race" research has developed over the past two decades, often focused on the experiences of individuals in North America and Britain (see, for example, Ifekwunigwe 2004; Parker and Song 2001; Root 1996; Shih and Sanchez 2009). As a profoundly gendered and historically power-laden concept, understandings of "mixed race" are intertwined closely with the social context of racial/ethnic relations, and have shifted over time. Recent research is notably interdisciplinary, with perspectives from psychology, sociology, geography, political science, history, cultural studies, philosophy and social work providing a diverse set of theoretical frameworks and focuses of study.

Theoretical approaches to "mixed race" are often grounded in the idea of difference, whether based in biology or culture. "Mixed race" has been and continues to be set apart: seen as linking separate worlds, pathologized as marginal and the worst of both worlds, or celebrated as the best of both worlds. Either way, the "worlds" are separated, and much "mixed race" research portrays "mixed" individuals as inherently in-between or out of place (Mahtani 2002b:470; Nakashima 1992). From a sociological point of view, different stages in the literature can be identified, highlighting both the historical context and motivations of research, and the theoretical underpinnings of each approach. Rockquemore et al. (2009:15) provide a useful framework for reviewing these shifts, as the *problem approach*, the *equivalent approach*, the *variant approach*, and the *ecological approach*. Each approach is linked to a specific historical and social context, reflecting the prevailing racial ideology of the time and the place.

Initial research on "mixed race" fell within the *problem approach*: research that positions "mixed race" identity as fundamentally problematic in a racialized world.

6 Finding the "mixed" in "mixed race"

Based in pseudo-biological explanations of racial difference and the racialized/gendered power differentials of colonization, "mixed race" was commonly pathologized in the nineteenth and early twentieth centuries (Ifekwunigwe 2001; Young 1995). It became the subject of increased sociological and anthropological concern in the early twentieth century, epitomized in Stonequist's work on the "marginal man": mixed individuals as caught between two worlds, never truly belonging in either one (Park 1928, 1931; Stonequist 1935, 1937). This idea of an individual torn in two has proven persistent, despite theoretical and methodological weaknesses. Marginality remains a common theoretical framework for research on "mixed race" and is often used to explain negative psychological and behavioural outcomes (Rockquemore and Brunsma 2008; Tizard and Phoenix 2002).

Shifting towards the intersection of the psychological and the sociological, research within the *equivalent approach* reflected developments within American racial politics in the 1960s and discourses of human rights. Based in the civil rights movement, this approach assumed that all racial identity development is equivalent, and that for reasons of political influence and identity "correctness", individuals of mixed parentage belong with the minority (black) side of their heritage (Rockquemore et al. 2009:17; Shih and Sanchez 2005:571). This approach brought together the personal and the political, with more recent research focusing on the political and moral imperatives of minority identification. Often within linear models of identity development, this approach emphasized the need for a dominant racial identity (Song 2010a), yet conflates biological, political, cultural and social notions of "mixed race", downplaying conceptions of difference.

The *variant approach* marked the beginning of an increase in research on "multiracial identity" from the 1980s, conceptualizing mixed identity as necessarily distinct – but not negatively so – in terms of psychological development and lived experience. This marked a shift from the marginalization of previous decades, as "mixed race" was no longer described as pathological (DaCosta 2007). With many researchers coming from mixed heritage and interdisciplinary backgrounds, this body of work explored how a mixed identity can be constituted and maintained, challenging both problematization and assumptions of sameness with minority groups (Kilson 2001; Root 1992). A number of models theorized the unique trajectory of "mixed race" identity development, exploring both psychological and societal factors influencing identity, while presuming a correct form of identity for a healthy "biracial" identity (see, for example, Poston 1990).

The most recent perspectives on "mixed race" take an *ecological approach*, drawing on an ecology of social factors (see Rockquemore et al. 2009). Such research can be fragmented: aiming to counter theories of marginalization while emphasizing uniqueness; highlighting both exclusion and new forms of belonging; and providing a framework to understand the fluidity of personal identity development while stressing the importance of social context and construction. However, this illustrates an important move away from previous models of marginality and fixed identity development, to better capture identity complexity.

The complexity of mixedness has been theorized in a number of ways, focusing on the fluidity of moving between different spheres, without identities necessarily competing. Four major identity options have been outlined (or placed on a continuum) by a number of theorists (notably Rockquemore 1998): individuals identify with either side of their ancestry (a *traditional* identity), with both in a hybrid identity (a *border* identity), with both on a situational basis (a *protean* identity) or with no racial category at all (a *transcendent* identity) (see also Binning et al. 2009; LaFromboise et al. 1993; Root 1999; Song 2010a; Ward 2006; Xie and Goyette 1997). Taking an ecological perspective allows for the complexity of "mixed race" identity to be more carefully explored, moving away from the pathologized and linear nature of historical research. However, this approach is particularly broad, lacking a single coherent framework and covering approaches from the social psychological to symbolic interactionist. Leaving behind identity analysis and typology, narratives and histories can instead be explored in a similar way: using the idea of ecology as a comprehensive and flexible standpoint from which to approach "mixed race".

Connecting the psychological and the sociological, an increasing amount of research explores the intersection between private identities and public validation and classification. Research on the "multiracial movement"[4] in the United States explores the impetus for a "multiracial" census category (a movement which ultimately failed), but often remains unconnected to the typologies of "mixed race" identities, highlighting a missing link between classification and identity. The concept of "mixed race" itself highlights the imprecise and arbitrary nature of racial categories, raising questions about whether race should be categorized at all, or whether "mixed race" should be a form of categorization in itself: both destabilizing and reinforcing existing racial frameworks (Goldberg 1997).

The classification of "mixed race" is particularly significant for individuals of mixed descent due to the frequent dissonance between racial categories and lived identities. Rather than representing a trivial, everyday form of organization, the lack of symbolic recognition effectively erases "mixedness" as a legitimate identity claim (Teng 2010). Different forms of racial and ethnic categorization can be seen at the state level. In Britain, with the recent inclusion of "mixed ethnicity" as a category in the census, the order of measurement (white, mixed [with white], Asian and black) clearly demonstrates the hierarchy of groups within society and the assumption that mixed implies "white and minority" (Aspinall 2003, Morning 2002, 2008, 2011). Brazil classifies individuals by colour categories, from white and yellow to brown and black (*branco* and *amarello*, *pardo* and *preto*): categories which are fluid, not necessarily based on ancestry, and which can change according to socioeconomic status (Silva and Reis 2011; Telles and Lim 1998). New Zealand allows for the selection of multiple ethnic groups, and has recently ceased to recategorize mixed groups into a single category, indicating a growing recognition of the fluidity and multiplicity of ethnicities in society (Callister 2004b, Didham and Callister 2012). Singapore has structured significant social policy around the Chinese-Malay-Indian-Other (CMIO) classification system, only in 2011 allowing for a symbolic recognition of hyphenated racial identities, while ensuring each individual maintains a primary race (Chua 2003; Immigration and Checkpoints Authority 2010). South Africa's racially divided history illustrates the role of "mixed race" in classification, drawing lines that became commonsense understandings between white, black and coloured (Maré 2001; Spencer 1997). Finally, the strength of a racially based ideology can also be seen in the American context, developing from a racially divided history and resulting in the 1977 Office of Management and Budget official classification standard for the measurement of race. This standard both reinforced and re-created the modern American racial hierarchy, becoming the target for advocacy for the multiracial movement. It was then altered to include the current acknowledgement of "mixed race" through the selection of multiple groups (Snipp 2003).

Different forms of categorization allow for the measurement of different understandings of race. As stressed by Harris and Sim (2002), each form of measurement reveals one aspect of the "mixed" population, rather than *the* "mixed" population. It is important to note that when official recognition does occur, it is often largely symbolic: providing a legitimated label which is then collapsed into broader statistical categories or overshadowed by group-based rights, as in the US, the UK, Singapore and New Zealand. The continuing dissonance between static racial/ethnic categories and the fluidity of lived identities highlights the interactions between personal identity, external identification and official categorization (Rockquemore et al. 2009:27). Such interaction illuminates the "in-between" spaces between categories, where a mixed identity can be described. The interplay between levels of identification shows evidence of both continuity and change, highlighting the ways in which public and private identities coincide and conflict.

Race, "mixed race" and racial formation

Omi and Winant's racial formation theory draws these factors together, looking at the tension between singular racial categories at the macro level, and complex and shifting identities at the micro. Racial formation theory highlights the centrality of race in social structures in many countries, and provides a lucid and analytically grounded framework with which to explore and analyze racial politics. The term *racial formation* describes the complex interrelationship between social, economic and political forces, in the creation of racialized categories, hierarchies and meanings. Racial categories, created and embedded within social structures and historical contexts, both dictate and reflect individual understandings of race. These are formed and contested at the intersection of "racial projects", where micro understandings meet macro structures (Omi and Winant 1986; Winant 2000a).

Central to this theory is a nuanced understanding of race as a social construction, grounded in historical context, with significant practical consequences. Race becomes the central point in analysis, highlighting the thread of racial signification across levels: from individual identity creation, to collective political action, to forms of state control. Looking at racial formations in different contexts provides a way to explore the continuous and complex interaction between the micro and macro, where signification and structure meet everyday experience, at the intersection of identity and society (Omi and Winant 2008:1565).

The numerous processes of racial formation are expressed at this intersection of structure and representation, described by Omi and Winant as a web of racial projects. These projects are the individual and institutional negotiations, conflicts and understandings of race in everyday life, and the day-to-day processes of how these meanings are formed and transformed. These projects range from state policies based on race, to collective action over racial meanings, to individuals' racial beliefs and experiences based on their own identity, connecting each to the other under contextual and historically racialized circumstances. It is through racial projects that racial meanings become institutionalized and bounded, and, conversely, that institutionalized racial meanings and boundaries are challenged and destabilized (Winant 2000b:186).

However, different forms of identity are not easily disentangled in theory or practice, and are never entirely separate for individuals or even groups. Any theory needs to conceive of individuals as more than simply "mixed race", bringing in gender, class, location, sexuality and age as equally defining. Anchoring theory in lived reality also remains a key concern. Much theorizing focuses entirely on the complexities and intricacies of "mixedness" as transcending race, overlooking the continued day-to-day reality of race and racial categories in everyday life (Song 2010a). Racial formation theory works towards addressing this, by providing a bridge between the individual and the structural, a way to theorize race as equally a matter of *descent* and *consent* (Ang 1999). Despite this, narratives of individual experience are lacking within this framework, leaving a significant gap when it comes to the intimate constructions and negotiations of identity, home and "mixed race". Racial formation theory is thus enriched by a narrative perspective: the storied dimension of racial formation draws out both dominant and subversive narratives at macro and micro levels, and highlights variation in subjectivities rather than a truth of mixedness. It is this combination – *narratives of racial formation* – that provides a unique angle from which to approach "mixed race".

Recasting national and personal stories as narratives of racial formation builds on the ecological school of thought, conceptualizing "mixed race" as inherently intersectional and grounded in contexualized narratives of identity. This combination positions "mixed race" at the centre of analysis: drawing out the relationship between classification and identity, and juxtaposing individual and state narratives of (mixed) racial formation. Moving outward from questions of individual identity, national narratives of race and belonging are counterposed with individual narratives of mixedness, illustrating how racial projects and racial narratives are interwoven across levels of analysis. Projects of racial formation at micro and macro levels can then be approached as forms of narrative, viewing narrative as actively constructing social reality. Rather than simply reflecting experience, individual, institutional and collective stories construct and give meaning to the social world (Ferber 2000:342).

Most importantly, a narrative understanding of racial formation allows for a novel approach to exploring the relationship between identity and structure. While individual narratives may be limited in terms of wider generalization, their very location within wider narrative constructions makes them sociologically valuable.

Personal narratives provide a window into difficult-to-define group identities and processes (see Phinney 2000), by exploring the commonalities and differences which emerge as individuals locate themselves inside or outside of wider narratives of belonging. A narrative perspective bridges the gap between individual experience and action, as individual stories constitute personal lives and experiences of the wider social world (Riessman 1993). Understanding racial formation as narrated provides a grounded link in the conceptualization of "mixed race", highlighting the parallels and divergences between personal, social and national narratives.

In the case of race and "mixed race" identity, the intertwining of narratives and power is particularly important, looking at the ways in which individual narratives can subvert or reinforce the status quo. Dominant historical narratives of "mixed race" have frequently been pathological, or have even erased "mixedness" from national narratives altogether. Collective racial identity is frequently based on narratives of exclusivity, stories of belonging to a single group with firm boundaries. Such narratives of strong and bounded racial communities may be embraced unproblematically by large segments of the population, with alternative narratives seen as dangerous and destabilizing. For those whose private narratives sit outside of dominant public narratives, adjustments must be made to situate the self within a wider social, cultural and institutional framework.

Rather than categorizing different forms of identity, this research instead characterizes and locates narratives of identity, in relation to wider contextual narratives. Racial projects and identity outcomes are characterized along narrative themes, rather than delimiting populations into typologies. This analysis of narrative rather than actor reflects the negotiation of affiliations inherent in identity construction and maintenance, analyzing the story through narrative research. A focus on narrative looks at how the story is framed, what is included and what is left out, how this relates to context and identity, and crucially, how personal stories fit into or break out of wider social narratives.

Narratives of "mixed race": Macro, meso and micro

The juxtaposition of narratives of racial formation across macro, meso and micro levels illustrates the storied process of (mixed) identity location, as described by Hall: ". . . identities are the names we give to the different ways we are positioned by, and position ourselves within, the narratives of the past" (1990:225). At the macro level, narratives of race are maintained through a complex system of racial projects which routinize and often normalize the pervasiveness of race as an organizing principle. Macro classifications and the resulting narratives are not about reproducing a social reality, but about creating a particular narrative of reality as common sense. Formalized identity categories, frozen in time, don't necessarily match lived and constantly changing identities, yet serve to shape the possibilities for individual narratives (Omi 1997:13).

National censuses provide a concrete example of social naming by a racially structured state. As a powerful and visible racial project, racial and ethnic questions in the census are an important means for the state to statistically describe collective identities. However, the narratives behind the census itself, as a tool of the state, are often overlooked, depicting the census as a neutral institution which merely *counts* – assuming that racial/ethnic categories exist in objective reality *to be counted* (Kertzer and Arel 2002, Nobles 2000).

The classification of race and ethnicity in the national census is particularly significant and often quite routine (Aspinall 2012). Both Singapore and New Zealand have British colonial pasts (albeit very different ones), and it is important to recognize the ways in which the colonial regime used categorization as a way of "imposing, reinforcing and extending the colonizers' racial and ethnic perceptions through categorization" (Nobles 2000:181). The colonial census was key in this process, creating categories and boundaries around racial groups with very real and practical consequences (Anderson 1991, Appadurai 1993). This form of categorization remains a significant organizing principle in many formerly colonized states, where the racial categories of the colonizers have been adopted, both bounding and creating identities. Colonial racial narratives have been reinvented as post-colonial, re-creating race in a way which influences everyday understandings of identity through bureaucratic practice and national narratives of belonging.

The positioning of "mixed race" in such narratives is complex and often contradictory. Despite singular bases for racial categorization, the lived reality of "mixed" and/or "unmixed" individuals continues to be infinitely more complex. Mixed identities represent the intersection of the biological and the social, and the dissonance between classificatory frameworks and personal identification highlights how individual and state racial projects can overlap, intersect and contradict. Definitions of race and "mixed race" are contextual and shifting, as attitudes towards measurement and the purposes of such measurement change[5]. Narratives of "mixed race" serve to critique the essentialized nature of racial categories, to subvert these categories in the assertion of hybridity, to bolster dominant narratives of categorization through promotion of the belief that distinct races exist to be mixed, or they can even be co-opted into state narratives of racialization.

Connecting macro narratives of racial formation to the personal and grounded level of individual narratives, we have an in-between space. As the institutions and communities linking the state to the individual, meso-level structures reveal the interconnections and dissonances between the individual and societal levels (Callister et al. 2009:9). As social interaction occurs within and between communities, the in-between positioning of individuals of mixed descent highlights a complexity of influences. In the case of minority/majority mixes, individuals locate themselves both within and between multiple communities, internalizing the racial narratives from the dominant majority, the ethnic minority, both communities simultaneously, or neither one in an attempt at dislocation. The meso level acts as a bridge between the two levels of analysis, connecting wider, impersonal narratives of state structure with individual stories.

At the individual, experiential level, racial projects and narratives are both personal and interactional. Located in a specific national and historical context, each individual formulates his or her own identity within a wider framework. Socially available labels and meanings shape individual racial projects of identification and interaction, with reference to understandings of race at the state and collective levels within society (Appiah 2009:670; Omi and Winant 1986). At the same time, individual racial projects can be tied to the projects of social movements or alternative institutional narratives, challenging the dominant racial meanings of the state.

Bringing together macro processes of racial formation and identity narration at the micro level, the racial narratives of individuals can be juxtaposed with wider-level narratives, illustrating different patterns through meso-level stories. Previous typologies of "mixed race" identity have been developed across levels: from micro-level psychological and therapeutic frameworks, to macro-level explanatory models of acculturation and assimilation. While useful explanatory frameworks, at all levels these models tend to reinforce the notion of distinct boundaries between racialized groups, lacking a coherent linkage between the micro and the macro, and often indirectly reinforcing negative stereotypes, such as pathologies of mixed blood or marginality.

Taking a narrative perspective, "mixed race" at the micro level can be explored through an understanding of narratives within narratives. The focus can be shifted from linear, deterministic understandings of identity, moving away from the idea that identities can be discretely categorized, or divided into parts. By looking instead at how individuals narrate their identities, we can emphasize the positioning of identities within the racial framework of the state: stories articulated in response to the available racial narratives. A narrative approach highlights the imposed and ascribed boundaries surrounding "mixed race", and the ways in which racialized identities are frequently understood as embodied. Narratives of mixedness, set against dominant narratives of singularity, show how conceptions of race and culture are complicated and redefined in everyday life, playing on meanings of difference and sameness, and alternative understandings of what it means to belong.

Four broad characterizations of narratives can be described around "mixed race" in New Zealand and Singapore. By looking at stories, and stories about identities, these highlight the themes and directions of such stories – not different types of identities. A characterization of narratives, rather than a categorization of identity, aims to highlight the fluidity and diversity of "mixed" identities, as illustrated and experienced by individuals in their daily lives. These narratives are characterized as follows:

Narratives of reinforcement, which support and reiterate the dominant racial narrative of singularity, matching categorization to personal identification and describing an active choice to live within a single racial label, potentially echoing "marginal" narratives of identity.

Narratives of accommodation, which fit unproblematically within state categorizations of race, accepting the racialized nature of state classification and policy outcomes. These narratives make a distinction between public and private identities, allowing for the coexistence of simplified identity labels within a state framework, and personal racial projects and narratives expressing mixedness.

Table 1.1 Narrative characterizations

	Working within state framework	Going against state framework
Acceptance of reality of the racial state (public/private division)	Accommodation	Transcendence
Active engagement in racial projects in/against state framework (matching public/private)	Reinforcement	Subversion

Narratives of transcendence, which accept the reality of racial categorization, but refuse practical engagement. These narratives instead maintain a non-racial identification (such as civic or religious) to distance personal narrative from public narratives.

Narratives of subversion, which actively oppose the categorization of dominant racial narratives through emphasis on mixedness, duality, or reclaiming formerly derogatory terms. These narratives seek to promote racial projects of mixedness in the public sphere, and push against the mismatch between public and private.

The four narratives characterized above (see table 1.1) seek to illustrate the different yet overlapping ways in which individuals of mixed descent actively construct their identities within a dominant narrative of racialized group membership. Growing out of (yet away from) previous identity typologies, this characterization focuses on the variety and inconsistency of individual racial projects, as constrained and enabled by context. Narratives describe processes of identification which can be described through stories, rather than a singular essence of identity to be mapped and analyzed (Hall 1996:2).

This characterization does not propose to firmly classify individuals, but rather to locate and explore the stories they tell. Individuals may position their stories within different narrative characterizations over time, or even several simultaneously. This fluidity highlights the flexibility and shifting nature of all forms of identity, allowing space for internal and external contradictions, changes and reinforcements. It also recognizes that there can be significant dissonance between how people want to be perceived, how they perceive themselves, how others perceive them, and how they fit themselves into wider classificatory frameworks. This framework of characterization focuses on "mixed" identity as a process, as a way of "moving through categories" (Mahtani 2005:90). "Mixed race" is shaped by issues of context and power: an identity negotiated by individual actions and beliefs, but firmly positioned within wider narratives and racial projects.

Forty men and women told stories that are presented in this volume: twenty in New Zealand and twenty in Singapore[6]. In seeking individuals from whom to elicit narratives, sampling was purposeful and selective, with interviews carried out in 2011. An important part of narrative inquiry was the interaction between myself (the interviewer) and the participants, as there is no research detached from the researcher[7]. This focus on personal narratives placed the individual at the centre of the story which I was to tell. Rather than describing an unchanging reality, these narratives were seen as shaping and describing individual perceptions of and assumptions about "reality". Narrative analysis thus added a further layer of analysis and reflexivity. As described by Chase: "Life stories embody what we need to study: the relation between this instance of social action (this particular life story) and the social world the narrator shares with others; the ways in which culture marks, shapes and/or constrains this narrative; and the ways in which this narrator makes use of cultural resources and struggles with cultural constraints" (1995:20).

In analyzing histories of racial formation in New Zealand and Singapore, personal narratives were used to illustrate the links between the personal and the institutional. This analysis focused on what people said, how they said it, and how their stories were structured in relation to wider social stories (Riessman 1993). I looked for both the particular and the general in each story, and the relationship between what was unique to the text, and common across groups, paying special attention to descriptions of categorization and identity/identification and other labels used to describe ethnic/racial heritage. The exact words used by participants were important to the analysis, as a particular choice of words can convey significant meaning, as interpreted both by the teller and the listener.

The narrative focus on data gathering and analysis sought to look further beyond the text, providing a way to conceptualize that ever-elusive link between agency and structure, micro and macro. Individual narratives were read and reread to produce new narrative fragments, without trivializing the particularities or commonalities of lived experiences. Wider narratives of racial formation provided the context in which to position individual narratives of identity, allowing insight into wider processes. Through a combination of a grounded theoretical framework and a reflexive and sensitive application of narrative analysis, the ultimate aim was to propose valid, well-founded and strong conclusions through methods that can be relied upon: seeking trustworthiness in research and in narrating the stories of others, rather than a simple truth (Richards 2005, Riessman 2008:189). This book explores narratives of (mixed) racial formation in Singapore and New Zealand, looking at the ways personal stories are created by and reflected in wider narratives of belonging. It keeps the constructed and shifting nature of identity at the centre of analysis, using narratives of racial formation to go beyond what people identify as (or with), to why they tell their stories as they do.

Notes

1 Although I understand "race" as a social construction rather than a biological reality, for clarity, scare quotes will henceforth not be used.
2 While mixedness is relevant for many groups in both countries, I chose to focus on this particular population to better illustrate the intersections of colonial legacies, racial hierarchies and present-day interactions. The terms "Chinese" and "European" were used, rather than "Asian" and "Caucasian", to avoid racially based and overly broad classifications. It must be acknowledged that as social classification is often based on phenotype (regardless of the biologically baseless nature of race), an element of defining the study population was related to an individual's perception of their appearance, their self-definition and the generalizations of others. These terms and groupings were chosen for their popular meanings and salience in both countries.

3 The idea of "racial mixing" is used here cautiously, based on social concepts of difference, with "interracial relationships" bridging a social and cultural gap (whether real or perceived).
4 Prior to the 2000 US census, a number of groups advocated to include a "multiracial" category in the census. Leaders suggested that due to a shared history of oppression and discrimination, and a common mixed heritage, the resulting sense of solidarity meant that the mixed population identified as a coherent group, and should be identified as such (DaCosta 2007; Spencer 1997). This movement was highly criticized, however, as the suggestion that the mixed population formed a coherent community was not substantiated (Nash 2004:217), potentially due to the heterogeneous nature of the mixed population (Harris 2001:14; Wallace 2004:197).
5 The purpose of classification and its importance at individual and state levels has shifted in a number of countries, including the US, Canada and the UK, as macro narratives of classification are increasingly associated with group legitimization and individual identification (DaCosta 2003; Morning 2002).
6 Further methodological details are available from the author upon request.
7 As described by Mahtani (2002b, 2012), my personal background is important to acknowledge, as I locate myself within the field of "mixed race studies" as both an involved insider and academic outsider (see also Khanna 2010). As a woman of mixed heritage, my research is necessarily grounded in my personal experiences and the assumptions drawn from this. Hence, I strove to carefully balance my roles and positionings as an insider and an outsider. I was also aware of a potentially positive bias towards my research topic, drawn from my own biography.

2 Histories of "mixed race" in New Zealand and Singapore[1]

Processes of racial formation in New Zealand and in Singapore have undergone significant shifts across different stages of nation-building. Although both countries were colonized by the British and can be broadly described as "post-colonial", the colonialisms experienced in either context varied greatly[2]. As described by much previous work, colonialism had powerful impacts on both the colonized and the colonizer (Gunew 2004; Stratton and Devadas 2010). In the case of these two countries, many of these impacts centred around the ideology of race. However, not all post-colonial states are the same, and New Zealand and Singapore represent key examples of the differences between *colonialism* and *settler colonialism*[3]. Each situation illustrates the power of experiences of colonization. In neither case are the legacies of colonialism entirely erased, and in both, race and racial ideology have had lingering effects.

In New Zealand, racial formations have moved from initial colonial understandings of racialized domination and hierarchy to the present-day complex narrative of a multicultural society within a bicultural national framework. Connecting these national narratives over time is a constant thread of racial differentiation, underpinning contemporary state and social understandings of race and mixed race. As a lingering colonial legacy, the idea of race as a means to structure, delimit and understand society remains pervasive and powerful. The political and socioeconomic dominance of Pakeha[4] and continuing institutional and social discrimination illustrate key intersections which perpetuate racialized hierarchies (Larner and Spoonley 1995:40). In parallel, as racial narratives have shifted over time, from colonialism and towards biculturalism, state, social and individual understandings of what it means to be "mixed race" in the New Zealand context have developed and changed.

Similarly, race and racial categories have long played a significant role in everyday life and state organization in Singapore. From colonization to independent statehood, narratives of racial distinctiveness and classification have underpinned processes of racial formation at macro and micro levels. While multiplicity and diversity are important characteristics of Singaporean society, Singapore's multiracial ideology is firmly based on separated, racialized groups, leaving little room for more complex racial projects. Multiracialism in Singapore has been described as "one of the nation's founding myths" (Benjamin 1976:116). In everyday life, the importance of race is simultaneously emphasized and downplayed, while at the same time dividing the population into distinct racial groups. Narratives of race in Singapore are highly visible, from the level of the state to the everyday lives of individuals, limiting even symbolic options for multiple racial identifications. While racial mixing has been a feature of Singaporean society for centuries, mixed identities have been marginalized, ignored, or even essentialized as a "new race", as in the case of the Eurasians.

New Zealand 1830–1947: colonization and nation-building

Race and racialized hierarchies were key in the British colonization of New Zealand, with pseudo-scientific understandings of race-based superiority providing justification for colonial policies of assimilation and dominance. Reliance on physical markers of difference and blood quantum made race an important organizing principle, defining the parameters for New Zealand's processes of nation-building (Salesa 2011). Both legal and social forms of discrimination were prominent, with state racial projects deliberately seeking to exclude non-white individuals, through restriction of immigration or policies of cultural marginalization and enforced assimilation. Initial racial relations were characterized by the power imbalances of the colonizer and the colonized, reinforcing the separation between white and non-white, and epitomized in the 1840 signing of the Treaty of Waitangi (Orange 1997; Spoonley 1993).

The categorization of the population along racial lines in the census was a crucial mechanism to elaborate this idea of race and racial separation. The first national census in 1851 included only the European population, providing a clear message as to which population counted (literally) in the nation-building process. A partial census of Maori was carried out in 1857–58, before full, regular, and separate censuses of Maori became institutionalized from 1867, with this separation in measurement continuing until 1951 (Statistics New Zealand 2004).

Racial measurement was directed particularly at those who were classified as "half-castes". This "half-caste" category was important to the state in monitoring both interracial relationships and the expected "amalgamation" of the indigenous Maori into the European population (Callister and Kukutai 2009). In contrast to many other colonial societies, the state closely monitored racial mixing and attempted to structure private lives through colonial policy, but never legally prohibited miscegenation (Wanhalla 2009). The Maori population was viewed as a "noble race", biologically "close" to the European settlers, and therefore intermarriage was seen as a viable method of social and biological assimilation, as well as of appropriation of land through biological claims (Freeman 2005). Interracial unions, as gendered crossings of racial boundaries, represented an important point of contact between the colonizers and the colonized, and a disruption of the racial hierarchy, particularly if they produced biological evidence of contact and amalgamation – the "half-caste" (Grimshaw 2002:12; Wanhalla 2009).

Importantly, colonial understandings and measurements of race differed significantly from how Maori defined identity and belonging. Traditionally, measurements of "blood" were not used to define "Maoriness", with such constructs imposed by the colonizing power. For Maori, being born with links to other Maori (*whakapapa*) makes an individual *mokopuna* of the *iwi* – grandchild of the tribe – regardless of blood percentage or other ancestral heritage, as a "part-grandchild" is an impossibility (Howard and Didham 2007; Jackson 2003:62). Official understandings and measurements of mixed race were then complex and often inconsistent – based on biological understandings of blood, but tempered by the realities of cultural practices.

Against this background, the Chinese in New Zealand were initially constructed and understood as the quintessential racial "other". Neither the colonizers nor the colonized, the Chinese were not included directly in the national narrative of identity, positioned instead as a racialized threat to New Zealand's national identity (Ip 2008; Ng 2003). From 1880, as in the United States and Australia, this notion of racial exclusion translated from social prejudice into economic and political action. The state aimed to combat the "Yellow Peril" and to preserve the racial purity of the country through ideological and physical exclusion. It enacted 21 separate bills over 39 years (including a poll tax), deliberately excluding the Chinese by preventing entry and isolating those already present from mainstream society (Murphy 2005; Sedgwick 1998).

Over the first half of the twentieth century, New Zealand's settler population continued to grow, and the dominant narrative of national identity remained intimately connected to race. This was reflected in the measurement of race, with Victorian understandings of race and racial fractions and the accompanying separation of populations emerging in census measurements (Kukutai 2007; Statistics New Zealand 2004:21). Such precise measurement indicated a declining tolerance for mixedness, as stated in the 1921 census report: "History has shown that the coalescence of the white and the so-called coloured races is not conducive to improvement in racial types" (cited in Murphy 2003:49). Against this backdrop, the institutional exclusion of and discrimination against the Chinese continued, until 1944, when the Labour government came into power and the poll tax was officially removed (Fong 1959; Ip 2003b). Institutional discrimination had begun to ease, although social exclusion remained common for the Chinese population.

Singapore 1819–1965: colonial race and pre-independence society

Singapore was established as a trading post for the British East India Company, before becoming part of British Malaya in 1867 (Goh 2007:122). As a British colony made up of a diverse population of settlers, it was also subject to organization informed by European racial theory, defining a racialized socioeconomic framework and hierarchy (Benjamin 1976; Hirschman 1986). As in New Zealand, ideology that justified key economic and political imperatives was put into practice through the administrative and practical divisions of the population along racial lines. In contrast to these neat delimitations, colonial Singaporean society was diverse and complicated, made up of groups that blurred at the edges[5].

The national census was a primary site of racialization in the face of this everyday ambiguity, as a powerful state racial project shaped by the colonizer's racial ideology. The earliest census categories were vague and multiple, while categories in later censuses became more particular, and importantly, more exclusively racialized. In delimiting and managing race, the colonial government also attempted to control "mixed race". Individuals who appeared to belong to multiple groups were reclassified within a single racial category – based on style of dress, religious belief or simply the least complicated option. The "Eurasian" category was an attempt to describe and encompass mixedness, providing a category into which European/Asian mixes[6] could be bundled without further discussion (PuruShotam 1998).

As an official marker of mixedness, Eurasian identity occupied a peculiar in-between position, suspended between the colonizers and the colonized. Eurasians subverted ideas of purity and authenticity, accepted by neither the Chinese nor the European community on the grounds of difference by blood and lineage (see Jayawardena 2007). In response to such racial hierarchy and exclusion, Eurasians in Singapore attempted to form a more coherent community. The Eurasian Association (EA) was formed in 1919, and as with other groups in Singapore, enclaves developed along ethnic lines (Braga-Blake 1992). Eurasian identity was consolidated around what was seen as unique to their community: mixed European/Asian descent (along patrilineal European lines), class, Christianity, and linguistic ability in English (Pereira 1997).

The Second World War and the Japanese occupation had significant effects on the strength of racial identities in Singapore, marking the end of British imperial legitimacy (Tremewan 1994). Against this background, a theory of multiracialism was developed, built on the racialized framework of colonial hierarchy, and proposed by English-educated intellectuals in the decade prior to independence (Hill and Lian 1995:92). The British granted internal self-government to Singapore in 1959, and in 1963, Malaya and Singapore became fully independent as a new nation: Malaysia. However, the two-year merger period was characterized by significant clashes between the central government and the Singaporean authorities on economic, political and social issues. While a number of issues contributed to the separation in 1965, a key disagreement involved the role of race in politics. Closely linked to the framework of multiracialism, the primacy of race for Singapore's position in Malaysia highlighted the continuing influence of colonial structures as strategies for independence and power were negotiated. The political discourse and heightened sensitivities of this period further promoted racialized identities, leading to instances of ethnic/racial violence within Singapore prior to the separation (Goh 2008a; Rahim 2009; Vasil 1995).

New Zealand 1947–1980: rebuilding, partnership and diversity

Domestically, the decades following the Second World War brought the beginnings of significant social change. With the increasing urbanization of the Maori population in the 1950s and 1960s, a consolidation and resurgence of Maori culture arose in opposition to the institutional racism in society. Parallel to this shift in social relations, dominant understandings of race were also in flux. Recognizing the institutionalized racism based on notions of racial hierarchies, the Race Relations Act was passed in 1971 and the Human Rights Commission was established in 1977, aiming to provide some form of protection and redress against explicit racism and discrimination (Spoonley 1993).

The measurement of race in the census also shifted: the term "race" was used until 1951, "race" and "descent" were used interchangeably until 1970, in 1971 the terms "descent" and "origin" replaced "race" entirely, and in 1976 "ethnic origin" was used for the first time (Callister et al. 2006; Callister and Kukutai 2009:19). The 1975 Statistics Act illustrated a shift away from the language of race, indicating that each census must ask a question on ethnic origin (understood as self-perceived). This was implemented in the 1976 census, which, as well as retaining the fractional division of "ethnic origin", also asked for statements of (full) European and (partial) Maori descent[7] by means of two tick boxes (Allan 2001; Khawaja et al. 2007). As illustrated by the insistence on fractions for measuring race/ethnicity/origin, monitoring and understanding "mixed race" remained a concern. Maori-Pakeha mixes were more socially acceptable than other racial combinations, but the health and social standing of these mixed children were of increasing interest as instances of intermarriage increased and diversified.

For the Chinese, legislative discrimination continued post-war, and despite the right to naturalization being restored in 1951 (Fong 1959), significant prejudice at the state level remained from the 1950s to the 1970s. A "white New Zealand" policy remained firmly in force: "Our immigration is based firmly on the principle that we are and intend to remain a country of European development. It is inevitably discriminatory against Asians – indeed against all persons who are not wholly of European race and colour. Whereas we have done much to encourage immigration from Europe, we do everything to discourage it from Asia" (1953 Department of External Affairs memorandum, cited in Murphy 2003:50).

For the small but increasingly established Chinese community already present in New Zealand, expectations were shifting in relation to generational change, balancing adaptation and tradition. The family was perceived as maintaining traditional values such as respect for elders, and many families achieved significant economic mobility through sustained hard work and persistence in the face of social and legislative discrimination. The second generation participated in dominant majority social and educational institutions, while certain traditions (such as arrangements and ceremonies of marriage) shifted to combine Western and Chinese cultural patterns, illustrating both upward mobility and a form of selective assimilation into New Zealand society (Fong 1959; Portes and Zhou 1993).

As in the United States, the Chinese in New Zealand became known as a "model minority": a minority group which assimilated adequately, maintained high standards of behaviour and didn't significantly challenge the racial hegemony (Ip 2003b:241; Yee 2003). As racial prejudice slowly began to diminish in the years following the war, intermarriage gradually became more accepted, but it was not commonplace or overtly approved of by either community. Given the small numbers of the Chinese community and the generational changes which were taking place, in 1959 Fong suggested that "... complete biological amalgamation, if and when it takes place, will be of no great benefit to either Pakeha or Chinese, for those of mixed ancestry will in time be indistinguishable from the *ordinary New Zealander*" (1959:128, emphasis added).

Singapore 1965–1980: independence, national identity and the PAP

After separation in 1965, Singapore found itself the only Chinese-majority population in the region, with many social, economic and political issues to address. To do this, the governing People's Action Party (PAP) took a survivalist approach to statehood, developing a narrative of legitimacy and struggle which encompassed the recent social unrest and wider geopolitical considerations. The government sought to tackle the legacies of colonialism: high unemployment, housing shortages, high birth rates, precarious economic viability, and a racialized, separated population without a unifying sense of national identity (Chua and Kuo 1990, Chua 2003, Lai 1995).

Multiracialism was a key aspect of self-definition in Singapore's new national narrative and an important tool for governance. Singapore became a constitutionally multiracial state with an overarching Singaporean identity, in an attempt to manage and bring together multiple racial groups in the process of nation-building. Carrying over inherited colonial categories, Prime Minister Lee Kuan Yew and his cabinet of ministers developed the multiracial framework into a managed form of organization, subsuming racial identities within the multiracial nation (Barr and Skrbis 2008:91). The ideals of multiracialism, multilingualism, multiculturalism and multireligiosity became the racialized framework of Chinese, Malay, Indian and Other (CMIO): separate, but equal, races making up a unique Singaporean identity (see Siddique 1989).

Without a shared history upon which to "imagine" a community, the state sought to create a nation through universal concepts which would transcend ethnic groupings, grounded in capitalist development and framed by a multiracial scaffolding. Each major racial grouping was conceived as a distinct and equal part of the new nation, to promote meritocracy in tandem with multiracialism (Chua 1998, Moore 2000). This reworking of diversity essentialized race as an integral feature of the population, linking the individual, society and the nation through a framework of racial singularity and belonging – belonging to the nation by identifying with one of the founding races. As seen in the transfer of racial categories, this framework to shape national belonging came directly from colonial understandings of race, providing a key thread of racialization across processes of decolonization. By continuing to classify in colonial categories, the boundaries, meanings and power dynamics of these racial categories were translated into the new state, with far-reaching consequences in terms of identity and practice.

Chinese, Malay, Indian, other

Under the CMIO system, all Singaporeans were categorized along patrilineal lines, leaving little room for more complex identifications. Each administrative group seamlessly linked descent, language, religion and custom to create essentialized, idealized versions of "separate but equal" racial groups (Chua 1998; Siddique 1989). Thus, in theory, the Chinese speak Mandarin, practice Buddhism and wear the *cheongsam*, the Malays speak Malay, practice Islam and wear the *sarong kebaya*, the Indians speak Tamil, practice Hinduism and wear the *sari*, and the Others speak English, practice Christianity and wear Western clothes (Benjamin 1976; Pereira 2006:12).

Multiracial categories served to simplify and homogenize, using race as shorthand for more complex identities, and glossing over linguistic, religious and cultural differences within each broad category. Race and culture were conflated, distilled and frozen in time by the multiracial framework – defining a racial essence and then pressuring groups to conform to the homogenous, simplified definition (Barr and Skrbis 2008; Chua 1998). With each group viewed as a component race of Singapore's multiracial society, the distinctiveness of each was emphasized, heightening differences to fit within the framework. Constant reiteration of this CMIO framework, from an individual's National Registration Identity Card (NRIC) to classification in the national census, reinforced this separation.

The CMIO framework was promoted by the state in a number of ways, from listing race on identity cards, to active promotion of racial practices and ethnic and religious festivals, reinforcing race as a visible and grounded form of identity. The population was also mapped along racial lines through the national census. The first post-independence census was taken in 1970, and thereafter at 10-year intervals (Sing and Lin 2009; Singapore Department of Statistics 2010b). Race was not utilized as a category on the census form itself, but responses to the question on ethnic/dialect group were reclassified according to the three main CMI groups, or as Others. As further specified in the census report:

> The concept of ethnic group used in the 1970 census is basically the same as that used in preceding censuses and connotes groups or communities belonging to the same stock or ethnological origin . . . it was observed in the 1931 census that this grouping is "in reality, a judicious blend for practical ends of the ideas of geographical and ethnological origin, political allegiance and racial and social affinities and sympathies"[8].
>
> (Arumainathan 1973:247)

The CMIO structure is clearly evident in this classification and practical definition, reflecting the colonial practice of conflating race, ethnicity, culture and nationality and relying on overarching racial categories under which lesser categories could be subsumed. Interestingly, the census report goes on to say:

> In recent years, the differences among communities have become even less pronounced due to intermingling and assimilation and the dialect or community subdivision no longer represents any distinct category or group.
>
> (Arumainathan 1973:247)

This assertion of the hybridity of the population then stands in sharp contrast to the insistence on these delimited groups for analysis and the fact that individuals of mixed parentage were categorized according to the ethnic group of the father. Eurasians were the exception, classified as a group under "Other", as:

> ... persons primarily of mixed European and Asian descent ... *do not belong to any specific ethnic grouping*. However, it has been the practice ... to treat them as a specific community and this practice has also been continued in the current census.
>
> (Arumainathan 1973:247, emphasis added)

The category of "Other" served to cover all those who did not fit into Chinese, Malay or Indian, encompassing significant complexity and, in an interesting shift, including all European ethnicities and nationalities as minority groups.

This form of racialization had significant consequences for Singaporean society. While multiracialism was ideal for administrative and organizational purposes, it both constrained and concealed the complexity of everyday life identities for Singaporeans. The blurring of boundaries between groups was deliberately ignored, as was the myriad of hybrid cultural practices of everyday life in Singapore. In addition, those who did not fit comfortably within the framework were marginalized as "Others", relabelled or excluded from dominant narratives of nation-building. Theoretical equality also masked the power dynamics of everyday life, as multiracial egalitarianism obscured the continued hierarchies along intersecting racial, religious and socioeconomic lines[9].

The CMIO framework was utilized to address numerous issues, including education, housing and welfare, by an openly interventionist government. Practically, the operationalization of multiracial ideology was highly successful, carrying over already instituted colonial categories into government policy and the everyday lives of citizens from the early 1960s onwards. Language was a central issue from the outset. Four official languages were established, providing a form of acknowledgement for each of the CMIO racial categories. The promotion of English was portrayed as essential to Singapore's economic development and global position, providing a further echo of colonial classification and racial/linguistic hierarchy. Mandarin, Malay and Tamil became compulsory second languages for each student, depending on their race: the "mother tongues"[10] and "cultural ballasts" which grounded individuals in their racial groupings (Chua 1995a:110).

The spatial distribution of the population was also affected by multiracial policy. The resettlement of the population into public housing estates and the clearing of *kampongs* around Singapore played a significant role in the development of the new state. These new estates and the accompanying demolition of villages were widely contested, as the new government sought to mold a diverse and disparate population into a manageable and measurable modern Singaporean nation (Loh 2009a, 2009b; Moore 2000). The new public housing estates were deliberately multiracial, breaking up racially based enclaves around the country as the population was resettled. This enforced diversity served as a safeguard for governance, to prevent large pockets of dissatisfaction from forming along racial and religious lines. Over 230,000 households were resettled into public housing estates, significantly altering the shape of Singaporean society and the communities and networks which had formed within it. The new housing estates became integral parts of nation-building and the consolidation of multiracial policy, as the government utilized inherited practices of control to manage the population (Goh 2008b, Loh 2009a).

"Mixed race" in independent Singapore

Multiracialism as a tool for policy and organization also had a significant impact on how "mixed race" was understood in Singapore. The multiracial framework left little space for racial boundary crossing and cultural hybridity. Such space was not seen as necessary, as in the words of then prime minister Lee Kuan Yew:

> "My expectation is that there will always be a small group of the adventurous in all the ethnic groups, perhaps those who are less egotistical, who marry across ethnic lines. But they will probably be in the minority. Therefore the chances are that if you come back to Singapore in a century from now, you would find people more or less the same."
>
> (Quoted in Siddique 1989:574)

Despite the strict divisions of multiracialism, intermarriage did occur in the 1960s and 1970s, and 4.4 per cent of all marriages in the 1970s occurred across ethnic/racial lines (Hassan and Benjamin 1973; Kuo and Hassan 1979). Racial and religious intersections proved particularly important in the case of intermarriage, with the most frequent intermarriages occurring between Malays and Indians, many of whom shared religious affiliations as Muslims. Both intermarriages and intramarriages could also be across religious lines, as well as across levels of socioeconomic status, as each racial group encompassed a diversity of religious beliefs and ethnic and linguistic origins.

Interracial relationships remained gendered in post-independence Singapore, with five times as many European men marrying across racial lines as women, and five times as many Chinese women marrying outside their categorized group (Hassan and Benjamin 1973:735). The gender discrepancy within the Chinese and European populations can be partly explained by the numbers of European men residing in Singapore, but also by the highly gendered notions of race for both groups. For the Europeans, women were viewed as the carriers of the race and signifiers of racial purity, leaving little space for intermixing with other groups. Men had significantly more freedom, and were additionally influenced by discourses of Asian women as sexual partners and companions. For the Chinese, notions of lineage and patrilineage meant that men carried on the family line and were less able to marry outside of approved groups. Women instead were more able to intermarry, crossing racial lines in much higher numbers (Hassan and Benjamin 1976).

The children of these crossings were constrained by the existing system of categorization. As race was determined along patrilineal lines, the children of interracial relationships were automatically assigned the race of the father. This quietly passed over complex backgrounds, and it rendered "mixed race" uncountable, reinforcing boundaries and the inviolability of racial groups. Hybrid groups, such as the Eurasians and the Peranakans, also lacked a defined space in the multiracial framework, being relegated to "Other" or subsumed under the broader category of "Chinese".

Post-1965, identification as Eurasian no longer brought particular privileges or higher status. This meant a significant shift for the Eurasian community, which did not make up one of the "founding races" or fit easily into the multiracial model. Being (literally) "othered" by the state had important consequences for the community, which was already culturally ambiguous and built on a history of hybridity. Defining "Eurasian" became increasingly difficult. Classification along patrilineal lines shifted the definition of Eurasian from mixed European and Asian, instead classifying as Eurasian those who had two Eurasian parents or a Eurasian father (Pereira 1997). "Eurasian" was seen less as mixed group in and of itself, but rather a minority ethnic group which could be classified as such. The Eurasian community was further marginalized, lacking both a distinctive identity and a claim to mixedness, adrift within a new national narrative which had little room for hybridity.

New Zealand 1980–2001: becoming bicultural and opening borders

In the 1980s, a range of far-reaching social and economic shifts occurred within New Zealand, based around neoliberal economic change and the dismantling of significant welfare systems. Against this background, debates about national identity continued, particularly in the face of persistent unequal outcomes for different groups within society, and especially the Maori population. With Maori activism gathering in strength, the emergent biculturalism of the 1970s served to reorient intergroup relations, with a number of progressive economic and social policies enacted in the 1980s which placed considerations of indigeneity at the fore (Bonilla-Silva 2000:202; Spoonley 2004).

Biculturalism as the dominant narrative of the nation grew stronger, positioning Maori and Pakeha as equal partners in nation-building. The idea of biculturalism gradually became institutionalized as a sociocultural partnership, based around shared values and institutional accountability. Theoretically, a narrative of biculturalism provided a powerful expression of united identity and (racial) inclusion. Yet, in practice, the very concept proved complex to adequately define and effectively translate into reality. Bicultural rhetoric and practice sat uneasily with the economic policies of the state, and the new orientation towards social justice and collective rights clashed with a growing focus on equity and efficiency (Larner and Spoonley 1995).

Immigration policy was also changed as part of the programme of reforms in the 1980s, counterposing allowances towards a multicultural society with a bicultural state framework. The 1987 Immigration Act removed the existing source country preferences for immigrants and aimed to attract skilled migrants to contribute to

26 *Histories of "mixed race"*

economic growth (Pearson and Ongley 1997). Further reforms facilitated immigration from Asia and transformed the character of immigration flows into New Zealand. In the 20 years following the legislative changes, immigration from Asia increased dramatically, with the Asian-born population increasing sevenfold and the Chinese ethnic group growing to become one of the largest in the country (Bedford and Ho 2008; Li 2009).

After a long history of racially restricted immigration, this new shift in immigration preference and the resultant impact on the population led to a rise in anti-immigration attitudes. Social cleavages and the precariousness of the national partnership between Maori and Pakeha became more evident, as (in)tolerance for immigration appeared to be closely linked to understandings of national identity. Illustrating Bonilla-Silva's "new racism" of the West, New Zealand's past racialized ideology resurfaced in debates surrounding immigration, multiculturalism and biculturalism, with racialized attitudes and assumptions loosely based in a language of culture rather than biology.

Immigration became increasingly politicized, drawing on a national history of racialized intolerance, aimed at different immigrant groups over time. Similar to the racism directed at Pacific Island immigrants after the Second World War, a racialized moral panic emerged in the late 1980s, as Asian immigration became a key target for political campaigning. The racialized base of anti-immigration sentiment was clear in the increasing conflation of the terms "immigrants" and "Asian immigrants". Immigration rhetoric revolved around discussions of the impacts of "Asians" on New Zealand society (ignoring immigrants from Britain and South Africa, for example), with all immigrants from the Asian region homogenized as a racial threat. The stereotypical images of antisocial behaviour, crime, isolation and lack of integration uncomfortably mirrored the concerns of immorality and corruption of one hundred years before (Palat 1996; Spoonley and Trlin 2004).

In reality, by the 1990s, the Chinese population made up 3.4 per cent of the total population and was increasingly diverse. Three distinct population groupings emerged, separating the established Chinese New Zealanders, the second-generation immigrants born to parents from abroad, and the newer immigrants who had arrived since 1987. The racialized nature of anti-immigration and anti-Asian sentiment meant that for the dominant population and in media portrayals, there was no significant differentiation between these groups, and discrimination increased for all sections of the Chinese population. For the longer established population, renewed discrimination highlighted the exclusion of the past and led to attempts at distancing from the newer immigrant population (Li 2009; Yee 2003).

In the face of continued controversy (and prior to the upcoming election), the national government introduced stricter immigration criteria. Following the 1996 election, immigration policies were relaxed for skilled migrants, a process which continued under the next Labour government. In an interesting shift, towards the end of the 1990s, the mainstream media became increasingly critical of the use of immigration as a political tool, and particularly the racialized nature of the debate. Open opposition to political anti-immigration rhetoric was found in editorials and articles by the late 1990s, and negative images began to be counterbalanced with messages of the positive economic impact and community benefits of immigration (Ng 2001; Spoonley and Trlin 2004).

Expanding the concept of race, moving towards ethnicity

In order to measure and accommodate an increasingly diverse population, state understandings of race shifted significantly in the 1980s and 1990s, laying the groundwork for a more fluid understanding of "ethnicity" rather than "race". As a reflection of this, the national census began to measure "ethnic groups"[11]. These categories were used in order to measure and assess the characteristics of community groups, as well as equity of access (and the corresponding allocation of funds) to services such as health, education and social welfare, for the Maori population in particular (Allan 2001:8; Kukutai and Didham 2009).

Two key changes marked this shift from race to ethnicity and highlighted an administrative acceptance of complex identities. From 1986, fractions were no longer used to measure racial heritage/ethnic origin in the census, and respondents were presented with a list of ethnic origin groups and asked to "tick the box or boxes that apply to you". The term "ethnic origin", with its connotation of ancestry and heritage, was abandoned in 1991, after a review suggested that respondents were becoming confused as to whether they were being asked about ancestry or cultural affiliation. "Ethnic origin" was replaced by "ethnic group" in the 1991 census, with a separate question about Maori ancestry (Statistics New Zealand 2004:22). This formal rejection of race as a meaningful marker of population differences set New Zealand apart from many other census-taking nations, although popular understandings of ethnicity varied and were often conflated with race and ancestry (Callister 2004a; Howard and Didham 2007).

Multiple, self-ascribed ethnic identities have then been explicitly measured by the national census since 1986. Over time, an increasing proportion of the population has selected multiple ethnic identifications, with fluctuations due to changed wording in the 1996 census. In 1991, 2001 and 2013, the question read: "*Which ethnic group do you belong to? Mark the box or boxes which apply to you*". The idea of multiple affiliations was much more prominent in the 1996 census, which asked: "*Tick as many circles as you need to show which ethnic group(s) you belong to*". Interestingly, this seemingly minor shift resulted in a spike in multiple responses in 1996 (up to 15.5 per cent from 4.3 per cent in 1991), which then decreased in 2001 (down to 9 per cent). This change illustrates that although multiple ethnicities are officially recognized, the choosing of multiple identities is not explicitly encouraged: the slight shift in wording in 1996 made the possibility of multiple options much more obvious, and it had such a dramatic impact on the resulting statistics that the change was reversed (Callister 2004a:120; Statistics New Zealand 2009a).

The measurement of multiple ethnicities created little controversy, but the process of recording multiple responses was more complex. Having dispensed with fractional identities, new methods of recording and simplifying data were needed. From 1986 to 1991, a system of prioritization was generally in use, reducing multiple ethnicities to one ethnicity to simplify the data. This was based on a priority coding system, which placed Maori at the top and New Zealand European/Pakeha at the bottom. However, as the multiple ethnicity population grew, this form of prioritization had a distorting effect on population statistics, leading to increasing consideration of other forms of counting[12]. These included total counts (where the total of all ethnicities would exceed the population), or a form of re-fractionalization (dividing multiple ethnicities into fractions to make each respondent count once) (Callister 2004a; Callister et al. 2006).

Measuring multiplicity has significant consequences for a national narrative of biculturalism and partnership. With increasingly blurred boundaries between identifications and groups, the underlying assumption of partnership between separate groups is harder to maintain. Measurement of Maori ethnicity in particular has practical consequences, due to ancestry-based commitments under the Treaty of Waitangi. Multiple ethnicities need to be carefully defined, taking into account the possibilities of situational ethnicities, self-prioritization, and the fact the recording multiple groups may mean identification with none of those groups entirely, but something in between (Callister and Kukutai 2009; Howard and Didham 2007). Furthermore, the very measurement of multiple ethnicities may in fact contribute to increasing identification with multiple categories, with census categories both recording and constructing social realities of individuals and groups (Callister 2004a:119).

Singapore 1980 onwards: returning to roots and Asian values

Multiracialism remained a core national narrative in Singapore post-1980, but with a shift in emphasis. As an attempt to balance Western influences and Asian heritage, the state sought to combine economic modernization with stronger cultural links. This led to a refocusing of multiracialism, seen in both policy and ideology (Barr and Skrbis 2008:92). Housing and Development Board (HDB) estates, already organized to prevent the formation of ethnic enclaves, were reorganized as a result of the 1989 ethnic integration policy. Interracial mixing in apartment allocation was enforced more firmly, through monitoring of quotas. This new policy ensured that no racial group was overrepresented, from the level of the entire estate, down to the building itself, micromanaging multiracialism and extending the reach of the government's control (Chua 1995a; Lai 1995).

In the sphere of social welfare, racial divisions became particularly important. In the absence of a universal state-provided welfare system, "self-help" groups were organized along racial and religious lines for the Malays, Chinese and Indians, based on the premise that each group would have issues best addressed by the group themselves (Kong and Yeoh 2003). MENDAKI was set up in 1981 for the Muslim population and provided with inaugural funding from the state. Originally *Majlis Pendidikan Anak-Anak Islam* (The Council of Education of Muslim Children), the group broadened its mandate to address poverty in the wider Malay community, reflecting the close associations between Malay categorization and Islamic identity. Following this, SINDA (the Singapore Indian Development Agency) and CDAC (the Chinese Development Assistance Council) were established in 1989 and 1992 respectively, providing a form of welfare for each major "racial" group (Chua 1998; Lai 1995).

The groups are funded primarily by member contributions – opt-out salary deductions for all designated members of a racial group – with some government assistance (Chua 1998; Pereira 2006). This organizational structure serves to crystallize racial boundaries and binds citizens into racial/religious groupings, while overlooking those who may not fit within the framework, such as Indian Muslims (Rahim 1998:236). While self-help groups are promoted as recognizing the importance of race for individuals and communities, they in fact reinscribe racial identities, and the accompanying assumptions of religion, custom, language and culture, onto the communities themselves. This illustrates the sometimes uncomfortable and potentially uneven outcomes of multiracial policy, which seeks to both emphasize racial differences and downplay national divisions (Moore 2000, Poon 2009).

The bilingual education system was also affected. The 1979 Goh Report both introduced educational streaming and intensified bilingual policy and had a significant impact on the meaning of race for the population (Barr and Skrbis 2008:121). In particular, the second language policy, which mandates the learning of an official "mother tongue", redefined linguistic ownership for individuals. A "natural" second language was ascribed based on patrilineal racial lines, whether or not the language was spoken within the family in question. Racial groups were understood as having a "true" racial essence, reflected in language and carried within each individual (Wee 2002).

This bilingual framework served to further essentialize racial groups and to mask significant complexities in the population. For a start, the official language for the race was frequently not the home language for families from the majority groups, who often spoke different languages or regional dialects. This effectively marginalized their actual "mother tongues" and created a linguistic hierarchy, as second language learning remained compulsory, regardless of prior knowledge. For individuals of mixed parentage, this problem also existed, as the "mother tongue" policy (like many others) generally assumed that both parents came from the same group. Hence, the language of the race of the father may not have had any resonance with their daily lives or their heritage (Chua 2003; Wee 2002).

A further dissonance between policy and reality was highlighted in the use of English. An increasing number of households spoke English as their primary language by the 1980s, including ethnically and linguistically mixed families and Eurasians. As the main language of education, and the neutral language for international and governmental communication, English could not be officially recognized as a "mother tongue". To tie it to a particular community would undermine the state narrative of neutrality and disrupt the bilingual framework of the education system. To combat the increasing everyday importance of English, the state chose to promote its bilingual framework still further, funding annual month-long

30 Histories of "mixed race"

campaigns to encourage the use of the three "mother tongue" languages (Chua 2005, Wee 2002).

Promoting Asian values and national identity

In the late 1980s and early 1990s, the emphasis on cultural heritage grew stronger. Singaporean multiracialism refocused on commonalities: using communal "Asian values" and "shared values" as a counterweight to the individualistic and material outcomes (and perceived Westernized excesses) of economic development and meritocratic policies (Hill and Lian 1995:102). With the PAP remaining in power, the leadership sought to reassure the population (particularly the Malay and Indian populations) that multiracial equality remained a founding principle of the nation. At the same time, racialized identities were increasingly promoted, as the population was encouraged to (re)discover their cultural heritage and traditional values. In reality, these "shared values" drew more from conceptions of Chinese culture than from the traditions of the remaining racial groups. The emphasis on Chinese values and Confucianism implicitly excluded minority groups and cast the ideal Singaporean as "Chinese Singaporean", subverting the initial understandings of a multiracial framework (Barr and Skrbis 2008).

Moreover, despite the confines of such a framework, intimate racial boundaries were crossed with increasing frequency in the last two decades of the twentieth century. In 1988, only 4.3 per cent of marriages under the Women's Charter and 16.4 per cent under the Muslim Law Act[13] were registered as interethnic (potentially due to the simplification of classifying children as the race of their father). By 1998, rates had climbed to 8.7 per cent and 20.0 per cent respectively, and in 2008, 13.8 per cent and 30.9 per cent (Singapore Department of Statistics 2008:7). In 2009, the numbers continued to increase, with 15.7 per cent Women's Charter and 32.8 per cent Muslim Law Act marriages classified as interethnic, or 18.4 per cent of all marriages in Singapore – almost one in five (Singapore Department of Statistics 2010b:54).

However, throughout the 1980s and 1990s, mixedness remained difficult to assert, particularly for individuals of mixed descent and for the Eurasian community. By 1980, Eurasian identity was largely excluded from dominant national narratives, not fitting easily into the multiracial model. To combat this marginalization, the Eurasian community attempted to assert its distinctiveness by recalling, consolidating, borrowing and even inventing unique aspects of culture which could then be labelled as typically and traditionally Eurasian. As a result, the government supported the community's efforts at self-definition. It co-opted the EA to act as the "self-help" group for the Eurasian community, and acknowledged the Eurasians as a distinct cultural group with official representation, both politically and symbolically (Pereira 1997, 2006). While Eurasian culture has been promoted and solidified in order to fit within the CMI(E)O framework, as for other racialized groups, the social reality of Eurasians remains much more complicated. This complexity is particularly important for a community which developed as a hybrid composition of heritages and practices and now finds itself with ascribed behaviours and identities (Pereira 1997).

Identity versus categorization: ". . . Every creed and every race, has its role and has its place."[14]

The relationship between ethnic/racial identity and categorization remains complex in modern-day Singapore. The CMIO framework is well entrenched in public and private life: almost all official forms have a section for race, and "what are you?" remains a common question in everyday interaction (PuruShotam 1998:53–54). Identities and action are closely linked to race and ethnic categorization, with the multiracial framework influencing all public institutions, from educational institutions to the press.

The continued essentialization of racial categories is also evident in the changing explanations for census categories. In the 2000 and 2010 censuses, as previously, race was not directly queried, asking instead for "ethnic/dialect group", but explaining:

> *Ethnic group refers to a person's race.* Those of mixed parentage are classified under the ethnic group of their fathers. The population is classified into the following four categories:
> Chinese: This refers to persons of Chinese origin such as Hokkiens, Teochews, Cantonese, Hakkas, Hainanese, Hockchias, Foochows, Henghuas, Shanghainese, etc.;
> Malays: This refers to persons of Malay or Indonesian origin such as Javanese, Boyanese, Bugis, etc.;
> Indians: This refers to persons of Indian, Pakistani, Bangladeshi or Sri Lankan origin such as Tamils, Malayalis, Punjabis, Bengalis, Singhalese, etc.;
> Other Ethnic Groups: This comprises all persons other than Chinese, Malays and Indians. They include Eurasians, Caucasians, Arabs, Japanese, etc.
> (Leow 2000:19, emphasis added)

The numerous racial/ethnic/dialect groups listed on the census form itself are then recategorized as above, into the CMIO groupings. In contrast to the longer explanation and disclaimers about blurring boundaries in the 1970 census, the 2000 and 2010 censuses then officially equated race and ethnicity, mirroring the colonial descriptions of race, and reinforcing the reduction of complexity.

Within this framework, individuals must therefore navigate being "raced" by a bureaucratic system, and align this administrative process to their personal experiences and construction of identity. Individuals of mixed descent are particularly affected by this tension, often being unable to identify with their allocated label, and being arbitrarily defined by phenotype. One study in 1990 suggested that some individuals resolved this tension by allowing for public and private differences and instead creating their own category of "mixed", which they used in informal settings (Siddique 1990). More public versions of CMIO subversion were noted in 1998, with individuals listing "homo sapien", "human", or simply "Singaporean" under the category of race (PuruShotam 1998).

Interestingly, in contrast to the rigidity of racial categories, everyday life and practices in Singapore are frequently multicultural, blurring official boundaries. Cultural hybridization can be seen as a marker of post-coloniality, and while uniquely Singaporean practices may not be officially acknowledged, Singaporean society has developed a *rojak*[15] everyday life culture (Chua 1995b; Velayutham 2007). Food, a particular preoccupation of the nation, is a good example of this lived hybridity. While Chinese, Indian and Malay cuisines are often essentialized and dishes attributed to distinct ethnic groups, in reality ". . . the three types of cuisines appropriate from each other, creating far greater culinary variety through hybridization" (Chua and Rajah 1997:2).

Hybridity is equally reflected in language, with *Singlish* used by much of the population: mixing English with parts of Chinese grammar and including vocabulary from Chinese, Malay, and Tamil. To the chagrin of the government, the language is often seen as a distinctive marker of Singaporean identity (Chua 2003; Ortmann 2009). Furthermore, certain lived experiences – those which are excluded from the national narratives of belonging – can be seen to form the commonality of what it means to be Singaporean. Chua (1998) stresses that shared experiences and traits are predominantly related to Singapore's economic development and political regime, including anxiety and pride, coming from a market-driven and interventionist form of capitalism and the country's economic success. Materialism is also seen as a strongly Singaporean trait by much of the population, manifested in the idea of *kiasu* – the fear of losing out to others (Ortmann 2009:35). These processes of cultural hybridization highlight both the power of the multiracial framework in Singaporean society, and its limitations in the face of growing hybridity and diversity.

New Zealand: a bicultural nation with a multicultural (mixed) people

Partly as a result of continuing immigration, the population of contemporary New Zealand is increasingly diverse: 74.0 per cent of the population identify as European, 14.9 per cent identify as Maori, 11.8 per cent of the population as Asian and 7.4 per cent as Pacific Peoples, while 11.2 per cent identify with more than one ethnic group (Statistics New Zealand 2014). With biculturalism remaining the dominant narrative and national framework for governance, the government finds itself attempting to reconcile this increasing diversity and multicultural immigration/naturalization policies with the idea of a bicultural nation based on treaty partnership (Ip 2008). The juxtaposition and coexistence of these two racial/ national projects is a key feature of present-day New Zealand politics and society. Concerns about this uneasy balance are expressed by many different groups in society: for Maori, a push towards multiculturalism and increased diversity can be seen as threatening their rights and position as the indigenous population; for Pakeha, ethnic diversity undermines the narrative of "we are all New Zealanders" which privileges Pakeha traditions and institutions; and for immigrants, new and old populations must negotiate a position between two often conflicting partners (Grbic 2010:131; Mok 2004).

Despite an official rhetoric of biculturalism and ethnicity as self-identified, relationships between ethnic groups (Maori-Pakeha in particular) continue to be labeled "race relations"[16]. This shifts the timbre of discussion away from the partnership, history and rights associated with indigeneity, towards biological characteristics of race and the assumption of individual attributes influencing socioeconomic positioning. In this context of "race relations", the government has tended to portray issues affecting Maori as separate from the rest of the population, further racializing the problem, the population and the potential solution, delineating "us" and "them" (Fraser and Kick 2000:18). This has led to resentment from both Maori and Pakeha, as Maori were seen as compartmentalized, with socioeconomic problems attributed to group shortcomings, while Pakeha resented socioeconomic assistance targeting the Maori population (Barber 2008).

Race remains a salient marker in New Zealand society in both official and popular narratives. The official understanding of self-ascribed ethnicity contrasts sharply with discussions of "race relations": seen in the existence of a Race Relations Office, the celebration of Race Relations Day and discussion of race in political rhetoric, particularly by the more conservative parties. In contrast, official data on ethnicity (potentially understood as race) is collected and utilized methodically by various government agencies, based on the rationale that socioeconomic inequality can be measured and addressed by (ethnic) group membership. Information on ethnicity is used to inform, plan and evaluate local and national government services, in order to better target policies and initiatives which focus on particular groups (Statistics New Zealand 2009a). Accompanying measurement, comparisons based on ethnicity are also common, often including statistics on crime, education and employment by ethnic group that are published in national media (Thomas and Nikora 1997:30).

Popular understandings of racially ascribed characteristics remain strong, and the ideology of bounded "racial groups" continues to exist in society and contemporary discourse (Callister and Didham 2009:63; UMR Research Limited 2009). Although skin colour and physical appearance are not officially measured by ethnicity statistics, phenotype remains a key, everyday marker of race for the majority of the population. Ethnic groups are often described by "racial" characteristics, and media discussions of Asian immigration have a serious racial dimension. Discussions of racial blood fractions can also be encountered occasionally, referring to an individual as "full-blooded", or suggesting that someone is a "half-blood" Maori, reflecting the legacy of fractional racial measurement (Cormack 2010; Thomas and Nikora 1997:30). Completely erasing the concept of race from government and social narratives of belonging has not been accomplished by replacing the word with "ethnicity". Despite an effort to acknowledge cultural affiliation, historical understandings of race and blood classification remain pervasive in the state and popular imaginary.

Measuring ethnicity

In an attempt to move away from measurements of race, Statistics New Zealand now measures ethnicity, as associated with voluntary cultural practices and beliefs:

> Ethnicity is the ethnic group or groups that people identify with or feel they belong to. Ethnicity is a measure of cultural affiliation, as opposed to race, ancestry, nationality or citizenship. Ethnicity is self perceived and people can belong to more than one ethnic group.
> (Statistics New Zealand 2005:2)

Primarily measured through the national census, ethnicity and membership in an ethnic group can be influenced by many factors, including name, ancestry, culture, location, place of birth, nationality, language, customs and religion (Statistics New Zealand 2009a).

This definition reflects an official attempt to align classificatory categories with lived realities and the changing dynamics of New Zealand society in a global context of increased individualism and human rights discourse. It focuses on self-identification for measurement, moving away from externally ascribed notions of race to better encompass the shifting, situational and often multiple aspects of ethnic identity (Keddell 2006). Classification occurs at four levels. The first level is commonly used for social science and policy-making purposes: European, Maori, Pacific Peoples, Asian, Middle Eastern/Latin American/African and Other[17]. The fourth level represents the highest level of detail, containing 233 categories describing detailed ethnic and subnational groups (Statistics New Zealand 2009b). Official ethnicity statistics are collected in New Zealand for similar reasons to countries such as the United States, the United Kingdom and Canada: to identify and address social and economic inequalities within society[18].

Importantly, official records continue to allow the selection of multiple ethnic groups, making New Zealand one of few countries to do so. While this remains domestically uncontroversial, there have been significant shifts in the way that this data is analyzed and presented since 2004. From 1986 to 1991, a system of prioritization was generally in use, reducing multiple ethnicities to one ethnicity to simplify the data, based on a priority coding system, which placed Maori at the top and New Zealand European/Pakeha at the bottom (Callister 2004a:123; Callister et al. 2006:9). The 2004 Review of the Measurement of Ethnicity highlighted the weaknesses and undercounting of minorities in this approach, replacing it with two standard outputs: total response data (individuals counted in all groups that they list) and single/combination data (counting individuals in unique categories, reflecting the mixture of their response) (Kukutai 2008; Statistics New Zealand 2004, 2009a).

As well as the question on ethnicity, the census asks for information on ancestry, but only for individuals with Maori ancestry. Collection of data on Maori descent is a requirement under the 1993 Electoral Act, and while ancestry does not require proof for the census, for resource, benefit or political claims, proof is often required (Callister 2004a:114). This difference highlights weaknesses in the official conceptualization of ethnicity, returning to the pervasive nature of race in the national narrative: self-identification of ethnicity is acceptable for national records, but proof of blood descent is required for practical outcomes. With ethnicity and Maori origin measured separately, the complexity of ethnicity/race/ancestry for individuals becomes apparent: more individuals record ancestry than identify with Maori ethnicity, and over 5,000 people identified as Maori but did not record Maori ancestry (Callister 2004a; Kukutai 2007).

Who is a "New Zealander"?

The idea of self-identified ethnicity faced an important test in the 2006 census. As a result of public debate and campaigns around ethnicity and national identity prior to the census, 429,429 people recorded "New Zealander" as their ethnicity, under the "Other" category. This represented a fivefold increase from the previous census, making "New Zealander" the third largest ethnic group in the population at 11.1 per cent (Statistics New Zealand 2009a). This was not repeated in the following census in 2013, where only 65,973 people chose "New Zealander". Analyses showed that the increase and subsequent decrease was due to "interethnic mobility", and primarily represented individuals who had been recorded in the New Zealand European category (Brown and Gray 2009:32; Statistics New Zealand 2009a, Statistics New Zealand 2014).

The debate over what it means to be a "New Zealander" is closely linked to understandings of race, illustrating the blurred boundaries between culture, race, ethnicity and nationality. The movement of individuals from the New Zealand European category reflected a long-standing discomfort with the label applied to the majority population – while stigmatized groups often attempt to change names, in this case, it is the majority population which seeks a clearer label reflecting its identity in an uncertain post-colonial setting (Grbic 2010; Liu et al. 1999). The two commonly used labels are problematic: "New Zealand European" is seen as overly reliant on links to Europe which do not exist for most people, while "Pakeha" is perceived as offensive by a section of the population who object to a non-English label and to the implied relationship with Maori[19]. Thus "New Zealander" is being substituted, merging ethnic and national identities and rejecting specific ethnic labeling. However, this move towards a civic identity does not merely suggest that "we are all New Zealanders", but rather that "some of us" are racialized New Zealanders.

Through this category, Pakeha culture and institutions are portrayed as the norm (assuming that there is a single Pakeha culture in the first place) from which "ethnic" groups deviate (Keddell 2006; Thomas and Nikora 1997). Being "just a New Zealander" becomes an option only for those who are not racially "othered". This is reflected also in the naming of state institutions, such as the "Office of Ethnic Communities" (previously Ethnic Affairs), which deals with those who are "ethnic" and distinguished from the majority population (see Gilbertson 2007; Sawicka et al. 2003).[20]

The significant increase and then decrease in "New Zealander" identifications reflected the continued importance of race in New Zealand society, in the way that ethnic groups are constructed and excluded from dominant narratives of belonging. It also highlights the limits of measurement of ethnicity as cultural affiliation, in a racialized context. While self-identification may come close to encompassing the dynamism of ethnic identity, individual and group understandings vary widely, combining aspects of identity such as culture, race, ancestry and nationality in different ways.

Hybridity, diversity and the Chinese in New Zealand

The contemporary Chinese communities in New Zealand remain divided by generational and immigration status, as immigration flows from Asia continue. While older communities are almost exclusively Cantonese from Guangdong Province in origin, newer groups have introduced significant diversity, with communities growing from Hong Kong, Taiwan and other countries in South East Asia. The vast majority of the Chinese population lives in major cities, in areas which are more likely to be diverse and to value cultural diversity (D. Ip 2011; Ng 1993).

The last country to abolish the poll tax on the Chinese in 1944, New Zealand was also the first to apologize for such exclusion. A formal apology was given by Helen Clark, the Labour prime minister in 2002 (Wong 2003:258), and a $5 million grant was provided to the Chinese Poll Tax Heritage Trust in 2005 (Department of Internal Affairs 2009). But even though legislative discrimination is no longer in place, the social context for the Chinese in New Zealand reflects a legacy of exclusion from the national narrative of belonging. Despite pronouncements that New Zealand is an Asian country, xenophobia exists throughout large sections of the population. Racially based discrimination and social perceptions of the Chinese as "undesirable aliens" continues to affect everyday life for many people. Although public perceptions may be shifting towards more positive perceptions, individuals of Asian descent are frequently regarded as "foreign" based on their physical characteristics (Asia New Zealand Foundation 2012; Human Rights Commission 2009). As in neighbouring Australia, the racialization of "Asians" is firmly entrenched in the dominant cultural imaginary, highlighting the continuing strength of race-based discourse to define and exclude the "other" (see Ang 2001).

From a broader point of view, both the established and newcomer Chinese populations sit uneasily with the national project of biculturalism. Diverse meanings of being Asian and being a New Zealander do not fit simply into this dual narrative, and this positioning as the "other" highlights unresolved tensions within biculturalism itself. Both Pakeha and Maori can perceive new (and old) immigrant communities as a threat – to Pakeha dominance and to indigenous rights respectively – with this third party allowing for the crystallization of New Zealand identity into a simplistic notion of being Pakeha versus being Maori. This in itself is highly complex, potentially portraying antagonism where it does not necessarily exist, fixing identities into polarizations which are more complex in everyday life (M. Ip 2011; Voci and Leckie 2011). Diverse Chinese communities struggle to find a visible and viable position within discussions of biculturalism, in the face of policies and agreements which focus largely on two bicultural partners (Ip 2003a; Li 2009; Spoonley 2005).

For the longer-established communities, different strategies have been adopted to deal with conflict between cultures, widespread racism and the ill-defined position of ethnic minorities within a bicultural partnership. As for all diasporic groups, "being Chinese" means a huge diversity of things, and "Chineseness" in New Zealand is under continual internal and external negotiation. Intermarriage highlights a form of integration into both the dominant Pakeha and the indigenous Maori communities. Continuing historical patterns of intermixing, increasing relationships between Maori and Chinese, and Pakeha and Chinese are being recorded, despite pressure from both sides for ethnic boundaries to be maintained (Callister et al. 2007; Ip 2008). New Zealand Chinese identities are becoming increasingly mixed, with 40 per cent of all Chinese born in New Zealand identifying with more than one ethnic group (Collins 2011; Didham 2009). As in the past, intermarriage has significant gender dimensions, with women identifying as Chinese being much more likely to have a European partner than Chinese men (Callister et al. 2007). The population of individuals identifying with both European and Chinese ethnicities is increasing, particularly for younger generations, with over 4,000 individuals over the age of 20 indicating mixed Asian/European ethnicities in 2006 (Statistics New Zealand 2006).

The future of multiracialism in Singapore: hyphenation and national identity

The national narrative of multiracialism remains central to Singaporean public policy, maintaining the visibility of race as both an essential part of cultural identity, and a potential source of conflict and division (Tan 2004). By elevating race within the private sphere and downplaying racial claims in the public sphere, the state portrays itself as neutral. It maintains the multiracial framework as a means of population control, to promote "racial harmony" and avoid "racial chauvinism". Multiracialism justifies a range of economic and social policies to promote such harmony, yet potentially leads to a constrained "racial harmony" based around simplification and stereotype (Chua 2003, 2005).

Singapore's model of cultural pluralism has then resulted in a hyphenated national narrative of sorts, through the promotion of hyphenated identities as essentially Singaporean. While the promotion of a unified national identity remains uppermost in the political considerations of the state, racial groups are not promoted equally and the benefits of development are not distributed equally, leaving Singaporean society highly racialized and divided (Barr and Skrbis 2008). Overall, many individuals remain uncomfortably situated in the dissonance between public and private identities.

In the face of this dissonance and increasingly diversity, hybridity has become a pressing issue to address. While the CMIO categories remain bureaucratically intact, the framework is showing signs of strain as boundaries shift and blur, and the category of "Other" encompasses more and more. Currently, the population is identified as 74.1 per cent Chinese, 13.4 per cent Malay, 9.2 per cent Indian and 3.3 per cent Others, and then divided into 95 ethnic and national subcategories (Neo 2010; Singapore Department of Statistics 2010a:10). For individuals of mixed descent, this framework creates a tension between personal, situational and externally imposed identities.

In an attempt to make classification more flexible, a number of changes have occurred over the past years under Prime Minister Lee Hsien Loong. In early 2010, a new policy required parents to register the race of their child at birth, but allowed "mixed" couples to register their children as the race of either parent (ending the patrilineal bias), or as Eurasian – a mix between races (Kok 2010b; Neo 2010). Shortly following this announcement, the government proposed that children of mixed descent could be registered as having "double-barrelled races", without having to select a single race (Henson 2010). This move caused significant debate, and it was further clarified that to fit within the established multiracial framework, individuals could indeed select "double-barrelled" classifications, but they must also select a primary race – the race before the hyphen.

This seemingly drastic change was thus tempered with the proviso that it was to be largely symbolic: a way to recognize hybrid identities, without allowing them to significantly disrupt the established system. In a response to the discussion generated by the change, Prime Minister Lee downplayed the shift, reassuring the media that as the majority of the population remained within singular racial groups, the numbers of those with "double-barrelled" classifications would be small (Popatial 2010).

Despite this reassurance, the idea of multiple racial classifications raised a number of concerns. For the self-help groups, this flexibility raised the question of which group would be called on to assist. Hence, the clarification that a primary race would still be mandated was welcomed, simplifying which self-help group would receive contributions and would assist if needed (see Lee 2010; Yong 2010). Changing classifications also have the potential to disrupt HDB quotas and apartment allocations. Fears that individuals of mixed descent would be able to selectively utilize different races to achieve better outcomes[21] were put to rest with the clarification that a primary race would be selected. But the question still remained: how would a primary race be selected? Parents were exhorted to carefully consider options when selecting a primary race, given the practical implications for education, language and housing.

"New" Eurasians and popular mixedness

The growing public discussions of "mixed race" and the suggestion that "Eurasian" could be used as a synonym for "mixed" brought debates about Eurasian identity to the fore. The Eurasian Association addressed the recent government moves, suggesting that the policy, combined with increasing immigration, could both increase the number of "new" Eurasians in the community and dilute the culture, or could deplete numbers, should individuals with a Eurasian parent choose to identify as non-Eurasian. The association then suggested that this could be mitigated by drawing "new" Eurasians into the community, while at the same time working to reinforce the existing culture and to retain existing members (Eurasian Association 2010). These concerns illustrate Pereira's point that although a highly distinctive Eurasian culture was created to fit within the multiracial framework, few (new) Eurasians identify with this culture, as it lacks salience in everyday life. And yet, despite this cultural construction, "Eurasian" continues to signify "mixed", both within and outside of the community: "Eurasians are natural born mixers. *It's in our blood.* We cross borders and transcend cultures naturally" (Eurasian Association 2010:7, emphasis added).

Mixedness and hybridity remained prominent in the national consciousness from 2010 to 2013, thanks to increased media coverage discussing the proposed classification changes and illustrating everyday mixedness in Singapore. Notably, a series of life stories were published in the main national newspaper just prior to National Day 2010, and again in early 2013 (see Ee 2010; Sim 2013). These stories described mixed identity through food, language and other cultural practices, stressing the possible diversity within a Singaporean identity. They linked mixedness and hybridity with the national narratives of diversity and multiracialism, highlighting the importance of national identity above all else. The individuals came from diverse backgrounds, Chinese/Indian, Japanese/Chinese, Italian/Chinese and British/Chinese, and each story raised issues which framed multiracialism, national identity and "shared values". Presenting "mixed race" in a less threatening light, and showing the "mixed" nature of Singapore as a whole, the stories discussed language and appearance, the importance of family values, heritage and national identity. The possibility of transcending race was highlighted, as was the importance of being colour-blind in everyday life and policy, reinforcing the meritocratic, multiracial framework of equality.

Symbolic recognition, practical consistency

The official change in policy came into force on 1 January 2011. As a result, parents can now classify their children as the race of either parent, as Eurasian, or as a hyphenated version of both races. As described by the ICA:

> This added flexibility of registering a double-barrelled race is in line with the Government's continual review of its policies in recognition of evolving societal changes. In this instance, we recognise that with the increasing number of inter-ethnic marriages in Singapore; the diversity of Singapore's racial demographics has accordingly also increased.
> (Immigration and Checkpoints Authority 2010)

The announcement stressed that there would not be any social or economic advantages in registering a "double-barrelled" race: as previously clarified, education and housing policy would use only the primary race, the race before the hyphen. Reinforcing the multiracial framework, the presentation of national statistics would continue to be based around the CMIO groupings, and the census would continue with a register-based approach[22]. Population statistics will therefore be published in the same format, incorporating hyphenated identities by using the first component of the "double-barrelled" race. In the first year of the policy change, only 16 per cent of children born to parents of different races were classified using the hyphenated system, with most listing the father's race as the primary race. The vast majority were instead listed as Eurasian or under a singular racial category (Tan 2012), reflecting both the newness of the system, and the ingrained nature of racial singularity in Singapore.

Despite the largely symbolic nature of the change, the official announcement emphasized the practical considerations of a "double-barrelled" identification: "Declaring or changing one's race is a serious matter that should not be taken lightly. If you are considering doing so, you will need to carefully deliberate the impact and implications of the change" (Immigration and Checkpoints Authority 2010). Further conditions were elaborated, highlighting the continued racial basis for organization, and reflecting a peculiar combination of biologically fixed and pragmatically fluid understandings of race:

1 "Double-barrelled" classification is based on ancestry, not simple social identification: individuals must have parents recorded as belonging to different races;
2 All siblings must have the same recorded race until the age of 21;
3 Children under the age of 21 must have consent of both parents to change races;
4 Singaporeans may change their race twice, by statutory declaration: once before the age of 21, and once after;
5 Changing the order of the hyphenated races counts as one change;
6 Only two races may be hyphenated – for parents of "mixed race", their children must be assigned a two-race combination of their four races. (Immigration and Checkpoints Authority 2010)

Hyphenated, mixed or unclassified?

The recent debates around "mixed race" also raised the question of the utility of racial classification in Singapore as a whole. An issue which has been raised in many census-taking countries, including the United States, the United Kingdom, Australia and New Zealand, race (or ethnicity) can be seen as a legitimate marker of belonging and a way to obtain important information about the population, or an outdated method of measurement, based along divisive notions of blood. In Singapore, the practical consequences of racial classification are much farther reaching. Certain commentators suggested that increasing intermarriage would make single-race classifications largely irrelevant, and an overt focus on race could prove disruptive to a cohesive sense of national identity (Kok 2010a). Shifting the focus away from race, emphasis could instead be placed on the nationality after the hyphen: Singaporean. This illustrates the point that growing numbers of

Singaporeans, particularly younger generations, are seeing themselves as Singaporean first, racial second. This form of identification had been particularly salient for individuals of mixed descent prior to the policy change, individuals who could not fit easily in the CMIO grid, and many of whom would describe themselves as simply Singaporean.

Despite this, official recognition of a solely Singaporean identity is not a realistic possibility in the current framework. This shift would sit outside of the CMIO categories, disrupting numerous social and economic systems. The multiracial framework and system of simplified race thinking is so deeply ingrained that non-racial classification is seen as ignoring reality, rather than accounting for changing identities: "Ethnic and cultural identities . . . are not going to disappear by doing away with it in our NRIC or providing an option for people to avoid stating their ethnicity . . . while race does not always equate to culture, it most often does. *Policy has to be based on the norm* and not the exceptions" (Law Minister K. Shanmugam, quoted in Chang 2009: emphasis added).

New Zealand: from "half-caste" to "mixed race" to "mixed ethnic identity"

In broadening the measurement of ethnicity, Statistics New Zealand has attempted to more accurately describe the multiplicity and changing nature of ethnic identities for increasing sections of the population. In the 2013 census, 11.2 per cent of the population identified with more than one ethnic group, a proportion that increased significantly for the younger generation (0–14 age group), which recorded 22.8 per cent belonging to two or more ethnic groups (Statistics New Zealand 2014). Other studies have shown even higher rates in some urban areas, where almost half of new babies are identified with more than one ethnicity (Collins 2010). Highlighting the state and socially understood break between ethnicity and ancestry, this number measures situational and temporally limited identification, given that a much greater proportion of the population could record multiple ethnic origins, or even more complex identifications. The number could be limited by the wording of the question (as seen by the discrepancy in numbers between 1991 and 1996), the tendency to simplify when filling out official surveys, a political identification with a particular group, or even the fact that ethnicity is not often requested or recorded in everyday life and is understood in different ways (Callister 2004a).

Increasing policy and social science research has been carried out in New Zealand over the past decade, exploring the identifications and characteristics of the "mixed" group, and the dual processes of constraint and acknowledgement created by the measurement of multiple ethnicities. It has been suggested that the very recognition of multiple ethnic identities encourages individual acknowledgement or even discovery of such identities, as measurement and ethnic group creation are mutually reinforcing processes. Multiple scholars stress that increasing official recognition and understandings of "mixedness" work to deconstruct limiting notions of race for both the state and society, recognizing the hybridity which characterizes evolving cultural identities in a diverse society (Callister 2003; Keddell

2006; Khawaja et al. 2007). With research exploring interactions and intermixing for individuals of Maori/Pakeha, Maori/Chinese and Pacific Island/Maori descent, conceptions of hybrid identities and dual/multiple identifications are increasingly removed from ideas of blood and ancestry and grounded in context and social interaction, strengthening the cultural affiliation understanding of ethnicity (see, for example, Ip 2008, 2009; Meredith 2000; Tupuola 2004; Ward 2006).

While the fluidity of hybrid ethnic identities is emphasized by the academic and (to some extent) the policy-making communities, wider social understandings of mixed identities as the practical outcome of mixed marriages remain fairly heavily circumscribed by notions of race. Mixed identities are seen as the product of interracial relationships, which cross socially maintained group boundaries. Among Pakeha in particular, racially based discourses remain common in describing both the relationships and the "mixed" children – using a rhetoric of concern rather than disapproval, by asking "What about the children?". Gibson (2006) found that previous notions of mixed children having "nowhere to belong" remained common, highlighting the fact that for many people, ethnic group boundaries seem rigid, even in the face of increasing discussions of hybridity.

While New Zealand maintains an innovative and potentially forward-looking method of measuring ethnic identification, this fluid categorization is sometimes constrained by the racially based framework of existing classification structures and dominant racial narratives. While individuals have the option to identify with multiple ethnicities, "mixedness" in and of itself is not explicitly recognized and is often rendered invisible in the public presentation of ethnicity data which highlights membership in bounded ethnic (racial) groups[23]. "Mixed race" is positioned within the bicultural/multicultural tension which characterizes "race relations" in New Zealand. Mixed identities for the individual can be seen as a reflection of the "mixed" nature of the state and society, with the narrative of a bicultural nation made up of two equal parts providing a macro-level depiction of a narrative of personal mixed race. This becomes more complicated at both macro and micro levels when the narrative of equal partnership and recognition is revealed to be closer to rhetoric than reality, as social and state understandings of ethnic identity remain heavily curtailed by traditional notions of race and belonging through blood.

Singapore: multiracialism, symbolic recognition and everyday hybridity

Reflecting historical processes of racial formation, identities in Singapore are bounded by a discourse of multiracialism which shapes state organization and individual practices. Drawn from a colonial past, Singapore's multiracial framework has ". . . institutionalized colonial racial identities and woven them into the fabric of political and social life to the extent that they constitute a common sense through which people conceive identities of themselves and others" (Goh and Holden 2009:2–3). The emphasis of multiracialism has shifted significantly over time, in accordance with government priorities and the particular emphasis of control. From initial narratives of national unity to concerted promotion of "Asian values", multiracialism has developed and become increasingly focused on the "racial" aspect. The management of race remains crucial in the story of Singapore, wound around ideas of descent, ancestry, belonging and blood.

While multiracialism as a racial project is based on the principle of enforcing racial equality, it has also had the practical effect of creating and reinforcing boundaries between groups through a reliance on racially based policies. Racialized communities have been imagined and commodified, simplifying culture to a few attributes of language and custom, reducing complexity to manageable traits and an inoffensive form of difference (Holden 2009; Kymlicka 2003). By focusing on such differences, and carrying over the colonial project of labelling and locating the "other", state multiracialism has depoliticized race on the one hand, and emphatically enforced its importance in the private sphere on the other. As opposed to Western versions of multiculturalism, in the multiracial model, groups are created, policed, and effectively disempowered politically, to maintain "racial harmony", equality, and state neutrality (Chua 1998:36).

Despite this rigidity, hybridity and subversion exist in Singaporean society. Cultural hybridity and personal projects of mixedness are both institutionally subversive and individually commonplace. Everyday experiences of mixedness and hybridity in interaction, intermarriage and emerging cultural practices are growing, allowing for a degree of informal identification as "Singaporean", rather than as a racialized Singaporean (Chua 1995b). Increasing numbers of individuals of mixed descent create their own labels of "mixed", while "double-barrelled" race classifications illustrate a state attempt to readjust inherited colonial structures to match an evolving reality. Nevertheless, multiracialism as ideology remains powerful at macro and micro levels, and the dissonance between political motivations for simplicity and individual experiences of complexity remains. While symbolic acknowledgement of "mixed race" brings hybridity back into the national narrative of belonging, Singapore continues to be structured as a hierarchical nation of distinctly racialized groups.

Notes

1 Sections of this chapter were published previously as: Rocha, Z. 2012b. "(Mixed) Racial Formation in Aotearoa/New Zealand: Framing Biculturalism and 'Mixed Race' through Categorization." *Kotuitui: New Zealand Journal of Social Sciences*. 7(1):1–13 (reused with the permission of the Royal Society of New Zealand) and Rocha, Z. 2012c. "Multiplicity within Singularity: Racial Categorization and Recognizing 'Mixed Race' in Singapore." *Journal of Current Southeast Asian Affairs*. 30(3):95–131.
2 By describing both countries as post-colonial, I am seeking to explore how colonialism affected identities in both countries, and how its legacy continues to affect individuals and institutions today (see Ahmed 2000; Pearson 2001).
3 *Colonialism*, as in Singapore, refers to a situation in which the colonial power relied on both the acquisition of land and the subjugation of peoples, prior to post-colonialism, leaving "newly independent states from which the colonial powers by and large 'went home'" (Prentice and Devadas 2008:1). *Settler colonialism*, as in New Zealand, describes a situation where the land was primarily desired, and the colonial power sought "the reproduction of one's own people through far settlement" (Belich 2009). Hence, in this post-(settler)-colonial experience, the colonial power remained, only now becoming part of the independent nation.

44   Histories of "mixed race"

4   A commonly used term to describe New Zealanders of European descent (the numerical majority). While frequently used by Maori and many Pakeha, the term is not without controversy, and it is rejected as discriminatory by some groups of European descent (see Bell 1996).
5   The Peranakans provide a good example of this complexity, as an ethnic group which traced its descent from seventeenth-century Chinese migrants who married local women in Southeast Asia (Beng 1993; Stokes-Rees 2007).
6   In keeping with the European understanding of racial hierarchy, much intermixing (particularly inter-Asian intermixing, such as the Peranakans) was left unrecorded and unremarked.
7   As stated on the census form: "If of *full* European descent, no matter where born, tick box" and "If you are a person of the Maori race, *or a descendent of such a person*, tick box" [emphasis added]. This wording reflects the 1974 Maori Amendment Act which defined as Maori a person of (any) Maori descent (Cormack 2010:14).
8   Although this definition was used for "race" in the 1931 report, rather than "ethnic/dialect group", showing both the pre-/post-colonial continuities and linguistic shifts.
9   This contradiction can be seen particularly in the example of the Malay community, as a marginalized group which remained on the periphery despite theories of equal opportunity and meritocracy (see Barr and Skrbis 2008; Rahim 1998).
10 "Mother tongue" is defined very particularly in this case, with interesting gendered implications: it is not the language first spoken with the mother, but rather, the official language of the assigned racial group, as determined by the father (Chua 2003:61; Wee 2002:285).
11 The national census shifted decisively away from race-based measurements to "cultural affiliation" and self-identification based on ethnicity following a 1983 research report. This Department of Statistics report showed that respondents were answering based on self-identification rather than racial ancestry, that increasing numbers of people questioned the validity of race, and that demographic change and intermarriage within the population meant that attempting to demarcate discrete racial groups had limited value (Allan 2001; Statistics New Zealand 2009a:9).
12 Although ethnic prioritization is no longer recommended for researchers and policy makers, it is still often used in the health research community, given its mathematical simplicity and ability to be used with previous data sets (Didham and Callister 2012).
13 Marriages in Singapore can be formalized either under the 1961 Women's Charter, or the Muslim Law Act of 1966. Sharing religious affiliation as Muslim has proved important as a factor in intermarriage, going some way to explaining why the proportion of interethnic Muslim Law marriages remains higher.
14 Lyrics from the 1994 National Day song, cited by PuruShotam 1998:53.
15 Malay for "mixture", and a popular mixed fruit and vegetable dish in Malaysia and Singapore.
16 This is also reflected in official discussions of "race-based" social policies, and the position of the Race Relations Commissioner in the Human Rights Commission (Callister and Didham 2009:63–64)
17 Statistics New Zealand notes that: "Although the ethnicity question is based on subjective self-identification, it's notable that 'New Zealand European' appears to be based on a concept of descent from European ancestors. In fact, all the response categories are legacies of previous race- and ancestry-based measures. Keeping them largely reflects a need to keep the measurement consistent and continuous through time" (Statistics New Zealand 2009a:10).
18 However, following the 2004/5 Mallard Review of Targeted Programmes, funding and programmes aimed along ethnic lines were reduced, shifting the focus for many sectors to need, not "race" (Cormack 2010:8; Mallard 2004).
19 There are also those who believe that the term is an offensive word in Maori (flea or pig), a theory which is contested by many scholars (see Bell 1996; Callister 2004b).

20 Interestingly, as in the United States, there is increasing research and questioning of what it means to be Pakeha, or white, and "non-ethnic", in the New Zealand context (see, for example, Pearson 2001; Gray et al. 2013.). Working to untangle questions of privilege, history and ethnicity/race, this research draws out the ways in which ethnic identification and associations around race may not always match up, and the ways that "whiteness" plays out in individual lives.
21 This is an interesting reflection of the continued discomfort and fear about "mixed race".
22 Personal communication, Statistician in Income, Expenditure and Population Statistics Division, Department of Statistics, 2011.
23 Personal communication, Kukutai 2009.

3 The personal in the political[1]

In everyday life, the legacies of race and racial classification are powerful. Race, with its reliance on the body, highlights the fact of phenotypical difference and brings with it the assumptions and hierarchies pertaining to that difference. However, context is key in the development of "mixed" identities. The sociohistorical context of majority and minority groups frames the positioning and ethnic options available to individuals of "mixed" descent, locating identities between forms of symbolic and reinforced ethnic and racial identities (Alba 1990; Gans 1979; Waters 1989). This interaction can be explored by looking at public and private identities, through the relationship between classification and identity.

Narratives exist across multiple levels, from the individual to the family, the community, and the nation. "Being mixed" takes numerous forms, across public and private spheres, macro, meso and micro levels. At the macro level of the state and public classifications, the complex and contextualized experiences of identity begin to emerge. Individual narratives and racial projects illustrate the multitude of ways in which mixedness is imagined and practised in daily life, challenging abstract theories of "mixed race" which cast identities as easily defined categories. Personal narratives are intricate and occasionally contradictory, as individuals located themselves in context. Narratives illustrate accommodation, subversion, reinforcement and transcendence, but not always in easily separable ways. The personal stories in this book were told and shaped within wider national narratives of belonging, but also worked to resist and reshape these very narratives.

Forty men and women shared their stories to make up this book: twenty in New Zealand, and twenty in Singapore, ranging from 19 to 64 years old. A summary of the interview participants is detailed in table 3.1 below.

Questions of classification

As a prominent expression of macro narratives of racial formation, racial categorizations framed personal stories. While identity is more intimately influenced by family and community relationships, these interactions are themselves

Table 3.1 Narrative participants

Singaporean (SG) group

Name[1]	Age	M/F	Location	Occupation	Mother[2]	Father
Amber Smith	19	F	Australia	Student	Singaporean Chinese	Anglo Australian
Sara Madeira	20	F	Singapore	Trainee customer service officer	Peranakan Chinese	Portuguese Eurasian
William Briggs	21	M	UK	Student	Singaporean Chinese	English
Richard Ong	22	M	Singapore	National serviceman	Singaporean Chinese	Anglo Australian
Susann Nasser	23	F	Singapore	Student	German	Indonesian Chinese
Skye Sia	23	F	Singapore	Student	Eurasian	Singaporean Chinese
Celine Chin	24	F	Switzerland	Intern	French	Singaporean Chinese
James Field	25	M	USA	Student/ company director	Singaporean Chinese	Anglo Australian
Terence Peaks	26	M	Singapore	Military instructor	Filipino Chinese	Anglo Australian
Katrina Henry	27	F	UK	Doctor	Singaporean Chinese	English
Alison Lijuan	27	F	Holland	Student	Russian Chinese/ Japanese	Hong Kong Chinese
Anne McNeil	27	F	Singapore	Teacher	Singaporean Chinese	British
Safiyah Matthews	28	F	Singapore	Librarian	Singaporean Chinese	New Zealand European
Alastair Jenkins	30	M	Singapore	Research engineer	Singaporean Chinese	Anglo Australian
Jeanne Goh	30	F	Singapore	Designer/ retail manager	French	Singaporean Chinese
Hannah Alley	33	F	Singapore	Trainer	Singaporean Chinese	Welsh
Sandra Pereira-Ivansson	36	F	Sweden	Account manager/ research fellow	Hakka/ Peranakan Chinese	Chinese and Portuguese
Andrew Wang-Jones	36	M	Singapore	PR executive	English and German	Eurasian
Francine Phillippe	37	F	Singapore	Administrator	Sikh/ Chinese	Eurasian
David Faulkner	64	M	Singapore	Airline pilot	Singaporean Chinese	White British

(Continued)

Table 3.1 (Continued)

New Zealand (NZ) group

Name	Age	M/F	Location	Occupation	Mother	Father
Angelina Ng	19	F	Auckland	Student	Pakeha New Zealander	Chinese New Zealander
Pamela McLane	20	F	Dunedin	Student	Singaporean Chinese	Pakeha/ Fijian/ Japanese
Andrea Wei	21	F	Auckland	Student/ coordinator	White American	American Chinese
Li Lin Zhen	22	F	Auckland	Student/ fashion designer	Pakeha New Zealander	Fijian Chinese
Rose Stein	22	F	Auckland	Student	Hong Kong Chinese	Dutch
Katie Murray	24	F	Wellington	Engineer	Malaysian Chinese	Scottish
Joel Andrews	24	M	Wellington	Doctor/artist	Chinese New Zealander	Pakeha New Zealander
Jacob Roberts	24	M	Auckland	Finance consultant	Malaysian Chinese	Pakeha New Zealander
Jenny Griffiths	25	F	Auckland	Nurse	Pakeha New Zealander	Chinese New Zealander
Jasmine Orana	25	F	Auckland	Violinist	Singaporean Chinese	Pakeha New Zealander
Melanie Townsend	30	F	China	Creative director	Taiwan Chinese	Pakeha New Zealander
Tai Feng	31	M	China	Teacher	Irish	Malaysian Chinese
Emmeline Tan	32	F	UK	Freelance designer	Pakeha New Zealander	Singaporean Chinese
Alexis Conrad	33	F	Auckland	Chartered accountant	Chinese New Zealander	New Zealand European
Nadine Moore	34	F	Wellington	Finance administrator (part time)	Pakeha New Zealander	Malaysian Chinese
Margaret Jenkins	35	F	Wellington	Immigration technical advisor	American Chinese	Pakeha New Zealander
Philippa Warner	38	F	Auckland	Physiotherapist (part time)	Pakeha New Zealander	Chinese New Zealander
Jason De Vries	39	M	Australia	Architectural draftsperson	Pakeha New Zealander	Chinese New Zealander
Nathan Fleming	39	M	Wellington	Entrepreneur	American Chinese	Pakeha New Zealander
Paul Moretti	48	M	Auckland	Executive	Chinese	Italian

[1] All names were changed, but the pseudonyms attempt to capture the cultural connotations of the original name, for example, Chinese first name and French last name.
[2] Parental designations are as given by the participant.

developed within the broader social and political milieu, as framed by classification. Questions of official classification were prominent in many narratives. Public discourse around race, ethnicity and belonging centred around categorization and form filling, shaping the way in which participants saw and described themselves (Katz 2012, Maré 2001). While the systems and histories of racial classification differ in Singapore and New Zealand, classification played an important role in both contexts, reflected in the labels people chose to use, avoid and invent.

For the Singaporean participants, race and racial classification loomed large in their everyday lives. In the Singaporean census, which lists a number of ethnic/dialect groups, as well as "Eurasian" and "Others", two thirds of interview participants chose "Eurasian" (see figure 3.1). However, the complexities around classification and lived reality, and particularly the term "Eurasian", came through more clearly in individual stories.

5. Ethnic/Dialect Group
- ☐ Hokkien
- ☐ Teochew
- ☐ Cantonese
- ☐ Hakka (Khek)
- ☐ Hainanese
- ☐ Others, pls specify _____
- ☐ Malay
- ☐ Javanese
- ☐ Boyanese
- ☐ Tamil
- ☐ Sikh
- ☐ Caucasian
- ☐ Filipino
- ☐ Eurasian
- ☐ Vietnamese
- ☐ Japanese

Figure 3.1 Singapore 2010 census question

A very present form of classification was the race listed on their identity cards (NRIC or IC), which did not always correspond to how they perceived themselves, nor to how they classified themselves on the census. One participant rebelled against the Caucasian classification on his IC, insisting to his friends that he was Chinese.

> Race, yeah, I don't know.
> On my card, it says I'm Caucasian.
> Which kind of sucks, like, can't I just be like both, Eurasian . . .
> but I had to follow what my dad is.
> And I used to get made fun of,
> because I would always pretend to be like, "guys, I'm all, I'm so Chinese",
> but they would just, all the local Singaporeans would just laugh at me [laughs].
> "No – it's not true", "oh okay, okay . . . maybe not entirely, but . . ."
> Race is not, well, I never thought it was that important to be honest.

But, I guess, because they ask for your race in Singapore, it means something.
[pause]
Which maybe isn't the same in London.
Like my European side, they don't really ask this kind of stuff.
I recently filled out a census form here [in the UK].
They have insane amounts of race, like, tick boxes.
It's like they spell it out for you, everything.
And I found it, it was more, it was easier to do here.
Than in Singapore.
Because they really, they just condense to like one . . .
I don't know.
Maybe, maybe Singapore should start considering, you know, stretching out the categories.

(William Briggs, SG, 21, male, Singaporean Chinese/English)

William's personal subversion of his official label was a way to assert his feelings of belonging, despite this claim not being recognized by his peers. The amused (and possible bemused) reaction of his friends highlighted the strength of racialized boundaries at both state and community levels. Although he mentioned this form of dislocation with a laugh, his concern with race and fitting in (to both boxes and social groups) and his use of "pretend" illustrated the importance of racial belonging to him, combining his subversion with a belief in distinct racial categories and stories of reinforcement. The dissonance between personal complexity and singular categorization became more apparent to him after leaving Singapore for London. The lack of flexibility in Singapore was particularly noticeable as he filled out the UK census, which allows for the selection of multiple ethnic groups. He found that he could fit himself more easily into multiple categories, rather than the singular selection available in Singapore, calling into question the rigidity of the Singaporean framework.

By way of contrast, a second participant was happy to have a singular racial category to identify with. As a child, Alison had always assumed she was Chinese, and was told only as a teenager of her mixed ancestry. The news of her ancestry was a shock for her, almost revealing a dark family secret. The knowledge of the potential for a complex racial identity had a significant effect on her, and she felt strongly that simple classification was better, reinforcing the CMIO framework in her personal life. The patrilineal rules of racial categorization were a relief for her, providing her with a simple way to classify herself, to not be highlighted as different.

Well, I never questioned. I always put Chinese.
Um, until my mum told me, and my sister . . .
then I knew.
But then I also looked up online,

I think I was applying for the identification card, that kind of the thing.
I think it says somewhere like if your father is Chinese, you just put Chinese.
So, yeah. I'm glad they made it easy for me.
I don't want to have to, on the form, think about what I have to fill in.
So, I just put Chinese, yeah.
And, I have a Chinese name, and I guess I look,
I think I look mostly Chinese, anyway, so . . .
I don't, I wouldn't want too many people asking so "what is Others?"
and "what Others do you mean?"
And that Others term is something that I would never want to fill in with.
It's a weird category.
Like, a alien, it's just not, not human or something,
I don't know, it's really strange.
I mean they can also do the same, like in the States, where they have tons of categories about,
I don't know,
what you are.
But . . . I guess Singapore, they decided to make it easy
and just put everything under the Chinese, Malay and Indian or Others.
Save time and space on the paper.

(Alison Lijuan, SG, 27, female, Russian Chinese
and Japanese/Hong Kong Chinese)

In contrast to the previous narrative, she saw the simplicity of Singapore's system as positive, allowing mixedness to be easily concealed. This reinforcement continued in her distaste for the category of "Other", which went against the neat categories, and to her, seemed a non-defined, or non-human (by being non-racial) category.

As well as seeking to assert mixedness or to overlook mixed heritage, some participants focused on "Eurasian" as a term that was both inclusive and exclusive. Eurasian provides a separately racialized category which encompasses a multitude of backgrounds and experiences (see, for example, Choo et al. 2007; Dickens 2010; Zimmern 2010). Participants used the term in both a casual sense to describe mixed ancestry, and in a more precise way, to illustrate the category of Eurasian within the government's classificatory framework. Some participants were very aware of the historical meaning of Eurasian in Singapore, and the essentialization of a distinct Eurasian identity within a racial framework.

Like I said, on my IC it's written Chinese.
I can't say I'm Eurasian because . . .
(although I am Eurasian)
because the term Eurasian defines the person half/half, Europe and Asian, right?
But in Singapore if you're Eurasian, it's not even what I am.
Because that group of people, that doesn't describe the kind of mix that I am.

So I can't really, that doesn't apply to me as well.
I'm not pure Chinese.
But it's written Chinese because I have a Chinese name after my father.

(Jeanne Goh, SG, 30, female, French/Singaporean Chinese)

For Jeanne, Eurasian was another racial category into which she did not easily fit. She highlighted her classification as Chinese, despite not being "pure Chinese", and her ancestry as European and Asian, although she didn't fit into Eurasian. The race of her father simplified her categorization, but left her personal identity at odds with her official label. Her narrative reflects accommodation around the term *Eurasian*, as she worked to accommodate the racial framework with a public/private divide.

Another woman focused on the private meaning of the term, and saw Eurasian as a distinct racial category for herself, and one with very precise boundaries. She described discovering the term as a young woman, and how this new label provided her with a sense of identification and belonging, as well as kindling an interest in racial heritage.

I think like when I was younger I just thought of myself as nothing.
Um, because um, yeah, I didn't discover Eurasian until year 9 [age 14].
Um, so until then, I guess I didn't really think about it, and um, it was sort of just nothing to me.
Like, I didn't acknowledge it like . . . um, I don't know. I guess I just didn't really think about it, and like . . .
But then, when I heard the term, like it was sort of all I thought about. Um, I guess.
I guess like when I was younger I wasn't interested in race and all that, but as I became older, like now I'm totally interested in it.
Yeah, like I guess, one of the things um, like when people are telling me a story, they're like "oh my friend like did this", and I'm like "what race were they?".
And, I don't know. It's sort of like, really like, I'm really interested in it now.

(Amber Smith, SG, 19, female, Singaporean Chinese/Anglo Australian)

For Amber, the term *Eurasian* referred to a particular biological combination, which was exclusively Asian and European. She saw Eurasian-ness in simultaneously personal and sweeping terms, as an important marker of personal identity, and a form of identification that could exist anywhere in the world, based on the assumption of the existence of separate races. The label enabled her to be more than "nothing", giving her a racial category in which to belong.

Others, however, saw Eurasian as a way to subvert singular racial categories, a form of recognizing mixedness (perhaps unintentionally) through the state framework. Richard used categorization to acknowledge personal mixedness, pushing for a Eurasian label to encompass both sides of his heritage. He utilized the category as a way to accommodate his feelings of belonging, while staying within the defined framework. His story of persuading a government official to change his assignment shows how he subverted expectations through humour, but also reflects a serious point: the power of external perceptions in reinforcing a racialized framework.

> Well, I'm proud to have Eurasian on my IC.
> 'Cause ah, back then when they gave me my IC at first, it said Chinese.
> And I was like "no, I'm not Chinese, can you change it?".
> And the lady looked at me and was "are you sure? Are you sure you're not Chinese?" and I was like "yeah, I think I am" [laughs].
> (Richard Ong, SG, 22, male, Singaporean Chinese/Anglo Australian)

For some, the distinction between the historical understanding of Eurasian in Singapore and the "new Eurasians" (those with one European and one Asian parent) heavily influenced their identification with Eurasian as a personal identity label, and as an administrative category. One man was not aware of the older meaning of Eurasian in Singaporean society, something which he discovered when he was taught about different cultures in Singapore during national service.

> I only realized that they had a really strong Eurasian community in national service, when they started like teaching everybody about, like cultures in Singapore.
> And apparently we have, Eurasians have special food [laughs], special games and all this kind of stuff.
> I was just kind of like, "I've never experienced that", and everyone starts looking at me like "really?".
> I don't think so [laughs].
> I don't recall this ever growing up.
> (William Briggs, SG, 21, male, Singaporean Chinese/English)

Although he had realized that his Eurasian experience did not include the cultural markers described as typically Eurasian, William did not make a distinction between the two definitions. Illustrating the shifting meaning of the term, he inferred a kind of commonality in being Eurasian, referring to all Eurasians as "we". For many others, however, the historical meaning of Eurasian meant that their personal experiences of mixedness did not automatically lead to identification with the community.

> I never really felt myself as a Eurasian in that sense. Yeah.
> Yeah. And when I first was contacted by the Eurasian Association, in Singapore,
> I mean, we looked through it, but I don't see a connection.
> Because . . . the, the Association was created by Eurasians,

> it was like second, third generation Eurasians who have been in Singapore for, for, at least 50, 60 years or more.
> And . . . it, they, it's different.
> And I guess the other problem is that Eurasian is a very vague term.
> Right? You are talking about Asian and . . .
> I mean, in your study, you're talking about Chinese and European, but in general the definition is more loose than that.
> You have Malays, Indians . . . and . . . and . . .
> So, the culture is also very different.
> So when I look at it, I read about it, it's like, yeah it's interesting,
> it's history, part of Singapore, but I, I don't relate with them.
>
> (Alastair Jenkins, SG, 30, male, Singaporean Chinese/Anglo Australian)

The oldest participant also described how this dissonance had existed prior to independence, recounting how Eurasian culture was significantly different to the cultures of his British father and Chinese mother.

> In fact, more often than not you would mix around with Eurasians – we call it the Portuguese Eurasians, the dark-skinned Pereiras and all that.
> And there was a difference, you know, it was . . . because they had a different culture,
> a significantly different culture from us and we didn't feel left out.
> We didn't, no, we didn't . . . don't . . .
> don't feel we were left out but it was not somebody you could have a close relationship with, you know,
> like an understanding of the culture,
> you have to start learning what their culture is.
> So my association with them would be just as good as a Chinese.
> That means I couldn't associate with both sides,
> like Chinese, Indian, whatever, Malays – doesn't make a difference.
> I did not feel a close affinity to the Eurasian community at that time.
> That's it.
>
> (David Faulkner, SG, 64, male, Singaporean Chinese/White British)

For David, Eurasian was another ethnic group from which he was excluded, as a result of being from a mixed family. His mention of Portuguese descent and "dark-skinned" also highlighted an important aspect of Eurasian identity – the divisions within the historical community along lines of colour and class. Several participants commented on these divisions as having existed in the past, particularly under British colonial rule, and having carried over to the present. One woman, Francine, described how "uppity" Eurasians would look down on those with darker skin, while another man used the terminology "upper ten and lower six" to elaborate on the intra-community divisions.

> I don't know what the upper ten and lower six, what the numbers mean exactly, but it's always been this phrase: "Ah, he or she is upper ten".
> Among the Eurasian community, upper tens refer to the fairer Eurasians.
> Those who have an Asian parent and have a European parent of fair descent so to speak, like Dutch, British, American, could be French, like Jeanne's case.
> And the lower six are those from, tend to be more tanned, those with more darker skin. I have trouble even saying that, like those who are tanned, and more darker, like the Portuguese Eurasians.
> Sometimes they even mistake them for Indians or Malays.
> And you find some Portuguese Eurasians in Singapore, of Portuguese descent, they also have Malay and Indian lineage. They take on Indian surnames.
> You find in the Eurasian community, they are Eurasians, but they're Muslims, or of Malay Muslim parents. So those are the lower six.
> In fact, within the Eurasian community, they are very fractious because of the upper ten and lower six distinction.
>
> (Andrew Wang-Jones, SG, 36, male, English and German/Eurasian)

Hence, despite having roots in hybridity, the administrative aspect of being Eurasian has defined cultural boundaries and it has developed sub-distinctions, creating a newly racialized (and even hierarchical) category. The present-day Eurasian Association has attempted to address this, in the face of dwindling membership. As a result, the term has been administratively broadened, drawing on the resurgence of the community in the 1980s, something Terence, Alastair and David commented on.

> 'Cause I mean, Eurasian is a very, Eurasian is a very broad term.
> And it's only recently that they, I think, made it more encompassing, ah.
> I think, it's more like, it's not like a specific domain or definition of people, it's more like an umbrella grouping now.
> Like, anyone . . . when you think about it, anyone can be Eurasian, ah.
> Yeah, so . . . it's a funny thing . . . me and my sister received an award from NUS, and they said "oh, yeah, you're, you're Eurasian", you know . . . "sure. . . ."
> I think because it's more, it's more loose, the term is more loose now, that it makes it easier to loosen things.
> 'Cause you're more inclusive as opposed to exclusive, ah.
> Most racial groups in Singapore, like, SINDA, MENDAKI, I think the tendency now is for them to become more inclusive.
> 'Cause, they like, if you don't become inclusive, you never grow, lah.
> If you grow means, if you grow means government gives you more money, lah.
> Gives you, 'cause you're addressing more, a larger group, ah.
>
> (Terence Peaks, SG, 26, male, Filipino Chinese/Anglo Australian)

Terence positions the association within the bureaucratic aspect of racialized groupings, noting the ways in which definitions of race can be used to access funding and resources. His narrative points to racial categories and groupings as largely constructed, broadening definitions as a way of becoming more inclusive. He accommodated his own mixedness and positioning within this framework of wider self-interest: recognizing the arbitrary nature of racial boundaries, but equally the administrative pervasiveness (and possible utility) of such boundaries.

Eurasian had a deeper symbolic meaning for some. For Amber, the acknowledgement of mixedness implicit in the term *Eurasian* was an important form of identity in itself. The category was repurposed, and re-racialized, as another group with clearly defined boundaries.

> I never tried to like fit into one or the other.
> Like, 'cause I notice that some . . .
> Like, back when *MySpace* was popular, you know it had the ethnicity drop-down menu.
> Um, I noticed like that one of my Eurasian friends then put "Asian".
> And that, I don't know, that really upset me.
> I didn't feel like . . .
> I never really like it when Eurasians sort of, classify themselves as one or the other.
> Because I feel like, really I'd like to have Eurasian as a recognizable third identity.
>
> (Amber Smith, SG, 19, female, Singaporean Chinese/Anglo Australian)

For her, denial of this identity was seen as a form of betrayal, choosing sides in choosing one racial identity over the other. As before, Amber used Eurasian as a broader, globalized term to describe a new form of identity, in effect racializing mixedness and creating a new race from component races. Her narrative highlights an interesting combination of both subversion and reinforcement: subverting singular racial narratives, but at the same time, promoting belonging in a single group as defined by racial background.

This subversive reinforcement was seen in another participant's attitude towards the new "double-barrelled" racial labels. He saw the recent shift towards hyphenation as divisive and unnecessary, pushing against greater fluidity or options for identification. For him, reinforcing the importance of race, a person is either Eurasian, or is not. Having grown up against a background where the CMIO framework was reinforced through the promotion of separate self-help groups and communities, his narrative centred around clearly defined racial groups. Further specification for him instead served to separate rather than acknowledge identity.

> Now, recently they came out with the double-barrelled thing.
> Which I think that's a bit rubbish, because you start segregating within the . . . if you're Eurasian, you're Eurasian, if not . . .

What's the point?
It's like taking the Chinese and separating them within the dialects, which . . . for a society which continually talks about cohesion, they are separating them even further.
So, I think I would like . . .
my IC says Eurasian and I'm fine with that. I wouldn't change it, anyway.

(Richard Ong, SG, 22, male,
Singaporean Chinese/Anglo Australian)

Eurasian then provided an interesting space in which participants in Singapore could manoeuvre. For some, the implications of a bounded, culturally specific Eurasian community provided another form of exclusion from a racialized framework. Yet for others, Eurasian could be repurposed into its component terms of European and Asian, allowing an acknowledgement of mixedness that could be accommodated within the state framework, even without identifying with the Eurasian community as a whole. Overall, in Singapore, classification was widely felt. Participants worked to accommodate their stories of mixedness in many different ways, sometimes deliberately subverting narratives of singularity, or even reinforcing existing classification structures through their own identifications.

Although classification formed a part of participants' narratives in New Zealand, the less pervasive nature of official classification meant that individuals were not always as aware of the officially available categories. The flexibility of the New Zealand system meant that individuals were able to select as many groups as they wished in the census, to better describe their identities and ancestries. Just over half of participants selected both European and Chinese, while the remainder selected "Other" and filled in the blank (see figure 3.2).

Figure 3.2 New Zealand 2006 census question

58 The personal in the political

Nevertheless, some found the categories themselves restrictive, particularly "New Zealand European", which implies a link to Europe. Reflecting the dominant nature of whiteness and "European" ethnicity in New Zealand, the link to Europe was seen as unnecessary, classifying New Zealander as unproblematically white. One woman clarified that whiteness was normal, and by default, all other groups were abnormal, in an interesting narrative of reinforcement. This unnoticed discussion of normality and racialized culture highlighted the lingering effects of racial categories, despite the flexibility of current categorizations.

While many participants saw race as unimportant in New Zealand society, not all were in agreement. One woman saw the hidden importance of race as a social construct that singled out minority groups.

> I don't know, I think it's kind of a social construct, and . . .
> I feel like . . . it's hard like, 'cause I feel like race only applies to like minorities, kind of.
> In New Zealand especially.
> Like if you're white, you're not a race.
> 'Cause there's . . . like if you're from Sweden or Germany or whatever, that you look the same, and people don't,
> they're not like "oh, where are you from?" you know?
> (Angelina Ng, NZ, 19, female, Pakeha New Zealander/Chinese New Zealander)

Another woman stressed the primacy of race, ethnicity and belonging, as a result of the public discourses of indigeneity and what it means to be a New Zealander.

> I mean, society uses that as an identifier right,
> so you're inevitably kind of plopped into a category, based on your race.
> I mean, during the time I lived in New Zealand, I didn't really feel that,
> but, in hindsight, and also talking to people, unfortunately New Zealand can be quite a discriminating country.
> Yeah. Yup, it's a bit unfortunate, but . . .
> I think also because, you know, the whole Maori identity is so, just pumped up and, and, you know, they feel a sense of privilege from that.
> So, that raises everybody's awareness of race. And ethnicity, I suppose.
> And, and, I don't know, maybe it's a result of that.
> So people really feel like they need to identify, with a certain race or ethnicity.
> (Melanie Townsend, NZ, 30, female, Taiwan Chinese/Pakeha New Zealander)

Melanie linked the dominant discussions between Maori and Pakeha to the racialization of other immigrant groups, emphasizing the roles of race and racism in discussions of national identity. Her questioning of race as an identifier suggested a form of transcendence, as she implied that national identity should not necessarily be predicated on racial belonging.

In both countries, participants were clear that official classifications of race simplified their more complex backgrounds into categories of convenience. One unexpected finding was how this simplification related to the categories used as part of this research, which focused on individuals with one Chinese and one European parent. Individuals defined "Chinese" and "European" for their parents in many different ways, and these categories did not accurately describe the ethnic, cultural and ancestral complexity of many family backgrounds. One man detailed his mother's background as predominantly European, but stressed that in Singapore, she is classified as Eurasian, having been born and brought up in Singapore.

> So my mother is actually, you could say predominantly, half English, half German.
> But she is considered Eurasian, because she's never been to Europe.
> So that's pretty odd.
> But in terms of . . . ethnicity, one would put it, she really doesn't have any Asian blood.
> I think there's a smattering, further up the line.
> I have really asked questions as to what this is,
> but when you look at my mother, she looks white.
> Although she is a true-blue Singaporean, quite Singlish, but speaks good plain English.
>
> (Andrew Wang-Jones, SG, 36, male, English and German/Eurasian)

One woman in New Zealand highlighted how the label of Chinese for her mother didn't fit easily with her mother's cultural background, as she was adopted by a European family. She stressed that the expected links between language, heritage and culture did not always apply, as her Chinese mother did not speak Chinese, while her Dutch father did.

> My mum is Chinese, she was brought up in Hong Kong.
> She's ethnically Chinese but she was adopted by an English and Irish couple.
> But they really wanted to impress upon her, her Chinese culture, by giving her Chinese lessons and stuff.
> That didn't quite stick [laughs].
> And my father is Dutch.
> He was born in Indonesia though.
> Yeah, and he, he speaks Cantonese.
> Yeah. So language is a bit weird for either parent.
>
> (Rose Stein, NZ, 22, female, Hong Kong Chinese/Dutch)

These descriptions show the dissonance between categories and lived reality, and the ways in which participants appropriated outside classifications to define the ancestries of their parents in meaningful ways. Their narratives encompassed complications and mixed heritage as everyday, unremarkable facts, reflecting the diversity of their experiences. Importantly, even a book on mixedness such as this can overlook the lived aspects of such complexity, using labels and categories that may have little meaning in everyday life.

Racialized categories became apparent when participants discussed their own feelings of identity, as the gap between social and state labels and personal reality came to the fore. This was particularly pointed for the Singaporean participants, who negotiated their sense of being "mixed" within pervasive categorization – on identity cards, at school, in the census. For some participants, labels had an impact on their lives and the way they had learned to describe themselves, but they were also able to make a clear distinction between public and private forms of identification. For one man, despite being labeled as Caucasian, he made a point of emphasizing his Chinese heritage, subverting expectations. Race categories were an administrative requirement, not a definition of identity, as he asserted a public/private divide.

> I was always labeled as Caucasian. That was it.
> But I'd always tell everyone I was Chinese [laughs].
> So, yeah.
> I don't know, it doesn't mean much to me to be honest.
> I wouldn't say it's a big deal.
> Mainly because it hasn't . . . I don't know.
> It's never been a massive deal to me.
> Like in Singapore, maybe to them, they would say,
> they would try and get race out of me,
> but I would never ask someone.
> Or it would never be important to me.
> They can say that, it was on my ID card that [laughs] um, Caucasian, whatever.
> Um, I mean it's not like I'm not, anyway.
> But obviously, it's . . . whatever.
> Whatever anyone wants to label me.
> 			(William Briggs, SG, 21, male, Singaporean Chinese/English)

For another participant, her personal feelings of mixedness overrode her classification as Chinese.

> I mean, it's fine to be classified under mixed . . .
> And I think being Eurasian is fine.
> Listing that category or the Others category. Yeah.
> But I mean, when filling out forms and stuff,
> I just instinctively tick Chinese, because it's stated Chinese on my IC.
> Yeah, because back then Singapore hasn't had the rule that you can state Eurasian.
> But now they have that rule. So if both parents are agreeable, it's fine.
> So my friends have told me "why don't you just go and change it?"

and I said "I don't want to spend the money changing my IC!"
Yeah, so I say it's alright.
It's not important what is stated on a form, as long as you know inside of you, where you are and what you are.
(Skye Sia, SG, 23, female, Eurasian/Singaporean Chinese)

The option to change her classification to Eurasian to acknowledge her heritage did not seem important to her, as external labels did not need to match her private sense of who (and, interestingly, *what*) she was. This reflected her personal accommodations of mixedness within a wider framework, accepting singular racial categories as public identification and a commonplace aspect of identity, while exploring her personal hybridity in a private way.

In contrast to those who seemed at ease with the dissonance between public and private, certain participants pushed against the idea of race as a categorizing principle, often comparing Singapore with other countries. The constant categorization felt constraining for some.

But there is this like, it's like . . . you know,
in Singapore they just brush over it,
well, let's not talk about it.
You know, you're aren't allowed to talk about racial issues.
But . . . we're going to box everybody up into a category before they've, as soon as they're born.
(Anne McNeil, SG, 27, female, Singaporean Chinese/English)

Anne fought against the racial label assigned to her, finding such singularity stifling. She sought to subvert the racial framework, criticizing its pervasiveness and strength. In this way, she sought to reconcile public and private identifications, hoping to allow for public forms of mixedness. Another woman, Katrina Henry, described how difference was only reinforced by an emphasis on racial classification, questioning the relevance of race as marker within the population, but not its reality. In doing so, she both reinforced the existence of racial divisions and pushed against the necessity of classification.

Overall, race was frequently questioned as an organizing principle by participants in Singapore. In New Zealand, race was much less present at an official level, with many participants finding the official ethnic categories unremarkable. Yet in both countries, participants spoke of race, ethnicity and culture in their narratives, and in doing so highlighted a number of varying understandings of mixedness, and an important thread of racialization. These included seeing race as bloodlines (reinforcement); separating race and ethnicity/culture (accommodation); viewing race, culture, nationality and ethnicity as interlinked (accommodation); understanding race as power (subversion); and questioning the basis of race itself (subversion/transcendence).

There were significant differences in talking about race between Singapore and New Zealand. Singaporean participants were much more comfortable speaking of race as genetic inheritance and ancestry, and the concept of race as blood came through strongly in the stories of many people.

> I think it's like, um . . . in your blood, I guess.
> Um . . . yeah, 'cause, um I don't think, I'm not sure that we're all the same.
> Like, because I think that if we were then we'd all look the same, but we don't.
> Like, um, yeah, like people are different colours and stuff.
> And it's obviously, it's obviously like something different in our genetics.
> To make us that way.
> Um, but I don't know. I think it, yeah, I think it's like something in your blood, and just genetics, and you're born with it.
> (Amber Smith, SG, 19, female, Singaporean Chinese/Anglo Australian)

This narrative fragment directly reinforces a racialized framework, as Amber positions herself in a racial view of the world. Her slight uncertainty highlighted her negotiations around this perception, as she built her story from her personal observations and experiences of exclusion. Her stories of mixedness were then grounded against this belief, essentializing "mixed race" as another racialized category.

The idea of race as blood was also found in the New Zealand context, with a small number of participants seeing race as encompassing everything from ancestry to culture. Race was most commonly described in the context of visibility: race was seen as visible ancestry, the colour of one's skin. It was not always linked to culture, personality or experience, potentially reflecting the official and academic push to replace concepts of race with that of voluntary ethnicity. The difference between ancestry (as race) and ethnicity (as lived experience and culture) was made clear by a number of participants in this context.

> Race to me is just the, the superficial façade of someone.
> Ethnicity to me is the way they live their lives, and the values of that particular culture.
> (Paul Moretti, NZ, 48, male, Chinese/Italian)

For many other New Zealand participants, race and culture were generally not seen as the same thing, and race (and racial classification) was often viewed as having a minimal impact on the identities and lives of individuals. Race and culture did not always have to align, and it was the practical aspect of ethnicity and culture that was seen as having the greatest impact.

In both countries, a small number of people viewed race primarily as an instrument of power: a way for the state to categorize and organize people, often through classification. From this perspective, race was seen as largely constructed, with broad racial categories glossing over the everyday differences between and within groups. One individual in Singapore was particularly pointed:

> Race is a means of government to stratify people and to implement policy, ah. I mean . . . there's no such thing as Chinese, as opposed . . . there's no such thing . . . Chinese is a very broad term. Indian is a very broad term.

> I mean, India, India as a nation itself is an artificial construct.
> China today is an artificial construct. It's a construct because of its own internal people ah.
> You have Han Chinese, you have the Uighurs, Muslims, I mean, yeah . . . the list can go on and on, lah.
> And . . . I mean, so, I mean it's an artificial . . . race is an artificial construct given by . . . it's an issue of power relations, ah.
> That's what I feel, ah. And, I subscribe to that argument, ah.
> (Terence Peaks, SG, 26, male, Filipino Chinese/Anglo Australian)

His understanding of race called into question the Singaporean CMIO framework and allowed him to develop his own personal narrative of transcendence. Race was administrative and meaningless in a practical sense in his narrative, with other forms of identity taking precedence. His narrative highlights a trend in both countries, where different aspects of identity were prioritized over, or even within, ideas of race. In both Singapore and New Zealand, nationality was often offered as an alternative or more important identity at the macro level. It was in these shifting understandings of national identity (inflected by race) that contextual and generational differences emerged more sharply.

Citizenship and its discontents

For all participants, citizenship and national identity were key in their descriptions of self. Both New Zealand and Singapore offered strong, civic identities, under which racial identities could be subsumed, but which also were linked with racialized beliefs about belonging. Tied with ideas of a geographical home, the nation provided an important space in which participants developed ideas of mixedness, linking place, culture, home and personal identity (Blunt 2005).

A number of participants in Singapore stressed the importance of a non-racial Singaporean identity, a way to identify primarily with the nation above any racial categories. An interesting generational shift was noted here. While the oldest participant lamented that Singaporean *should be* available as a non-racial identity, younger participants described themselves as though it *were already* available.

> Maybe in the next generation or in the future generations
> there will be a time they will say, "I'm a Singaporean," rather than a . . .
> Because when you think about it an Indian refers to someone that comes from India. Chinese someone comes from China.
> But when it comes to Singapore, you're born in Singapore and you're not a Singaporean?
> You know, can't you be called a Singaporean?
> (David Faulkner, SG, 64, male, Singaporean Chinese/White British)

> In my pink IC there's, the state has called me a Caucasian,
> because my father is Caucasian.

But in my military IC it calls me European, because . . . I don't know why also.
I guess the way they classify, ah.
So inherently, at times, I think it doesn't matter.
Yeah, I subscribe to the fact that it doesn't matter who I am racially,
but it matters who I am, which country I stand for, lah.
So I'm Singaporean, lah.

(Terence Peaks, SG, 26, male,
Filipino Chinese/Anglo Australian)

This shift in perspective reflected the differences in social context around mixedness and belonging, as experienced by the 64-year-old David Faulkner and the 26-year-old Terence Peaks. State narratives around race and antipathy towards mixedness were strong during David's childhood and young adult years. Terence grew up as national identity was increasingly emphasized above race, allowing him to transcend racial labels in a personal way. This difference reinforces Siddique's (1990) claim that younger individuals in Singapore are choosing national identity over racialized labels. As a form of transcendence, this means that some individuals, such as Terence, see themselves as national first, over and above the CMIO system. For him, classification was administrative and abstract, while his sense of belonging to Singapore was practical and demonstrated in his personal identification. This civic identification as *just Singaporean* was echoed by several of the younger male participants, as they described race as a public classification that had little personal meaning. National identity was perceived as a way to belong to the nation, transcending racialized categories.

This highlights an interesting intertwining between gender, race and nationality in the Singaporean context, closely related to the compulsory military service for men when they reach 18 years old. James Field chose to leave Singapore, renouncing his Singaporean citizenship and his military service obligations. However, several others stayed in Singapore and undertook their training. Terence Peaks joined the military professionally, and for him, military service cut across divides of race and ethnicity, creating a higher-level Singaporean identity. Being Singaporean, as expressed through national duty and military service, was a key form of identity for several of the young men. "Serving the nation" became a way to belong, regardless of race, and provided a way of expressing feelings of loyalty.

And I think it's because I love Singapore this much, that's why decided to sign on.
And give up my Australian citizenship. And . . . why . . .
I mean some people ask, "oh, do you regret?" and I say "no."
Uh, 'cause at the end of the day,
I think home is a function of where your emotional connections are, and where everything is, ah.
Logically, you may feel that, from a pragmatic side,
it might be better to be Australian because, oh, the welfare system is there, ah,
it's more relaxed pace of life, it's slower.
But I think at the end of the day, home is where your family is,

home is where your friends is, lah.
And your entire history is in a place called Singapore,
then your home is naturally Singapore. Yeah.

(Terence Peaks, SG, 26, male,
Filipino Chinese/Anglo Australian)

For a second man, national service emphasized the dissonance between his personal feelings of belonging, and his exclusion from Singaporean citizenship. As Singapore does not allow dual citizenship, participants with parents from two different countries are required to choose between the two once they reach 21 years old, even after having finished national service.

The fact that they're trying to take it away from me,
it's like making me really like "ugh".
Really, angry.
But . . . more disappointed in the fact that it's probably going to happen.
Like, I can't really do anything about it.
I think so. Citizenship . . .
I have both now, but obviously I'm going to have to give up one.
But I mean, Singapore's making me give up one.
The UK doesn't really care [laughs].
Just so, like what, what, why?
Yeah. Yeah. I think so.
Citizenship is important,
for me [laughs].

(William Briggs, SG, 21, male,
Singaporean Chinese/English)

Having to choose felt like a denial of his identity for William, after his sense of belonging was strengthened during his two-year national service period. Although he laughed as he talked about his choice, his sense of belonging to the nation was at odds with his exclusion from Singaporean citizenship.

Citizenship was seen as an important form of identity, a way to belong outside of racial categories. However, this forced choice illustrated the limits of transcendence as a practical identity, creating another form of singularity into which individuals of mixed descent did not always easily fit. Along with race, national identity involved intimate and complicated connections, which singular forms of belonging could not encompass. This sentiment was echoed by a third participant, Andrew. He felt that wider Singaporean society did not provide space for multiplicity, nor for him.

I think there's a double frustration,
because I continue to serve every year, as part of my national service obligation.
As long as you're able, you have to serve 40 days a year.
And I feel I've served, I've done a very heavy commitment with the military,

I've completed this until today, and as an officer,
I serve a lot more than the average Singaporean.
Yet people continue to mistake me for [a foreigner] ...
I've served my time. And I get a bit passionate, and very angry about this.
[...]
Because I feel like I'm a son of the soil.
I served my national service willingly,
and yet people continue to treat me like a foreigner.
I continuously have to justify my identity, or identify myself.
Each and every day.

(Andrew Wang-Jones, SG, 36, male,
English and German/Eurasian)

After significant service with the military, Andrew felt that his connections to Singapore should not be denied. Yet his sense of being Singaporean was both challenged by those who perceived him as "the other" and reinforced by his civic obligations to the Singaporean government. For young men of mixed descent in Singapore, narratives of transcendence around national identity and national service were common, but such identities were often constrained. National service evoked feelings of both belonging and dislocation and, either way, forced a choice regarding national loyalty.

While Singaporean was a strong form of identity and a way to transcend racial categories, this was not a simple or uncontested form of belonging. Rather than unquestioningly subscribing to a national identity, many participants questioned what it meant to be Singaporean. One woman felt that Singaporean was a constraining rather than an enabling form of identification, and she chose to disassociate herself as much as possible.

I find myself rebelling a lot in Singapore.
You know, it's like, it's like if I could get,
if I could get a massive like "fuck you, fucking idiot" like pasted on my body
so that I could show it to anybody, you know, like ... I would.
Because I just feel like, you're so closed, they're so closed minded here.
And it's like, oh my god, you can't possibly do that,
because you're not this, this, this.
You know, and I'm just like – you limit yourself so much. And you ...
You put people in these boxes that you don't want to deal with,
and you know, and why are you doing that?
And ... therefore ... I don't think I'll ever, I feel like I won't ever belong here.

(Anne McNeil, SG, 27, female,
Singaporean Chinese/English)

Anne saw the idea of a civic identity based strongly on categorization and its associations with an authoritarian form of governance as limited and closed-minded. She separated herself from Singapore in her narrative, describing how "they" are, underlining her feelings of not belonging. She keenly felt the lack of acceptance of her mixed background and described how she sought to break out of the Singaporean framework, subverting both national and racial belonging as identities she could not subscribe to. She sought instead to bring together ideas of race and nationality:

> And, you know race shouldn't just be about the colour of your skin.
> You know, somebody's race is, it's the entire community and culture that they come from. And they are you know . . . and that they are a part of.
> And everybody's race in Singapore is Singaporean.
> You know, like you come from an entire culture where your entire lives are intertwined with other people's cultures and other people's beliefs, and you know, other people's religions, and it's great!
> And there shouldn't be any kind of like, you're this, you're that, you're the other, and that's it.
> You know, because, because you're not.
> You come from a world, you come from a country where you are lucky enough to be surrounded by everybody of different, you know, ethnicities, and cultures and vibrancies . . .
> and instead of seeing that, you see the colour of their skin.
> (Anne McNeil, SG, 27, female, Singaporean Chinese/English)

Her narrative is particularly subversive, questioning the basis for both racial and national belonging, and suggesting that each be a question of experience and culture. She distanced herself from the wider framework, as she saw it, using her in-between positioning to step outside of concepts of race, and to challenge and change meanings.

Returning to Andrew, he made a distinction between feeling Singaporean and holding Singaporean citizenship, separating the administrative practice of citizenship and the felt connection of national identity.

> So I think, I don't want to be clever, but for me,
> to live with myself and in order to be, to sleep well at night,
> when people ask me "are you Singaporean?",
> maybe I come out with a very wise-ass answer.
> I say "no, I'm not Singaporean, but I'm a Singaporean citizen".
> Because I don't feel Singaporean, in terms of my, of the nation at large.
> I don't think I can identify with that.
> But I'm happy to say that I'm a citizen of this country, and I enjoy the privileges of being a citizen here.
> (Andrew Wang-Jones, SG, 36, male, English and German/Eurasian)

His reaction to citizenship is closely related to his experiences of national service, as compared to his experiences of discrimination and social displacement.

He asserted his citizenship on paper, but stressed that being Singaporean was not something that he identified with, primarily because he did not feel as though he belonged within the racialized structures. For him, race and racial categories remained an important part of Singaporean identity, and as someone who did not fit into these categories neatly, he felt rejected and distanced from Singapore as a nation. National identity was not a viable way to transcend racial identity as a result, and his efforts at subversion in order to align the public and the private left him frustrated.

The importance of the racialized base for Singaporean identity was echoed in the stories of a number of other participants, who explored the interplay and conflation of race and nationality. As in the CMIO framework, some participants described being both racially and nationally identified, without being able to separate one from the other: they felt unable to be Singaporean without also being racialized, reinforcing wider narratives of race. Racial classification and national identity often came through when describing exclusion. A number of people described a sense of dislocation as a result of not fitting within strict categorization systems, and not being seen as an authentic Singaporean. One participant highlighted the primacy of the four-race framework and narrative of CMIO belonging in detailing her and her husband's mixed backgrounds.

> I think it will be quite interesting.
> Because actually my husband is also somewhat mixed, but he is Malay and North Indian. Yeah, I used to joke that okay,
> we have Chinese, we have Caucasian, and then Malay and Indian,
> so our kids will be like true blue Singaporeans.
> Like, can't get more Singaporean. [laughs]
>
> (Safiyah Matthews, SG, 28, female, Singaporean Chinese/New Zealand European)

Brought together in the identities of their future children, their ancestry would encompass all four CMIO groups, creating an interesting paradox: a reinforcement and the epitome of Singaporean-ness as a mix of all four races, but at the same time a subversion of the separate but equal framework, in which each race is distinct from the others.

Race and nationality were often difficult to separate in participants' descriptions of their identifications and the identifications of their parents. Most participants specified Chinese Singaporean or Singaporean Chinese, identifying as a racial Singaporean. A small number used just Singaporean when referring to ancestral or racial identifications, equating Singaporean with Singaporean Chinese. For Amber, race was particularly important in her stories of belonging, but when describing herself, she used national terms of belonging: Australian for her father's family and Singaporean for her mother's. For her, her Chinese side was intertwined with her mother's identity as Singaporean, linking race and nation in her personal narrative and reinforcing narratives of race. She went on to elaborate how she tried to balance her acknowledgement of national identity to include both sides of her heritage.

I feel like if I say Singapore, then they'll know that I'm like Asian,
like mixed Asian or whatever . . .
but then I feel like sort of bad after I say it, because,
I feel like sort of I'm denying my "Australian-ism" or whatever.
And, well because, like it kind of feels like a lie in a way, 'cause I'm not,
I don't know if I could call myself Singaporean.
Like I do have like a Singaporean passport and like nationality and everything,
but even, when I went on to Singapore on holiday like I used my Australian passport.
So, I don't know [. . .]
I guess like, I don't know, it depends if I call myself Australian or Singaporean, and I've never really embraced either.

(Amber Smith, SG, 19, female,
Singaporean Chinese/Anglo Australian)

Nationality was strongly connected to race and heritage, as she emphasized her Asian heritage through identification with Singapore. This also contributed to her feeling out of place in Australia, as Australian became equated with European or "white" culture, excluding mixed heritages and identities. Her feelings of belonging, or not belonging, were further complicated through her passports, which she described as symbols of belonging, as she had not yet had to choose between them. Thus, national identity in Singapore and narratives of national belonging encompassed issues of race, experience, gender and generation. Nationality could be understood as a wider form of non-racial belonging for some participants, as seen in narratives of transcendence, but also as an exclusionary form of identity based along ancestral and racial lines, drawing clear lines as to who does and does not belong.

For men and women in New Zealand, race and nation were equally intertwined, but in different ways. Over half of participants described themselves as New Zealanders *first*, portraying a civic identity that encompassed a multitude of ethnic, cultural and racial identifications. Being a New Zealander was understood as a different form of identity, a non-racial transcendence in a context where race was less important, although still pertinent. For one woman, Pamela McLane, her narrative was entirely based around transcendence, as race was not something which she thought about in her day-to-day life, preferring to identify herself only as Kiwi. A second woman spoke more of accommodation, and illustrated the conflations and confusions between race, ethnicity and nationality.

So nationality is the nation state that you belong to, so I'd be a New Zealander.
Race and ethnicity, I get confused.
I think ethnicity is something to do with your blood. Is that right?
Well, I guess to me, ethnicity would be more what's your bloodline, and race would be more cultural, but I really don't know [laughs].
But there's definitely a difference between the bloodline and the culture, and the nationality, you know, which country you think you belong to.
Even though culturally, you're not necessarily aligned with that country,

but I think you can live in a country and see it as home
but still be culturally something else.

(Alexis Conrad, NZ, 33, female, Chinese New Zealander/New Zealand European)

For her, race and ethnicity meant culture and blood (in an interesting reversal of common understandings), and nationality provided the vessel in which these other identities can be kept. She accommodated the reality of race and ideas of belonging, while separating what it meant to be at home and to belong somewhere. In her narrative, nationality could act as an overarching identity that aligned better with cultural belonging for some than for others.

For another participant, her sense of belonging to New Zealand was tempered by the reality of racial hierarchies and how she viewed (and was viewed by) the dominant Pakeha group in society.

Um . . . definitely [I belong] in New Zealand.
Um . . . oh when I've traveled other places in the world, definitely don't feel like I belong there.
Even if it was China, or . . . anything, anywhere else, no.
And . . . but, at the same, I guess, I mean, it's okay in New Zealand
'cause there's so many different cultures here, that a lot of people do fit in, because we are very multicultural.
But at the same time, I think the dominant race will always be European New Zealanders.
So . . . I don't think I entirely fit in, no.
And I don't, yeah I don't really think that anyone . . .
well, yeah, I don't really think that anyone, unless you're white in New Zealand, fits in completely.
'Cause that was, that's like the dominant race here, I feel. Yeah.

(Jenny Griffiths, NZ, 25, female, Pakeha New Zealander/Chinese New Zealander)

Jenny's story highlighted uncertainty around questions of belonging and fitting in, with marked hesitations and negative statements. She made a distinction between where she felt she belonged, and how she thought she fit in, as a New Zealander. For her, New Zealand identity had a definite racial dimension and was not available as way to transcend racial categories entirely. Whiteness trumped a civic form of identity, leaving her excluded from what she perceived as New Zealand identity. Her narrative illustrated the limits to civic transcendence, as she found herself dislocated by both racial and national belonging.

Several other participants elaborated on this interplay between race and nationality, but more in terms of accommodating difference within nationality. Paul used his identity as a New Zealander to encompass and transcend the multiple aspects of his heritage. At the same time, he allowed for uncertainty in this identity, by describing the broader label of New Zealander as "whatever that kind of means".

The label then became a flexible and open identifier, into which he could mix all aspects of his identities.

> I see myself as a New Zealander, with Chinese and Italian heritage.
> I don't see myself as a Chinese New Zealander, or an Italian New Zealander, I see it the other way around.
> I think about Italy and I think about China, but I really don't see myself as either one.
> I used to think for many years "I need to be more Chinese" or "I need to be more Italian". And I need to immerse myself even more . . .
> But I've come to the conclusion now that that's actually the wrong thing.
> Because I'm actually neither.
> I'm actually a New Zealander, whatever that kind of means.
> (Paul Moretti, NZ, 48, male, Chinese/Italian)

Another participant made a distinction between heritage and national identity, emphasizing the importance of a civic identification, while acknowledging the reality of race and physical differences in New Zealand society.

> I would describe myself as a Kiwi and . . .
> and ah, a Kiwi. With Chinese heritage.
> And a person that likes, likes culture. Someone that . . .
> like I like to travel for that reason, I like to see cultures and things like that.
> Yeah. I don't really know where to go with it . . .
> Um . . . [pause]
> But definitely as Kiwi. I don't really see myself being Chinese.
> That's not a word that I would really associate with myself.
> Unless . . . but I'm obviously more Chinese than,
> than other people that are just, you know, New Zealand European. Yeah.
> (Joel Andrews, NZ, 24, male, Chinese New Zealander/Pakeha New Zealander)

This illustrates both transcendence and accommodation, as he stressed his connections as a Kiwi, but acknowledged that his Chinese heritage marked him as different, regardless of the strength of his identifications. Joel experienced a public/private dissonance in his identifications, something that another participant, Nathan, sought to avoid. Nathan further complicated understandings of nationality with dual American/New Zealand citizenship.

> Well, first and foremost, I'm a Kiwi. A New Zealander.
> Don't see myself as ah . . . all that American.
> Even though I hold a passport, still I don't . . . I probably view Americans the same as any Kiwi does, you know.
> In terms of Chinese, yeah, belonging to China – no, I don't, I don't identify with China too much.

Because we get a lot of negative press over here about China, um you know, human rights issues and stuff like that. Yeah.
Even though I share some genetic link years ago.
How do I feel? Yeah . . .
What was the original question? Where do I belong?
I think, I think as a New Zealand Kiwi really, more European if anything.
I, we do have Chinese here, a lot of them.
And you'll notice the fresh ones stick to themselves, so they don't mix. I don't identify with being one of them.
Um, their next generation will definitely mix, will be quite Kiwi.
I think they call them bananas, yeah yellow on the outside, white on the inside.
Um, but because we come from America, maybe I also don't, yeah, I also don't . . .
oh mind you though, I do have a friend who's Chinese
and we have, we have quips to each other over Facebook, and that's purely because we are Chinese, I mean.
So I guess yeah, in some regard we do have a bit of a bond there.
Yeah, and if I meet a half Chineser, I'll mention it, and have a bit of a joke about it.

(Nathan Fleming, NZ, 39, male, American Chinese/Pakeha New Zealander)

He viewed national identification with the United States as administrative and symbolically unimportant, much on the same level as his national/ethnic identifications with China. New Zealand national identity was primary for him, over and above racial identifications. He linked his citizenship with his experiences of growing up and feelings of belonging to the nation, as opposed to his lack of connection with the United States. The Chinese were very much "the other" for him, seen in terms of the Chinese state and immigration, and he distanced himself from the newer Chinese immigrants in New Zealand by asserting his Kiwi identity and the authenticity of his belonging. His affinity for being "European" aligned with his identifications as Kiwi, together with his discussion of "bananas", and reinforced wider narratives of racial belonging. Yet at the same time, he felt some commonality with his friends of Chinese descent, and more particularly, people who are half Chinese: "half Chineser", a way of reconciling difference within New Zealand identity.

Similarly, other participants stressed the importance of their upbringing and childhood experiences in New Zealand, factors that made them identify strongly with the country. Participants also noted that their feelings of belonging differed from their parents, given their experiences growing up. Two participants, Katie Murray and Paul Moretti, who each had two migrant parents, highlighted that they felt a sense of ownership in New Zealand, as compared to their parents who had experienced feelings of dislocation[2].

New Zealand identity thus seemed flexible for most participants, a way to bring together various strands within an identity based around experience and culture. Several participants used New Zealander as a broad signifier, which could be altered to include differences in ancestry and race/ethnicity, or seen as a continuum of authentic "Kiwiness". As described by two women:

> I'd probably say Kiwi with like a little bit of difference.
> (Angelina Ng, NZ, 19, female, Pakeha New Zealander/Chinese New Zealander)

> But I still consider myself Kiwi,
> but not maybe as Kiwi as some people might think of themselves.
> But I can't really say, you know, I'm Singaporean 'cause I didn't grow up there, and I don't know as much and all that . . .
> so I guess maybe Kiwi with a dashing of other stuff [laughs].
> (Pamela McLane, NZ, 20, female, Singaporean Chinese/Pakeha, Fijian and Japanese)

Such narratives highlight both the perceived flexibility of being Kiwi, and how belonging in New Zealand is inflected by race yet allows some room to manouevre. National identity in New Zealand was related to conceptions of race, ancestry and belonging, and belonging as a Kiwi provided both freedoms and constraints. National belonging was often reflected in narratives of transcendence or even accommodation. Such narratives allowed space for individuals of mixed heritage to redefine categories and stretch boundaries, perhaps reflecting the flexible categorizations of ethnicity rather than race within the state framework.

Classification, national identity and belonging

As seen in the stories above, the personal and the political were intricately involved in both Singapore and New Zealand. Individuals of mixed descent located themselves in national frameworks of classification, and national identity provided a strong potential sense of belonging in both cases. However, the embeddedness of the four-race framework meant that being Singaporean had strong racial connotations. Narratives highlighted the possibility for transcendence but also its limitations, while individuals discussed subversive and accommodating tactics in the face of public/private dissonance. Race influenced national identity in New Zealand, but greater flexibility appeared to allow for more space to negotiate being Kiwi as a non-racial form of identity. Transcendence was then more feasible, and accommodation required less of a shift between the public and the private in order to align identities.

In both contexts, national identity was often something that participants were required to defend. Public and private dissonances were made very explicit in the question "where are you from?". A common finding in qualitative studies of "mixed race", this question highlights how difference and potential ambiguity are emphasized through questions of belonging and identity. Paragg describes this questioning as an external gaze that "others" (2011:143), positioning individuals of mixed heritage as outsiders, who need to legitimize their feelings of belonging to the (racialized) nation (see also Cheryan and Monin 2005; Mahtani 2002a; Root 1998; Song 2003).

74 *The personal in the political*

Participants in both countries discussed being asked this question in various guises, being asked directly about race, or in a more roundabout way, asking about background, heritage, language or parents. Several of the Singaporean participants who had lived overseas mentioned that they encountered this kind of questioning much more frequently in Singapore, as their backgrounds transgressed the familiar race/language/culture framework. Men and women narrated the different ways in which people tried to position them along familiar racial lines, guessing their backgrounds based on their appearance or accent. The wide variety of these guesses highlighted how ambiguous appearance or accent confounded expectations about racial characteristics: some suggestions included Spanish, Brazilian, Scottish, Polynesian, Filipino, Maori or Korean.

Participants responded to these questions in very different ways. As seen in previous research, individuals used a number of strategies to cope with questions that they often felt were intrusive, unnecessary, alienating, or even just wearying. Strategies included forms of accommodation, such as giving a short summary of their background; transcendence, such as asserting uncomplicated national (or other non-racial) belonging; or subversion, such as using humour to deflect the question, answering in excessive detail, or deliberately misunderstanding the question to confuse the questioner.

In Singapore, Andrew suggested that he could assert his sense of belonging by showing his Singaporean identity card to people that he met, while Hannah avoided the question by asserting her feelings of being a global citizen. She also suggested humourous ways of pre-empting the question:

> But the one thing that people always do, is they ask you what mix you are, where are you from.
> All the time. All the time!
> I tell them what it is. But I always felt tempted to wear a T-shirt that says Welsh-Chinese, and then explain to them where Wales, Wales is, because nobody knows.
> Then I would, I would tell them. I thought a faster way was to do it via Facebook [laughs].
> And then I can understand the draw, because every time you see someone mixed, you want to know as well.
> What's their mix? You know, Portuguese, Italian, what? What?
>
> (Hannah Alley, SG, 33, female, Singaporean Chinese/Welsh)

In New Zealand, one woman was often perceived as Maori, and she played on this ambiguity by being particularly involved in Maori activities at school.

> I mean like I've been really used to people asking me where I'm from. Like ... forever.
> 'Cause people can't tell, you know, being half/half and then having freckles and you know, just ... people like just haven't got a clue, most of the time.
> Like I got away with being the leader of the Kapa Haka [Maori performing arts] groups at school [laughs].

And people were like "oh, what tribe are you from?" and like "um . . . I haven't got any Maori . . ."
And no, no, and sometimes I'd go "oh, I'm half Chinese" because I, you know, assumed that they'd guess the other half.
But "oh, half Chinese and half Maori?" . . . "no . . ." [laughs] "half Chinese and half Pakeha", they're like "oh okay . . ."

(Jasmine Orana, NZ, 25, female, Singaporean Chinese/Pakeha New Zealander)

For Jasmine, being "difficult to place" allowed her to participate in different groups and underlined her sense of belonging to New Zealand through being mistaken as indigenous. Her answer to the question "where are you from?" often confounded the questioner, as she subverted expectations by culturally identifying with a group outside of her heritage.

In both countries, individuals experienced these questions in different ways, with some brushing them off, or even enjoying the shock value of their answers, and a small number being deeply affected by the continual questioning of their right to belong. For those who answered questions at face value, providing nationality rather than ethnic background for example, a follow-up question was often asked: "where are you *really* from?". People found this question particularly offensive, implying that they belonged somewhere else and excluding them from being "real" Singaporeans or New Zealanders because of racialized assumptions. One woman described how she used to deliberately misunderstand these questions, confronting the questioner with the fact of her belonging:

I would always get asked where I was from. And I used to get quite facetious, I used to say things like "Oh, I'm from Wellington".
And they'd be like "No, where are you from?"
"Oh, do you mean like where I was born? Oh, I was born in Upper Hutt."
And they'd just get really frustrated, like "Oh, where are your genes from?" and I'd just say, "Oh, they're Lee jeans". Or just . . .
Oh, I used to get angry about it, and now I don't get angry about it 'cause I just realized that people are just curious, and I'd just answer them. When I was [laughs] it used to be so difficult, yeah . . .
And I think I still resent the question "where are you from?" because it's kind of like, it's like accusing like you should be from somewhere else.
And it's like "I'm from this place. I have no problem with that [laughs].
I don't know what your problem is."

(Nadine Moore, NZ, 34, female, Pakeha New Zealander/Malaysian Chinese)

Whilst having some sympathy for this type of curiosity, she asserted that it remained profoundly dislocating for her as a New Zealander. Her attitude turned the question back around to the questioner in a form of subversion, suggesting that belonging in New Zealand could mean many different things, and it is the questioner who has misunderstood.

Locating the self in structure

The relationships between classification, nationality and racial/ethnic forms of belonging were complex in both Singapore and New Zealand. Differential processes of racial formation resulted in macro narratives that both constrained and enabled personal stories of mixedness around transcendence, accommodation and reinforcement. Unsurprisingly, in both countries, the power of history was brought out in individual narratives, as participants constructed their identities within a national story shaped by colonial and post-colonial processes of social, political, and economic organization.

Classification along racial lines, past and present, affected participants in both countries, but it influenced narratives more strongly in Singapore as a result of practical impacts. Race and racial categorization remained real and everyday, shaping the ways in which individuals identified themselves and reinforced narratives within and around these categories (see Song 2010a:266). The strength and established nature of racial classification in Singapore came through strongly in individual stories, reflecting the personal within the political. Participants were very aware of race and acceptable racial categories, as well as how these categories combined to structure the narrative of the nation. Such stories were reflected in how individuals spoke of blood, racial traits and belonging (or not belonging) to a racial group, highlighting a strong thread of racialization and reinforcement in the Singaporean context. While Singaporean participants were very conscious of racial labeling and the practical consequences and constraints of this, they were also very aware of the ways in which they, and many others, did not fit easily into categories. Racial singularity was not seen as particularly accurate in describing everyday identities, and one fifth of participants felt that such singular classification should be abolished altogether. Race was understood as a way to belong in the Singaporean context, but also as a way of dividing the population along arbitrary lines, seen in stories of reinforcement and subversion.

Race appeared less present in New Zealand, with participants being less conscious of state classifications of race and ethnicity. Official classifications based around voluntary ethnicity allowed individuals to adjust categories to their own backgrounds. This meant that for the majority of participants, such fluid classification was seen as potentially officially useful, and easier to accommodate. A key difference with the Singaporean context was the lack of state-sanctioned material consequences of classification in New Zealand, as racial and ethnic categories were understood as more personal, social and interactional, rather than top-down and singular. Despite this, a racialized past continued to echo in contemporary New Zealand narratives, as participants discussed whiteness as normality, and the ways in which their ancestral differences marked them as abnormal as a result.

Interestingly, racialized discourses came through particularly strongly in Singapore when looking at the relationships between race and heritage. The framework of being located as a racialized Singaporean meant that participants spoke of positioning themselves within racial groups, and mixedness as related to blood and ancestry, as well as culture. Non-singular options such as "Other" and Eurasian were often seen as unsatisfactory ways to acknowledge mixedness within this framework: Eurasian was seen as very specific and even re-racialized in its hybridity, while "Other" was sometimes perceived as non-human through being non-racial. In New Zealand, race was more associated with visibility, with visible minorities being racialized within a wider framework of ethnic belonging. Understandings of race, ethnicity and culture were often separated in the New Zealand context, with participants describing these identifications as not necessarily linked in predictable ways. For the Singaporean participants, this break was more difficult to make in the public domain, against expectations of a seamless alignment of race, culture, language and tradition. Drawing on colonial histories of classification, race was inseparable from notions of power in both contexts, and linked to concepts of normality in either country. In Singapore, a singular race was seen as normal, and mixedness transgressed this framework. In New Zealand, whiteness was unproblematic and normal, with ethnic/racial forms of difference (mixed or not) representing the transgression.

National identity offered an alternative (or transcendent), but often racialized, form of identity for participants, reflected in narratives of inclusion and exclusion, and in attitudes towards external questioning. Questions of national belonging as related to race highlighted key differences between the two countries. A national Singaporean identity was perceived as both racialized and non-racial, with evidence of generational change. Singaporean as a non-racial identity was more practical for younger participants, several of whom saw themselves as Singaporean first, racial second. The majority of participants located their connections to Singapore within a wider racialized framework, exploring the limits of transcendence as they experienced exclusion and disconnection by not identifying as a singularly raced Singaporean. Racial hierarchies were also evident in narratives, as participants often conflated Singaporean and Singaporean Chinese, with other groups seen as less Singaporean, or not authentically Singaporean at all. This was resolved by some participants in separating civic identity from feelings of belonging, and accommodating a public/private dissonance by allowing oneself to be administratively Singaporean, without identifying with wider national narratives. For others, this dissonance illustrated contrasts in how they identified themselves, how they were identified by others and how they were classified by the state, particularly when looking at national service and the intersections of race, gender and nationality. As a result, a number of Singaporean participants described how their backgrounds meant that they did not fit anywhere, set outside of the race/nationality framework.

In contrast, a non-racial, transcendent New Zealand identity seemed more of a lived reality for participants, with over half talking about themselves as New Zealanders first. This did not mean that race was unimportant for national identity, and the strength of whiteness and legacies of racialized hierarchies also came through strongly, as individuals spoke of European culture and appearance as just being normal. Despite this background of racialization, being a New Zealander did appear to be flexible for many people, as a civic identity which was able to stretch to include differences in heritage, culture and ethnicity. The strength of such an identity also illustrated generational change, as participants described how they felt strongly connected to the country, as opposed to their migrant parents who felt excluded from narratives of national belonging. Illustrating a possible impact of minimal classification and redefinition of ethnicity as voluntary, participants' descriptions of Kiwiness were often shifting and open. Although structural constraints certainly existed in day-to-day life, many individuals were able to reconcile public and private forms of identity within a less constricting framework.

In both countries, individuals stressed the public/private dissonances of identity and identification as they told stories of accommodation, looking at how external perceptions shaped personal understandings of self and belonging. Questions such as "Where are you from?" highlighted disconnects from wider narratives of race and national belonging. Such dissonances were experienced in Singapore and in New Zealand, with a greater focus on the state aspect of public identifications in Singapore, given the pervasiveness of state classification in this context. In New Zealand, public identifications could also diverge from personal feelings of connection, relating more to wider social groups and the accompanying narratives of what it meant to be a New Zealander. Interestingly, as in recent British studies, such public/private dissonances were not always experienced and internalized in the same way (see Song and Aspinall 2012). Some participants felt profoundly misrecognized and dislocated, whereas others were indifferent or even positive about the ambiguity and flexibility in the perceptions of others.

In both contexts, then, personal narratives of mixedness and difference stood outside of national narratives of race, belonging and national identity. National stories formed the narrative space within which micro stories of belonging and dislocation emerged, through strategies of subversion, accommodation, transcendence and reinforcement. Participants' stories highlighted how racial classification, no matter how fluid, could not easily account for cultural influences and life experience, locating mixed identities as counter narratives in both Singapore and New Zealand (see Ip 2008; LeFlore-Muñoz 2010). Race and heritage were complicated by individual stories juxtaposed against national histories, as individuals both adopted and questioned official categories. The limitations of governmental racialization came to the fore particularly in the stories of Singaporean participants. Individual perceptions of macro-level processes and identities then provided the backdrop against which participants experienced more personal constructions of being Chinese, European and mixed, as lived within the family and community.

Notes

1 Sections of this and the following chapters were previously published as Rocha, Z. 2012a. "Identity, Dislocation and Belonging: Chinese/European Narratives of 'Mixed' Identity in Aotearoa/New Zealand." *Identities: Global Studies in Culture and Power*. 19(6): 673–690 and Rocha, Z. 2014. "Stretching out the Categories: Chinese/European Narratives of Mixedness, Belonging and Home in Singapore." *Ethnicities*, 14(2):279–302.
2 This dislocation is interesting, relating more to the symbolic and felt aspects of citizenship and belonging. Practically, permanent residents in New Zealand have very similar rights to citizens, including the right to vote and the right to remain indefinitely. See www.oag.govt.nz/2013/citizenship/part3.htm for more details.

4 Being and belonging

Intermezzo: learning who to be and where to belong

Linking the micro level of identity and macro level of social structure can be analytically difficult. It is easy to obscure the flexible interconnections between identity, community and structure at the meso level. Previous research has connected individual identity choices with a variety of meso-level factors, including family context, generation, socioeconomic status, neighbourhood, religious affiliation, educational experiences and community group membership (Khanna 2004; Tyler 2005; Waters 1990). A focus on group-level experiences and contexts for mixedness sheds light on the connections between various forms of identity, identification and categorization. Importantly, individual stories are influenced by and told around social groups and contexts, bringing together macro narratives of racial formation with meso narratives of community belonging. The meso level acts as a bridge, an intermezzo, between the two levels of analysis, connecting wider, impersonal narratives of state structure with the intimate and half-hidden stories that individuals tell themselves in order to make sense of the world.

Locating the self in the family

Family was particularly important in participants' narratives, in both countries. In all contexts, parents play a key role in shaping how children view their identities and the cultural backgrounds of the family (Childs 2002): teaching children "... who 'we' are and who 'they' are and how 'we' and 'they' ought to relate" (Murad 2005:480). The family is an important site of socialization, with family narratives shaping personal stories and being shaped by the wider narratives in which they are located. Families serve to both reproduce and contest dominant narratives of race, sometimes reinscribing categories through intimate actions of reinforcement and sometimes challenging dominant hierarchies by transcending race.

Participants illustrated how the family provided a microcosm for identity negotiations, as a unit that had to contend with the constraints and contradictions of macro narratives of race. Family meant different things to different participants. Some families were large, some small, and many illustrated the complexity of kinship through the roles of extended family, adoption, divorce, and remarriage. Understandings of race and "mixed race" within families were equally diverse,

80 *Being and belonging*

and many described unique family cultures based around particular stories and memories (see also Rocha 2010).

Participants frequently set the scene for talking about family by talking about their parents. The family background to the marriage illustrated the social context in which their relationship developed and showed the changing attitudes to mixed marriages over time. While some extended families welcomed the idea of a culturally mixed relationship, family opposition proved to be common in both countries. For both sides of the family, mixed marriages were particularly threatening, as unknown quantities and historically stigmatized boundary crossings. In Singapore, the families of some Chinese sons and daughters often had fairly extreme reactions to the impending marriage, to the point where family members would be disowned for disloyalty. One woman described the reaction of her Chinese grandfather:

> Um, they got married in 1980.
> And at that time I think it was still very odd, still very not done, to be married.
> So my mother's father saw it as, ah, losing face.
> To marry a, a Caucasian man, who was older and had been married once before.
> So he did not approve of the marriage.
> So the first time that my um, that my dad went to go and visit, like to pay respects to the father, he was chased out with a chopping knife. Yeah.
> So, um, he never went back to see my, my grandfather.
> Um, we, my mother ended up eloping to England, got married in England, and then they came back.
> But my grandfather made it very clear that if she was to get married, then he wanted nothing more to do with us. So, that was it really.
> Um, he's now passed away, so I don't have . . .
> and um, since then my grandmother has said it was very silly and, you know,
> at that time he was a Chinese man, and you know, he, it, face was very important.
>
> (Katrina Henry, SG, 27, female, Singaporean Chinese/English)

This story made clear the strength of the boundaries crossed by her parents. Her grandfather saw their relationship as shameful, causing him to "lose face", a particularly Asian sentiment, which may not have been easily understandable to her English father. The importance of "face" is highlighted by the grandfather's strong reaction, chasing her father out of the house with a knife, effectively severing ties with his daughter with the same action. His reaction was in keeping with ideas of lineage and ancestral notions of what it means to be Chinese, as marrying outside the cultural group threatened his understanding of "Chineseness" as descent (see Dikotter 1996, 1997:32).

New Zealand provided a similarly hostile context for intermarriage, invoking parallel ideas of race, blood and purity on both sides. Against a background of anti-Asian sentiment and historical condescension for "half-castes", mixed marriages were unusual and viewed with suspicion by both the immigrant Chinese families and the New Zealand European families. Despite this, several participants described cultural boundary crossings which facilitated family relations, particularly when it came to language. Melanie's father seemed less foreign to her mother's family, and potentially less threatening, due to his linguistic ability. Language provided a point of commonality against a background of difference, allowing for flexibility on both sides.

> On mum's side, um, you know I think at first my grandparents were probably a bit dubious about dad.
> But because he spoke Chinese and you know,
> he's a very just sort of nice, solid man, and they saw that, and they knew that you know, he would be good for mum, so um . . .
> And to be honest, maybe there was more resistance, but they didn't really tell me.
> But I was sure that it was, 'cause it was something totally new to them.
> No one in the family had ever married, had ever had a cross-racial marriage, so . . . um . . .
> But I think the fact that he spoke Chinese was a big thing,
> and you know, he had an understanding of Chinese culture as well.
> (Melanie Townsend, NZ, 30, female, Taiwan Chinese/Pakeha New Zealander)

Interestingly, participants highlighted opposition from their Chinese families more than from their European families. This was surprising, as given New Zealand's history with anti-Asian sentiment and policies, it seemed more likely that the European family would veto the relationship. From the experiences of the interviewees, the families from the dominant European group may have experienced trepidation, but this was either expressed less obviously or not seen by participants as an important part of their stories. One woman shared this surprise:

> I've asked my mum about this quite a few times,
> 'cause I always imagine that my, my white grandfather would have been like "no", but . . .
> Um especially 'cause they grew up in a time in New Zealand where . . .
> Um, like just, I did history, I do history and stuff at uni
> and just learning about like Asian immigration, like just the propaganda and posters surrounding that . . .
> and like, I mean, you see posters with like white girls, and it's like, do you, you don't want your white girl marrying this like oriental, yeah.
> So, yeah, even coming, I guess those sort of posters would have been around when my grandparents were younger,
> but um, my grandfather was totally accepting of my dad, which is really cool.

> And yeah, like, liked him more than some of my mum's previous like white boyfriends.
> Um, but on my dad's side, I think like they'd already lined up like a girl that they quite wanted my father to marry.
> And so I don't think they really understood that.
> But . . . now it's fine.
> And I mean . . . 'cause my grandma on my dad's side, my Chinese grandma, she lives in New Zealand and she can only speak Cantonese.
> So she's lived here for about, like 60 years maybe, but she still doesn't really speak English.
> But my mum's time in Hong Kong meant that she learned Chinese, so now they're able to communicate,
> so I think my grandma quite likes her now, because of that [laughs].
> (Angelina Ng, NZ, 19, female, Pakeha New Zealander/ Chinese New Zealander)

Overall, while the New Zealand participants described instances of opposition, such opposition often seemed to abate over time for both sides of the family. This was in contrast to some of the Singaporean stories, where family disapproval lasted until the parent died. This emphasizes the twin strength and permeability of racialized boundaries in both countries, as personal relationships were shaped by histories of race and belonging.

The roles of both parents proved important to participants, with gendered parenting roles emerging as influential, but in different ways. For the Singaporean group, many more mothers were of Chinese descent and fathers of European descent than vice versa. For the New Zealand group, the gender/ethnicity ratio was more even, with roughly the same numbers of Chinese mothers and European fathers, and Chinese fathers and European mothers. Previous research has explored gender roles and racial identification, suggesting that the mother's role as the primary nurturer is more influential in transmitting culture (Wilson 1987), or that as a result of patrilineal emphasis, coupled with the father's inherited surname as a signifier of culture, the father will be the stronger influence (Qian 2004; Waters 1989; Xie and Goyette 1997)[1]. Individual stories showed an interesting combination of both, often related to the relationship of the parents. Participants discussed how divorce and separation affected their families, showing that the physical separation and dislocation of parents splitting up created more of a dissonance than any perceived cultural gap. The parent (usually the mother) who took the role of the primary caregiver after the split unsurprisingly had more of an impact on the described cultural identity of participants. William felt strongly connected to his mother's culture as a result.

> And um, yeah, they're not together anymore,
> so I have like two different worlds again, kind of thing.
> And like so I spend most of my time in Europe with my dad

and I stay in Singapore with my mum.
So it's, it's quite different . . . [laughs].
Um, my dad moved around quite a bit.
He didn't stay in Singapore all the time. Um, he moved to different parts of Europe and yeah.
My mum always stayed there, in Singapore. And raised us.
So I guess, again, it's quite strongly towards the whole Chinese culture that I have.

(William Briggs, SG, 21, male, Singaporean Chinese/English)

When exploring childhood memories and experiences, the intersections between ancestry, culture and family were prominent. While many participants in both countries were born and/or raised in two-parent, biological families, some had to reconcile experiences of adoption and blended families. Two of the Singaporean participants had parents who were adopted into families that were culturally different to their birth families. As a result, these parents were raised within another culture, adopting the traditions, language and religion, despite being ethnically identified as Chinese. One of the participants, Safiyah, saw her mother's adopted culture as her own, practicing Islam and feeling at ease in the Malay community of her mother's adopted family. The other, Sandra, reacted very differently, saying:

I'm very aware of the fact that on my mother's side, it's the adopted family right, so they're not blood related.
And to that extent, I'm unsentimental.
I'm really a person, I mean I've done personality tests and all that,
and I'm really somebody that's more logic than emotion,
and quite unsentimental in the sense that I see things as they are,
and on my mother's side, I grew up with what you would call cousins and aunts and uncles that I knew were not blood related.
And whose values I shared very little of, actually.
Um, I tended more to question their beliefs and their, their way of thinking, more than anything else.
On my father's side, I would say that I felt more comfortable,
but maybe it's a biased perception because I know that they are blood related.
I know that I wanted to identify with them.
I mean, I chose to identify with the Portuguese side,
being Eurasian rather than Chinese.

(Sandra Pereira-Ivansson, SG, 36, female, Hakka and Peranakan Chinese/Chinese and Portuguese)

She drew a sharp line between blood and non-blood relatives, expressing a belief in lineage and biological descent as constitutive of identity: a strong narrative of reinforcement. Her focus on blood as belonging highlighted the emphasis on race in Singapore, as she placed race in the category of logic. The choice to emphasize her European side reflected the legacy of racialized hierarchy, privileging European heritage, particularly within the Eurasian community.

Narratives of blood and belonging were also found in New Zealand. One man was adopted himself, the son of a Chinese New Zealand man and a Pakeha woman, raised in a Pakeha family.

> I was adopted
> and I grew up in a Pakeha family,
> I pretty much identify with that side
> much more than the Chinese side,
> because I didn't grow up with that side of the culture [. . .]
> Um, and the interesting thing from the adopted point of view, the whole nature versus nurture thing.
> Um, how really similar we are to, um, our genetic families.
> Um, whereas, this whole nature side of things, ah nurture side of things, where we've like,
> okay there's values and so on that have been instilled,
> but from a personality point of view, we're so different from our adopted parents.
> And very similar to our birth families.
> Yeah, so . . . and I hadn't, I hadn't really grown up with the Asian side,
> but as I've grown [inaudible] I've developed a real interest in it.
> And from doing martial arts and so on,
> when I was younger and a lot of it now, um,
> for some reason I identify more with Japanese culture than Chinese.
> Um, but yeah, developed that interest in a whole lot of things Asian.
>
> (Jason De Vries, NZ, 39, male,
> Pakeha New Zealander/Chinese New Zealander)

Jason described the strong impact of the culture of his adoptive family, while also questioning the relationship between nature and nurture, and the reality of racial descent. As someone who perceived himself as biologically rather than culturally mixed, his story intertwined both transcendence and reinforcement: he identified with his Pakeha family, while also stressing his sense of connection to his Asian roots, through his Chinese heritage. Interestingly, for him, Asian identity in a broader sense held more interest than solely Chinese identity. This reflected his understanding of general "Asianness" through practice (martial arts in his case), as a point of difference to identify with and draw upon.

Location and dislocation

Personal experiences were key in participants' stories, and these stories were always located in a particular context of family, community and neighbourhood. A number of studies around the world have emphasized the importance of local context as having a powerful impact on how individuals see their own identities and their place within the wider community (Jimenez 2004; Motoyoshi 1990; Oikawa and Yoshida 2007; Stephan and Stephan 1989; Wilson 1987). For participants in this research, the location in which they grew up and the circumstances of their upbringing had important effects on how they saw themselves, both in terms of belonging to the nation and in their connections to national and/or cultural groups elsewhere.

Geographical location and relocation were important themes, interweaving stories of descent, parental background, childhood and migration into wider narratives of identity. In Singapore, the distinction between local and expat, Singaporean and foreign, shaped many peoples' childhood experiences and, as a consequence, how they saw themselves within Singapore. James and Katrina described how they felt primarily expat Singaporean, having vastly different experiences at school and within their families to how they perceived "local" Singaporeans.

> I don't think I ever fitted in with the . . . I didn't,
> like my father still lives in a very Caucasian world, like we don't go to, we don't go to local hawker centres, or we don't do . . .
> or he doesn't anyway, and that point I was listening to him,
> so you'd go to school, you'd come back from school, we played in the condominium, or the apartment blocks where most of my neighbours were Caucasians anyway.
> And then on the weekends it's church.
> But it was quite . . . you had . . .
> and then if we went out for dinner, we'd go to the Dutch club, or the British club, or the American club, you know the Tanglin club.
> So there wasn't any of this going to eat in the middle of the night you know, or shopping in some neighbourhoods.
>
> (Katrina Henry, SG, 27, female, Singaporean Chinese/English)

The majority of participants positioned themselves somewhere in-between local and expat, often related to the schools they went to and the neighbourhoods in which they grew up. William described how he felt like an expat as a child, and then identified strongly as a local Singaporean during his national service.

> I, at the beginning, obviously as I said,
> I was in international school, really Westernized, like most everything I did and all my friends, although we had similar backgrounds . . .
> I lived a bit of an expat life at the beginning, and that's very different to what you see with the locals, and they do, they tell me
> and towards the end, when I really, well the end of the time I was in Singapore, like during national service, I really felt quite local.
>
> (William Briggs, SG, 21, male, Singaporean Chinese/English)

Location within Singapore itself continued to be important for many people as they grew up. Living in a private condo or a public HDB block, in the centre of the city or an outer suburb, was something that affected people in terms of how they perceived the diversity of the area and their position within it. Many lived in "heartland" suburbs and felt that they and their families were quite prominent and unusual in such areas. Andrew felt quite isolated as a result, and sought an area where ethnic diversity would be more common.

> And Jeanne and I, right now, we live in this area.
> It's really a Chinese heartland. A Singaporean heartland.
> When we say a heartland, the heartland, we really mean the Chinese Singapore.
> People here speak a lot of dialect, they don't speak Mandarin. Hardly speak English. Huge problem for us.
> And we want to move away from that.
> We're not ashamed of being in this area.
> We are part Chinese. She, her surname is Goh, I have Wang as part of my surname, but we want to go to a place where there is more ethnic diversity.
> And just one week ago we went to ah, Arab street, where the mosque is, and um, we had a sigh of relief really.
> It was . . . we had this load lifted off us, just being in the area where you don't see Chinese people. It's so odd to say.
> (Andrew Wang-Jones, SG, 36, male, English and German/Eurasian)

He positioned himself as both a Singaporean and an outsider, feeling connected to Singapore as a nation, but excluded by racialized groupings within the country. His story highlighted his feelings of exclusion, conflicting with where he felt at home, reinforcing narratives of racial belonging. Somewhere in the middle of the expat/local dichotomy, he struggled to position himself symbolically and physically as a racialized Singaporean.

In New Zealand, the expat/local division did not exist in the same way. While diversity was important for participants in how and where they located themselves, external perceptions focused around an immigrant/non-immigrant divide, which was not replicated in how individuals saw themselves. Participants often spoke of belonging to New Zealand through an attachment to place, something which would not necessarily be recognized by others, but which formed an important part of personal identities. Melanie and Alexis talked about the importance of literal personal location: knowing your way around as a way to not feel lost, both physically and symbolically.

> Um, I also really like to explore, you know, the city, I think.
> Um, I want to, you know, know the roads, and where I'm going, and just familiarize yourself with directions and stuff.

That's really important for me, to feel like I belong somewhere.

Um, I mean it sounds like a given, but it's amazing how many people I know, just, you know, hop in a cab, and wherever, they don't know where they're going.

Or they don't know how to get there. You know? Or they have a driver that just takes them.

And, they don't know the routes, and they don't know where this road and that road is, and I just can't, I can't be like that [laughs].

(Melanie Townsend, NZ, 30, female,
Taiwan Chinese/Pakeha New Zealander)

Melanie's narrative was simply about locating herself in physical space in order to feel at home, a subversive way to belong outside of traditional categories and groupings. Her story set private feelings of belonging outside of public perceptions, allowing her to determine her own locations of home. Another woman indicated that her feelings of belonging were more of process, a personal location that developed over time and experience. For Philippa, belonging grew out of connections and experiences. She felt that she could locate herself in a community that she worked to contribute to, which was not necessarily defined along ethnic lines. Her story was more accommodating, as she built her own sense of belonging through networks and shared understandings.

Um, I think it's, from my point of view, it's having stayed in one place for a long time and starting to build up relationships with um, people in that area.

Um, you know you can walk along the street, and you can say hello to a few people.

You can go to the shops, and they know you.

Um . . . you, you know, as an adult, you have friends that you can go and have dinner with, and the kids can play.

Um . . . which you kind of need, when you've got kids my age, and you're starting to kind of get back a life. And you can start to go out.

'Cause I, I've kind of shifted round a little bit.

And when you get to a place and you don't know anyone, you have to make those connections.

But it takes a while.

And when you've been in the same, in you know one place, and you're starting to get all those connections, I think that's what it feels like to be belonging.

Belong somewhere.

(Philippa Warner, NZ, 38, female,
Pakeha New Zealander/Chinese New Zealander)

Importantly, participants from both Singapore and New Zealand often located themselves in multiple places, describing experiences and links to a number of countries and communities. Rather than portraying a diasporic connection to an ancestral homeland, many participants talked about how they felt connected to places they had lived in and travelled to, where they felt at home. Seven of the Singaporean participants and four from New Zealand were currently living outside of the country, with many participants having lived in or travelled to multiple countries throughout their lives. For some, travel was a way of life growing up, separating them from their peers. As a result, they described how they felt comfortable around diversity and multiplicity, enjoying both the cultural variety and the relative anonymity of not standing out.

James and Sandra made a point of emphasizing that they felt the need to keep moving around the world, as they were attracted to diverse and populous cities. Skye and William indicated that leaving Singapore once they had finished their secondary education was something they had always assumed they would do, to experience other cultures and continue the habit of travel that they had grown up with. For these individuals, their links to multiple places and cultures gave them the option to locate themselves differently, perhaps with their more fluid connections to Singapore allowing them to move around more easily. Sandra drew on discourses of reinforcement, biology and racial traits, suggesting that the desire to travel was in her blood, as she was descended from immigrants. On the flipside, Terence equated his mixed heritage with an increasing propensity to travel, suggesting that "mixed race" was a result of social and historical processes of immigration and globalization. He located his mixedness as part of a wider social trend, seeing his background as less about racial differences, and more about migration and meetings.

> It just means that you're different. And that you're just, you're a function of globalization, ah.
> Um, yeah, people tend to move more. And people move more, they have greater access to transportation, it just means that um, you have greater opportunity to meet other people, ah. And then, just . . .
> I mean, they're just part of a trend, lah.
> The trend today is people are more, there are more interracial marriages. And because there are more interracial marriages, interracial kids.
> And you're just part of this trend, ah.
> (Terence Peaks, SG, 26, male, Filipino Chinese/Anglo Australian)

Participants in New Zealand also described significant travel over the course of their lives, something which they felt set them apart. Most participants would travel to see friends and family as they grew up, and as for the Singaporeans, many felt that these experiences had instilled a sense of possibility in them: seeing the world and living outside of New Zealand had shaped how they positioned themselves both in New Zealand and elsewhere. One woman felt that she belonged anywhere but New Zealand:

[I belong] Overseas [laughs].
Um . . . I like Auckland, but, New Zealand's . . .
I find 'cause I've had that exposure to travelling and things, and new ideas . . .
it's um, I find New Zealand culture very isolating, and quite small. Very um, parochial, I think.
And I . . . I want to just go overseas, and bring my experience, and just take it all in, and go to different places and sample and taste . . . different cultures.
I find New Zealand quite limiting.
Although, I like, I love New Zealand.
My, I think, I was trying to explain this to a friend the other day.
It's the kind of place where you go and have your family, 'cause it's so isolated, and safe, and calm. And you know, you know the lay of the land.
But I think there's more, um, sort of world. Well there is, and you should go and experience it.
And knowing what's out there, I can't just live here, and not go out and want to try it, at least.
So . . . um, I guess, physically that's where I am. But, I don't know.

(Rose Stein, NZ, 22, female,
Hong Kong Chinese/Dutch)

Her story portrayed a dual sense of belonging: here and elsewhere. She described New Zealand as limited in its culture and possibilities, and sought to locate herself somewhere more diverse. Interestingly, this illustrated the strength of her connection to New Zealand, as she felt too comfortable and at home, seeking adventure elsewhere. Another woman, Emmeline, felt at home in diversity and cosmopolitanism, something which she found New Zealand lacked. For her, travel had opened up possibilities of places to locate herself, in order to enjoy her uniqueness rather than feeling compelled to conform. One man spoke of locations and differences within New Zealand itself:

And, um, yeah, I do remember, like I really had a kind of a . . .
I kind of resented it to start with.
Like for many years when I was a child.
And I, like I mentioned, it's simply because I stood out,
because it was so, um, culturally like,
the Caucasian population was by far the largest part of the population in Blenheim.
Um, so yeah, I did, I was quite ashamed for many years.
And it gradually sort of faded towards the end of high school.
Um, to the point that, like I mentioned, in my 20s,
especially down in Dunedin, where there's, there is that diversity.
I think that that is the secret, like just having, seeing there's a lot of other people that are different.

(Jason De Vries, NZ, 39, male,
Pakeha New Zealander/Chinese New Zealander)

90 *Being and belonging*

As in Singapore, different locations within the country affected how participants viewed their identities, and how they belonged. Jason's narrative illuminated the different contexts within New Zealand itself in terms of diversity: contrasting small towns and larger cities, the North and the South Islands. His narrative drew out a sense of belonging through difference, both reinforcing racial differences, and accommodating his own sense of difference within diversity.

Travelling and movement around the country and the world had different impacts on participants. Some felt that they were able to live in and adapt to multiple environments fairly easily, and others struggled to feel like they belonged easily in any one place. Individuals in both contexts spoke of the positives and negatives of changing locations frequently: discovering a sense of identity distinct from wider notions of belonging, while simultaneously feeling that they did not fit in anywhere.

> Um, but it's never really been important to me, and it's never really been, um, it's never, I've never felt,
> while I've never felt like I was part of a greater clique, you know, I've never felt I was Singaporean, I've never felt I was Australian,
> and I never felt that I was part of something pretty, you know, and I should probably have mentioned this before, I'm also not religious.
> Um, so I've never felt like I've been part of a big cultural, or ethnic, or religious or national group, but I've never ever, I've never missed it.
> I've not missed being part of that.
> Um, does that make me more individual? I don't know. Maybe . . .
> Um, but I also kind of like the idea that I am a bit sort of transnational, you know?
>
> (James Field, SG, 25, male, Singaporean Chinese/Anglo Australian)

James linked this sense of isolation to a feeling of exclusion from any community, be it ethnic, national, cultural or religious. His narrative transcended these traditional ways to belong, as he searched for alternatives. For him, this lack of community was not something that he sought to remedy, as it had become a part of his sense of individual identity. He instead negotiated *not belonging* as a way to belong and locate himself.

Location was also linked to experiences of racism and discrimination. Many participants in both countries told stories of discrimination and exclusion, particularly at school. Name-calling was common, and participants often found themselves the target of teasing, or in the uncomfortable position of witnessing race-based bullying but with others not realizing their backgrounds. In Singapore, participants at local schools spoke of standing out due to their European heritage.

> You know, you have the name-calling.
> No, that's fine, it becomes a term of endearment after a while, with your friends. Because . . . the local slang for you know, for Caucasians is Ang

Mo, which is red haired. And that kind of stuff, it's either that or Kangaroo. Yeah, it's been throughout, so 11 years of that, you get used to it.

(Richard Ong, SG, 22, male,
Singaporean Chinese/Anglo Australian)

As in Richard's narrative, several people mentioned that these were just names, and did not have a serious impact on how they saw themselves. However, for others, the constant questioning and bullying had more lasting impacts, particularly when they were involved in more serious or physical instances of racism.

'Cause since primary school I've always had a problem.
I've had kids, my classmates, in very broken English, say to me, ah, "Hey you, Italy boy, ah!" "Are you from America, ah?"
Once I remember, when I was in primary 4, age of, ah, what would that be? 10, or 11, I suppose.
I remember I was walking by a sidewalk, and a school bus passed by with Singaporean kids, and they were saying, "British bulldog go home!"
Threw stones at me and stuff. Very weird.

(Andrew Wang-Jones, SG, 36, male,
English and German/Eurasian)

The New Zealand participants had many more stories of race-based discrimination and bullying at school, experiences which centred around their Chinese heritage and their visible difference from the majority population. Many found this dislocating, as people questioned their place in New Zealand along racialized lines.

Like even though my school was quite multicultural, I was definitely exposed to quite a lot of racism, even from a young age.
And I still remember it.
'Cause, you know, you're like bullied and things like that, and I always feel, I remember feeling out of place, because I wasn't like, um . . .
I wasn't like the typical Asian primary school kid that was definitely like, had just come to New Zealand type thing.
I was like, I thought of myself as being like a New Zealander, and being like I've been brought up in a Western way.
But yet, people would obviously see, you can tell obviously that I'm not European, and I definitely look Asian, and so I used to get teased a lot when I was at primary school, which was never nice.

(Jenny Griffiths, NZ, 25, female,
Pakeha New Zealander/Chinese New Zealander)

Jenny's story reinforced her impressions of New Zealander as primarily European, stemming from her experiences of exclusion based on her appearance. She sought to reconcile her own feelings of belonging with how she believed that others saw her. Yet she also made a point of distinguishing herself, as a New Zealander, from the new Asian immigrants.

Other participants narrated how their physical appearance was a point of difference which others made fun of, but which didn't necessarily affect how they felt about themselves. Joel and Nathan discussed bullying at school, but downplayed its seriousness and effects.

> I was teased, because they said my dad's the postman, you know. . . .
> But um . . . hmmm . . . I know my brother was probably teased a little bit more, but having said that, he's the most confident one. And pretty tough.
> You know there's a chant that goes round school . . . what was it, I don't know if you've heard and seen that, have you?
> With the Chinese Japanese thing? Well it goes [laughs] . . .
> you pull you eyes downwards for Chinese, you go "Chinese, Japanese" and pull you eyes up "Chinese, Japanese, blah, blah, blah and look what's happened to me" and then you sort of mix your eyes up and down, something like that.
> And you get a lot of this sort of stuff, and chink, and all sorts of slang for Chinese.
> Yeah, it wasn't too bad.
>
> (Nathan Fleming, NZ, 39, male, American Chinese/Pakeha New Zealander)

Despite the overtly racist connotations of his experiences, Nathan mentioned that it "wasn't too bad", laughing in discomfort at a rhyme around both Asian appearance and "mixed race". He talked about himself and his brother, stressing their (male) resilience to the teasing, although for different reasons. His own experiences were based around how different he looked to his family, while his brother was seen as Asian, and treated as such. His sister noticed the differences in experiences, commenting on the impacts of gender and race in terms of discrimination and vulnerability.

> And I think, you know guys' experiences are always going to be different to what women's experiences are going to be, growing up.
> I mean I don't know.
> I don't think Nath would have been given any crap for being Asian because he doesn't look it. . . .
> Nathan the milkman's boy. Yeah.
>
> (Margaret Jenkins, NZ, 35, female, American Chinese/Pakeha New Zealander)

Several women had the opposite reaction to their school experiences, and Jenny offered a similar gender-based explanation for why some people were affected more than others by discrimination at school.

I do think that, like, because of your experiences when you're younger, it . . . it totally influences how you perceive, like your perception of life in general.

Like if I had never had had any racist comments when I was little, I probably would never be so self-conscious about my . . . who I am, and my ethnic background.

But because I had multiple negative experiences when I was at primary school, I just distinctly . . .

like I've always been super self-conscious about . . . about what I look like, and . . . where I belong and the fact that my dad's Chinese and my mum's white,

but I only really identify with being white, and oh my god, what's going on . . . so . . . I think it's . . . yeah.

Whereas I think my brothers probably didn't . . . like you know also guys, boys are usually more thick-skinned than girls, so they probably don't take to heart as much things as females do half the time.

So that could also partly be why.

(Jenny Griffiths, NZ, 25, female, Pakeha New Zealander/Chinese New Zealander)

Similarly, another woman was so affected by the chants and the teasing that she had recurring nightmares as a child.

Yeah, so they used to do the whole [pulls eyes] "Hi, my mum's Japanese, my dad's Chinese, whatever, whatever" . . .

and um, a lot of them were blond, blue-eyed at my school, and they were like "oh, you're so ugly, you've got brown hair, your eyes are the colour of poo" [laughs] [. . .]

I think my mum used to . . . um, find me in the middle of the night having nightmares. It's what she tells me now, as an adult.

And I was like reliving all the mean things that people were saying to me at school.

But I'd never tell her about it when I was awake, so she only knew because she heard my nightmares [laughs]. Yeah. . . .

I don't remember those nightmares though, so it's okay.

(Alexis Conrad, NZ, 33, female, Chinese New Zealander/New Zealand European)

As for Alexis and Jenny, those who spoke of being most affected by racism at school were women. Some also spoke about wishing they could have changed their appearance when they were younger – reflecting the intersections between judgments of physical appearance, race and the pressures of gendered expectations of beauty and belonging.

Participants also explored issues of race and racism in wider society, reflected in the microcosm of school. In both countries, the age range of participants provided an interesting comparison of social attitudes towards "mixed race" and levels of racism over time. In Singapore, mixing was not encouraged, and those who were mixed were initially seen as "not correct":

> I think in the early part, the mixing was not so easy and it tended . . . here I've got to be careful . . .
> it tended to feel that people who were mixed weren't correct in the early days.
> That means the Chinese were, you know, the Chinese . . . and for example I was dating a girl – Chinese girl – for a couple of years but we knew we weren't going to marry.
> The parents would say, "No, that's definite, you won't marry."
> And that . . . that is kind of the environment that we grew up in, you know, there was no crossing of lines.
> You're . . . the boundaries are there. Even now there are religions and that kind of problems, but that's clear.
> We . . . we understand those religions like Muslims or Catholics, you know, that kind of stuff. That's clear.
> But in those days how hard it was, you know, how difficult it was to cross over.
>
> (David Faulkner, SG, 64, male, Singaporean Chinese/White British)

David's narrative, as the oldest Singaporean participant, was particularly interesting as he remarked on the difficulties of mixed relationships in the past. He was cautious about how he described this, illustrating the taboos around boundary crossing that linger on. He presented a personal narrative of accommodation, allowing his own experiences of mixedness to exist alongside these external opinions. While many people (including David) mentioned how Singapore had changed to become more tolerant, particularly in the last decade, Anne and Andrew were adamant that racism still existed, but was now just more hidden than before.

> And that's . . . and it's something that . . . it really irks me because there's so much racism in Singapore. But it's not obvious.
> You know . . . and it's so, like, quiet, and subversive, and like, okay we're not going to talk about it.
> We're just going to pretend everything's fine and dandy. And it's not. [. . .]
> And it's . . . that is what Singapore is like to me. It's like, on the outside it looks so good, and you know, everybody says they believe these things.
> But on the inside, they don't believe them. And the inside of the country doesn't look good.
>
> (Anne McNeil, SG, 27, female, Singaporean Chinese/English)

The New Zealand participants described a similar trajectory, moving from an obviously racist society towards greater tolerance, yet also continued prejudice. One participant, Jason De Vries, stressed that location was key, as more diverse contexts tended to be more tolerant. He saw a significant difference in the populations of the North and South Islands, as the North has much more diversity and is the destination for most immigrants arriving from Asia. Paul Moretti, the oldest participant from the New Zealand sample, highlighted the changing attitudes in society over time. He talked about racism as he grew up, and New Zealand's isolation in terms of food and diversity. He used details of difference in his story, centring on food as a marker of difference for him and his family.

> Um . . . New Zealand in the 1960s and 70s was a racist place, I believe.
> Um . . . it was, it was strange for me because my father was Italian, so an Italian name, and my mother was Chinese.
> And so for some people I look Chinese. And for other people they're not quite sure what I am. [. . .]
> Um . . . New Zealand was a very closeted place in those days.
> I mean, I can remember my mother and father having to travel into Auckland City to buy bags of rice, 'cause you couldn't buy rice in supermarkets, and you couldn't buy garlic, you couldn't buy ginger, all the simple things.
> Or soy sauce . . . all those sorts of things.
> (Paul Moretti, NZ, 48, male, Chinese/Italian)

In contrast, for several young women in their twenties and thirties, change hadn't been significant enough to prevent racism from playing a significant role in their lives.

> Like, I think it made me feel quite . . . quite sort of vulnerable when that sort of thing happened when I was small.
> And then things got quite . . . well, things didn't ever get bad for me personally at high school but when there were a lot of migrants who came in there was a massive backlash at my school anyway.
> People were really racist and horrible and it constantly, like, everywhere you go, everyone was just constantly talking about, "Oh, those fucking Asians, those gooks I wish they'd just all, like, go home."
> And they . . . they used to put, like, massive racist graffiti in the bathrooms and I remember just kind of not really knowing what to do 'cause I kind of felt like I didn't identify with, um, the migrants but then I really didn't like what those people were saying.
> But then I didn't also want them to think that I was one of them.
> (Emmeline Tan, NZ, 32, female, Pakeha New Zealander/Singaporean Chinese)

Emmeline's story was caught in social attitudes towards immigration and national belonging. She found herself trapped between wanting to belong as an uncomplicated, (non-)racial New Zealander, and feeling for the Asian groups being targeted. This was an interesting narrative of accommodation, as she positioned herself as both insider and outsider, shifting her sense of loyalty as a result of her experiences. Another woman felt that racism existed for both minority and majority groups, and as she had connections to both, she felt caught in the middle.

> I just feel that I, I also feel that um, people in general, especially,
> well, not especially, but . . . but yeah.
> People are always racist wherever you go.
> And being of mixed ethnicity, it's like an internal struggle,
> 'cause like, I often hear white people being racist against Asian people, all the time.
> And I think a lot of my friends and things, and people in general treat me as, like not the, like not Asian, because I'm so Westernized.
> But then, you also hear Asian people being quite racist towards white people.
> And because I sit in the middle, I feel . . .
> like it feels like an internal kind of strife.
>
> (Jenny Griffiths, NZ, 25, female,
> Pakeha New Zealander/Chinese New Zealander)

Racism was an important part of Jenny's reality, and was something that impacted her everyday life in a negative way, despite the increasing tolerance described by other participants. She reinforced racial groupings by narrating herself as caught in-between, facing exclusion from both sides. The changing context of immigration and the shifting demographic profile of New Zealand society in the 1980s and 1990s meant that these women felt caught up in the backlash, as racialized discrimination brushed over differences of ancestry, culture, generation and immigration status.

Belonging and not belonging

Against these backgrounds, participants negotiated ways of belonging as Chinese, European and both at once. Moving away from family and location, participants described the more personal ways in which their heritages made them feel both in and out of place. Ethnic and racial communities provided important markers as they positioned themselves in relation to their parent's ancestries, both within and outside of socially defined groups. As individuals with family links to more than one background, race as a social identity was complex, requiring considerable thought and negotiation, as well as a balance between personal and external conceptions of culture and belonging. The available narratives of cultural belonging provided a base for identification, as understandings of "European" and "Chinese" identity in Singapore and New Zealand shaped the narratives of participants.

Descriptions of ethnic and racial belonging were central in personal stories, illustrating the selective, shifting and situational options available to participants as they described their identities. Similar to previous research on approaches to mixedness, most individuals described how they identified in different ways with both sides of their ancestry, even if this self-perception was not reinforced by others. Traditional, singular racial identities were not often used as personal labels, in contrast to many previous studies done in the North American context, particularly when looking at black/white mixes. Labelling was therefore complex, and it was through personal stories that individuals were better able to express what being (or not being) Chinese and European meant to them.

Chineseness and belonging

Despite the majority of participants asserting that they felt both Chinese and European, it was "Chineseness" that came to the fore in narratives. Theoretically, the category of Chinese is extremely broad and difficult to define, linked to nationality, ethnic group, ancestry, diaspora, traditions and cultures (Chow 1998; Matthews 2002). For participants, being Chinese meant many different things. For the Singaporean participants, Chineseness was linked closely to linguistic ability and cultural upbringing: practices and family traditions which would reinforce assertions of cultural authenticity. This question of authenticity was key for William, as he sought to position a complex identity within a singular framework:

> [I say] "I'm as Chinese as all of you!", but they don't believe me [laughs].
> They just laugh.
> Which is kind of why I want to learn Chinese as well,
> just to kind of support everything that I'm saying.
> 'Cause I can't just go around and "yeah, I'm Chinese"
> without being able to speak Chinese,
> or even look as Chinese as everyone else.
> Just, just yeah.
> An arsenal of, just, just to back up whatever I'm saying.
> (William Briggs, SG, 21, male,
> Singaporean Chinese/English)

His narrative centred around being demonstrably Chinese, using language as a real and tangible marker of identity. For him, symbolic identity left a gap between his private feelings and his friends' public acknowledgements, showing the cultural practices around race in the Singaporean context.

Interestingly, Chineseness was discussed and asserted particularly by the New Zealand participants, reflecting the need to describe and perhaps defend a minority identity in a largely white society. Being Chinese was held up in opposition to just being a "normal Kiwi", and was a key point of difference to be emphasized or downplayed. A large number of participants mentioned "Chinese" traits in their upbringing or their personalities, illustrating how their heritage had influenced who they were. Several people discussed how they felt that financial security and family obligation were particularly Chinese traits, often in combination with respect for elders. One woman saw this perspective as having significantly influenced her life choices and her role in her family.

> I originally wanted to do fashion design.
> And I was, I was actually studying at the London School of Fashion,
> and I got so much pressure to come back, and "that was a terrible decision"
> and "what are you thinking?"
> and I was sort of halfway thinking the same thing . . .
> And so that's, that's definitely a Chinese thing.
> Needing to know, as well, that I can look after my parents if I need to.
> And I did, I looked after my father,
> and I made sure that I had everything in place to make sure that he was okay.
> I think that's a Chinese thing as well.
> I don't really see that for many of my other friends, that very strong sense of responsibility to the parents.
>
> (Alexis Conrad, NZ, 33, female,
> Chinese New Zealander/New Zealand European)

In her case, her Chinese ancestry came through in feelings of loyalty to her family, and her financial responsibility, reinforcing links between culture and biology. She narrated being Chinese as being different from her friends, seeking personality traits that reflected how she perceived Chineseness. For others, being Chinese was heavily influenced by food and family culture, as well as attitudes to academic learning and inherent predispositions, such as suggesting that their mathematical ability came from their ancestry. For Paul, the oldest New Zealand participant, his childhood was very shaped by what he saw as his mother's traditional Chinese practices, many of which centred on food and her role as a mother around language and care.

For other participants in both countries, however, being Chinese was less a matter of practised behaviour and more a feeling of connection. For one adopted participant, Jason, his Chinese background was of greater importance symbolically than his European background, despite his lack of cultural knowledge. Another woman felt that she was connected to China because of how other people treated her, even though she didn't feel any personal affinity for the culture or the country.

> I feel like, somehow, I have a connection with China.
> Even though I've never been there.
> Whereas he [brother] thinks it's quite weird for someone to ask him what it's like to . . . what Chinese culture is.
> Um . . . so . . . I don't know, maybe, I feel like I have more of a connection than they [siblings] do. I'm not sure.

Just because people have always treated me that way.

(Andrea Wei, NZ, 21, female,
White American/American Chinese)

Her story reflected the power of external perceptions in shaping internal identifications, as her feelings of connection came largely from the expectations of others. This narrative reflected an interesting form of accommodation, as she worked to reconcile the internal and the external, taking on an identity which was assigned to her. As both her parents were raised in the United States, her link to China was several generations removed, and she connected China as a country with how she understood being Chinese.

Another participant was more distanced from how he saw his Chineseness, making a distinction between cultural practices which were part of his everyday life, and those which were enforced by his parents.

> But, there was definitely like an influence from my parents that wanted to keep um, this Chinese culture going.
> So you know, they would, we'd go to festivals and um, eat Chinese food, and . . . go to language schools and things like that, learn lion dancing.
> Um, yeah so . . . and it, but it was more a superficial way of pushing culture.
> Like I never thought as a Chinese person would think.
> Um, it was more just the superficial things. Yeah.
>
> (Joel Andrews, NZ, 24, male,
> Chinese New Zealander/Pakeha New Zealander)

Joel saw his Chinese culture as superficial, or even symbolic. It was not a major part of who he was as a person, despite external pressures and activities to reinforce that aspect of himself. He saw himself as definitively not "a Chinese person", marking a clear divide as he described a sense of belonging in New Zealand, delicately inflected by a Chinese heritage.

Chinese identity was therefore extremely variable, and was not a form of identity which could be taken for granted. As well as describing practical instances of being Chinese, participants often placed weight on what they felt was Chinese about themselves: a more symbolic, emotional form of connection. Yet, in addition to looking inwards for what being Chinese meant, participants looked outwards for definitions. In both Singapore and New Zealand, nationality, upbringing and immigration status were important distinctions. For the Singaporeans, being Singaporean Chinese was markedly different from being Chinese from mainland China, with significant cultural differences between the two. In New Zealand, differences were pointed out between New Zealand Chinese and recent immigrants from China. The New Zealand Chinese were seen as more culturally acceptable, more authentically Kiwi, given the length of time their families had been in the country.

The New Zealand participants often referred to their Chinese parent and that parent's attitude to their heritage. The majority of parents had immigrated to New Zealand themselves, and they had taken different routes to reconciling a new national identity with different forms of cultural heritage. Most parents had immersed themselves in their new country, with some even distancing or disassociating themselves from their Chinese heritage as a way to strengthen their bonds to New Zealand.

> But, um . . . it's funny as well, my mum has been here so long, like, um . . .
> she was driving one day, and um, you know some Asian driver pulled out in front of her. And she goes "bloody Chink!" [laughs]
> And me and my brothers were like "you're a Chink too!" [laughs]
> She's like "no, I'm not a Chink like that Chink!" [laughs]
> (Jasmine Orana, NZ, 25, female, Singaporean Chinese/Pakeha New Zealander)

Jasmine's story showed how her Chinese mother had taken on some of the common stereotypes about Chinese immigrants in New Zealand, stressing her belonging as a New Zealander. This narrative highlighted the complexity of categories and the different ways of being Chinese and Asian as a minority identity. Her mother both subverted expectations and reinforced stereotypes, in a complex negotiation of belonging.

For two other women, their fathers' lack of identification with their Chinese backgrounds had a significant effect on their own feelings about their heritage. One woman, Andrea, felt that her father's negative attitude had encouraged a superficial practice of Chinese culture and a negative attitude towards being Chinese. A second woman, Jenny, saw her father as Westernized but felt that his lack of acknowledgement for his heritage left her without a cultural anchor on her Chinese side.

> Um . . . he [father] . . . he's really Westernized. Like 'cause he came to New Zealand when he was one.
> So, even his Cantonese is like the ability of an eight-year-old.
> He doesn't do anything Chinese at all except for eat Chinese food every now and then.
> And other than that, nothing.
> So . . . I guess that in itself, like could make me quite confused as well.
> 'Cause he never, he doesn't even acknowledge his Asian roots anymore.
> Which is fine, I mean, he might not feel, he probably doesn't feel he's Chinese either, 'cause he's grown up in New Zealand.
> But . . . when people look at him, or look at me, they think "oh wow, she's definitely not a Kiwi".
> (Jenny Griffiths, NZ, 25, female, Pakeha New Zealander/Chinese New Zealander)

Her sense of not being Chinese was then closely linked to how she saw her father. She acknowledged that he must have felt a similar public/private dissonance to her, as his appearance and his cultural/national affiliations did not match in a simplistic way. The strength of external perceptions heavily informed her narrative, as she struggled to reconcile the public and the private. Her story illustrated her feelings of exclusion from being a "proper" New Zealander, while at the same time highlighting her search for a way to identify as Chinese.

On not being Chinese

Generation, immigration status and nationality were all key distinctions in how participants understood being Chinese, for themselves, their families and others. For many participants, their sense of *being Chinese* was balanced by how they felt they were not Chinese, as *not being Chinese* proved to be an important aspect of identity. Rather than *being European*, participants described how they did not feel Chinese, meaning that the idea of "whiteness" was conspicuous in its absence in descriptions of identity.

Seven of the New Zealand participants (Angelina, Li Lin, Jacob, Jenny, Melanie, Tai and Paul) and one of the Singaporean participants (James) had visited or lived in China at some point in their lives, sometimes because of a perceived connection through their ancestry. Some participants talked about the experience as "going back", despite never having visited before. Others had expected to feel Chinese and "at home" in China, but the reality of their experiences was significantly different. Tai had moved to Shanghai, and he found that the local population did not treat him as Chinese, despite his background.

> I guess previously I thought I was Chinese.
> And I certainly thought, well, at least half-Chinese.
> And I certainly thought my dad was Chinese, 'cause he always identified himself as Chinese.
> But, here I realized that, um, it's quite different.
> I mean, the Chinese people here, culture, and society and everything, is quite different to Chinese people that, you know, like me or my father, or anything. And um, yeah.
> And ah, and I, it made me think, like the Chinese people outside China are very, um, they're often very, kind of, um, feel very strongly about, um, they think they're so Chinese.
> And um, you know they're really super proud of being Chinese.
> And like Chinese people in China don't seem to make such a big deal of it [. . .]
> I think overseas Chinese, you know they're not as Chinese as they think.
> (Tai Feng, NZ, 31, male, Irish/Malaysian Chinese)

This led him to reassess what it meant to be Chinese, and to question why the label *Chinese* often seemed to trump other identity labels for people of Chinese descent outside of China. This was especially apparent in the experiences of his father, who had always described himself as Chinese, but saw himself as an outsider when he visited his son in China. His narrative highlighted conflations and breaks between national identity, culture and belonging, as he stressed the importance of experience and context in identification.

James made a distinction between Singaporean Chinese identity and Chinese identity when describing his reasons for going "back". His mother felt that her symbolic connection to China would provide meaning for her son's identity, but in reality, he felt disconnected and isolated.

> And it was interesting going back because, well, not going back, but going there, I was sort of pushed.
> The idea to move to China sort of originated with my mother, who, who, who is Chinese,
> who is Singaporean Chinese in that very Singaporean Chinese way of being very proud to be Chinese.
> But yet, she herself would never ever go to China or live in China, you know, she's quite happy in Singapore.
> Um, I don't know, Singaporean Chinese have this strange affinity with the China, the Chinese of China, because, you know, China is rising and they own half the world, and they're proving that there's a Chinese spirit that's there, and blah blah blah. [. . .]
> So I moved there in order to sort of, I don't know,
> somehow find some affinity with the Chinese in me.
> You know, and I found about as much as I wanted to find,
> and realized that I'd actually found it and I think I'd rather live in the south of Italy, than in China! [laughs]
>
> (James Field, SG, 25, male, Singaporean Chinese/Anglo Australian)

His narrative drew on the meaning of "Chinese" in Singapore, comparing the symbolic connections to China felt by his mother's family, and what he saw as the reality of Singaporean Chinese identity. He questioned the strength and relevance of diasporic identifications, finding himself distanced from being Chinese, in any sense of the term. His sense of identity seemed to transcend this ancestral connection, as he grounded himself more in his experiences.

Four of the New Zealand participants went to China deliberately to explore their roots, often visiting regions where their grandparents or earlier ancestors had come from. For the two individuals, Jenny and Li Lin, who had undertaken an organized trip for New Zealand Chinese, experiences were mixed. Li Lin was surprised at the level of connection that she felt when she saw her grandparents' villages, and how she could recognize the origins of some of her current family traditions, accommodating both heritage and practice in her story. However, she also realized the significant cultural and generational differences, and the multitude of ways in which she did not feel Chinese. Jenny found the trip "back to her roots" an isolating and disconnecting experience, primarily because it emphasized the fact that she was not culturally or ancestrally "full Chinese", reinforcing narratives of racial belonging. For her, it put the fact that she did not feel Chinese in contrast with her connection to New Zealand and New Zealand culture, and left her feeling rootless, rather than rooted.

For a number of participants then, *not being Chinese* was an important part of how they described their identities, as though holding up their ancestry against the reality of their experiences. Some participants identified Chinese traits and then illustrated how these traits did not apply to them, while a number of them highlighted linguistic barriers as a marker of their lack of connection with being Chinese. Margaret stated that her lack of cultural and linguistic fluency meant that her Chinese heritage would mean less to the next generation.

Many participants, both in Singapore and New Zealand, described a connection to being European as a way of not being Chinese, but did not often explain what "European culture" entailed. In New Zealand, Pakeha culture is often an unnoticed norm, held up in opposition to indigenous or minority groups, or anything "ethnic". Chinese identity provided a symbolic identity which could be illustrated or disavowed by participants through traits and practices in opposition to the dominant culture in which they grew up, as "European" ethnicity is conspicuously absent. "Whiteness" was seen less as an identity, and more as a positioning against which being Chinese could be described (Bettez 2011; Storrs 1999). Paul, as well as going to China to learn about his heritage, also went to Italy to learn about the other side of his heritage. In doing this, he was in a minority, and for most interviewees the European side of their families fitted in easily with the wider New Zealand context, often passing unnoticed in their descriptions of themselves and their cultural backgrounds.

For the Singaporeans, European culture and ethnicity was in the minority, but carried with it historical associations of colonialism and privilege. Socioeconomic status influenced participants' experiences with diversity and their attitudes to their backgrounds (as in Butler-Sweet 2011; Mahtani 2002a; Tyler 2011). Some participants felt separate from the wider Singaporean population due to their socioeconomic positioning, which was often fairly privileged, particularly when the European parent worked for an international company. Choice of school illustrated this distinction, given the high fees for international schools, as well as the availability of overseas travel and family pastimes which would be out of reach for the majority of Singaporeans. James described how where he lived influenced how he saw himself within Singapore. Living in private housing, he found himself around many others with international backgrounds, and as such, felt distanced from "local" Singaporeans.

Socioeconomic positioning was equally important in New Zealand, but in different ways. The Chinese populations of New Zealand are not as socioeconomically differentiated as the European populations in Singapore, and participants' experiences varied depending on their parents' occupations and their locations around the country. Many participants, such as Paul, described experiences of hardship, as their newly immigrant parents settled and raised a family, while others, such as

Katie, with parents in professions such as medicine and law, were more aware of their privilege in society.

In both countries, intermarriage cut across socioeconomic sectors, and identities based around mixed heritage were not necessarily perceived as more important than other lines of gender, class and location. One woman in New Zealand felt that where she had grown up had influenced her more than her cultural heritage.

> In a way I think your lifestyle growing up and stuff like that has more of an impact on who you are and how, how you see yourself and other people.
> Like, um, because there's plenty of, plenty of Asians that have come from really well off families, and have a way different outlook to life.
> And . . . my family wasn't that well off, and so, I suppose I identified more with the people of that area, where people are not so well off. Yeah, so. Around here, it's like quite multicultural.
>
> (Jasmine Orana, NZ, 25, female, Singaporean Chinese/Pakeha New Zealander)

Jasmine's story highlighted that her childhood lifestyle, combined with her geographical and socioeconomic experiences, meant that she felt a strong connection to the place she was living, as opposed to a symbolic connection to her Asian heritage. For her, and for others, lived experience overtook ethnic identification in importance when she considered her practices in day-to-day life.

Being Chinese *and* European

In describing the ways in which they felt Chinese and European (and both at once), participants spoke of symbolic connections and practical expressions of culture. Experiences and knowledge of language, traditions, food and festivals were important manifestations of culture for individuals in both countries. As in previous literature, such cultural practices and memories of cultural exposure had an important impact on participants' identities, and particularly how they viewed their connections to either side of their heritage.

Language was a particularly influential practice linked with cultural connection. Participant groups differed when it came to linguistic ability. Two thirds of participants in Singapore spoke both English and either Mandarin, Cantonese or another language. In New Zealand, only four people spoke both English and Mandarin or Cantonese, with two thirds speaking only English. The majority of the Singapore group was most comfortable in English, with one quarter feeling comfortably bilingual. The number of bilingual individuals in New Zealand was much smaller. These differences reflect, to a large extent, the language policies of the respective education systems in each country – in Singapore, a second language is compulsory from primary school, and is ostensibly based along racial lines ("the mother tongue" of the race). Despite this, English was the comfortable language for the majority of respondents in both countries, and was often a taken-for-granted link to national and cultural identity. One man described his connections between culture, language and family:

> As much as I hate to say it, I don't really know my mum's side very well. I prefer going on holidays with my dad's side than my mum's side.
> That's purely from . . . I guess I never . . . the language barrier's a big thing for me.
> And, 'cause you can't get over the language barrier, you just can't relate to people.
> But . . . I kind of wish I did know the language 'cause I could get to know my mum's side better.
> (Jacob Roberts, NZ, 24, male, Malaysian Chinese/Pakeha New Zealander)

He highlighted what many participants mentioned: the power of language in strengthening a familial bond. His story presented a "barrier" between him and his extended family, the cultural differences that have come to be represented in his language ability. For him, and for others, speaking the language of the family in question meant that participants could feel a stronger bond, using language as a demonstration of belonging and cultural connection.

In Singapore, more participants spoke of negotiating multiple languages. For some families, it was a conscious decision to stick to one language, usually English, within the family. For others, English was the dominant language by default. The lack of a second language was felt by these participants, who often expressed regret at not being bilingual. Speaking Mandarin particularly was seen as an important link to Chinese culture, and a way to back up a symbolic link to heritage. It was also seen as a connection to Singapore, and a way to practically demonstrate feelings of being authentically Asian, reflecting the success of the "Speak Mandarin" campaign. One woman, Amber, saw language as a way to assert the reality of her Asian heritage and "prove" to others that she was half Chinese and connected to her heritage. For her, being a "proper Eurasian" meant exhibiting characteristics that were both authentically Asian and authentically European, and most importantly, having other people believe her. Other individuals were bilingual, and moved easily between English and Cantonese or Mandarin, code-switching depending on context. This allowed for a closer connection to both sides of the family for many people.

Bilingualism also involved other languages. Two participants spoke fluent French and English, both having Singaporean fathers and French mothers. One woman spoke English and Indonesian, as the language of her Indonesian Chinese father. Singlish, as a local dialect, was an important language in the Singaporean context. Many participants described switching between English and Singlish with their families, friends and in local neighbourhoods. Some participants mentioned that others would not expect them to speak Singlish, assuming that their backgrounds excluded them from this Singaporean marker of identity.

In the New Zealand context, far fewer participants were able to switch easily between two languages. One woman, Melanie Townsend, was fluent in both Mandarin and English, and attributed this to both her parents being fluent in both languages. Several others described understanding basic words in a second language and having language classes as children, but stressed that in the context they grew up in, they never needed to speak another language. For participants whose Chinese parent had grown up in New Zealand, their language skills were often limited, and it was less natural for them to pass on the language to their children. Similar to the Singaporean examples, many participants expressed the desire to speak Mandarin or Cantonese better, particularly as they grew older and began to consider passing on heritage to the next generation.

Language was an important part of fitting in to the wider social context in both countries. In New Zealand, participants or their parents often attempted to minimize difference by focusing on speaking English to better blend in. In Singapore, language carried with it another set of connotations, drawing on the shifting government policies on language, racial identity and national belonging. The oldest participant in Singapore grew up speaking English, with some exposure to Cantonese.

> So I got familiar with Cantonese because that was the . . . the language spoken in the house and I think in general you either grew up in a Cantonese environment or a Hokkien or a Teochew, what do you call those,
> Kampongs or whatever.
> Until the Mandarin issue came in then everyone went haywire.
> Even now today when I go to Hong Kong, it sounds very familiar.
> The . . . the words sound familiar because we grew up listening to those kind of words and I don't . . .
> I don't feel threatened but if I feel . . .
> I walk down in Taiwan or whatever I would not know what they were talking about. China also I wouldn't know and to a certain extent even here.
> In . . . in some housing estates I don't know what they are saying.
> I can walk there, I have no clue what they are talking about.
> They're talking in Mandarin and I have no way of understanding and it feels very . . . I would say threatening, you know, because you do not know what they are saying.
> They could be saying anything, you know, that's the trouble.
>
> (David Faulkner, SG, 64, male, Singaporean Chinese/White British)

For David, the later government emphasis on speaking Mandarin left him feeling excluded and foreign, particularly in certain neighbourhoods. He described the minimization of other dialects by the "Speak Mandarin" campaign, as well as the ambiguous role of English as an overarching official language, not associated with a particular group, delegitimizing his "mother tongue" by default. His story highlighted his exclusion from the language/race alignment in the CMIO framework, and the way in which he felt othered, and even threatened, by language as a marker of belonging.

The predominance of Mandarin in everyday life was also difficult for Andrew, who felt that speaking English was a point of pride, and an important part of his identity.

> I will speak Mandarin with people sometimes, and I will stop and refuse to speak it.
> I want to speak English.
> And then, it makes it more difficult for me, so I create my own difficulty.
> And then some people say why don't you just speak Mandarin, it's easier for us, I don't want to do that, you see.
> I feel as if, I'm caving in to the expectations of the majority.
> In order to blend in, you've got to speak Mandarin.
> In Singapore English is the working language, and it should be the language that cuts across the ethnic groups.
> And it has for a long time.
> So for, I don't know why, I'm proud of speaking English.
> So, I would like my children to be armed with Mandarin,
> and Jeanne says they must learn French.
> So her French culture and her French heritage is very strong.
> So I think we will have to do that.
> She says that she wants to speak to our children in French, and I'll speak to them in Mandarin, and English,
> we'll speak to them in order to get them to learn those languages as much as possible.
> (Andrew Wang-Jones, SG, 36, male, English and German/Eurasian)

He saw a disconnect between the emphasis on Mandarin and the status of English in Singapore, making him feel that he needed to uphold English for himself. Tellingly, he spoke of needing to "arm" his children with Mandarin, providing them with the necessary tools to fit in and belong in Singapore – something that he continued to struggle with. Language for him was something of a battle, a negotiation between the public and private aspects of his identity.

The emphasis on language as connected to heritage in Singapore was emphasized by the requirement to learn a "mother tongue" at school. For participants who spoke English at home, the requirement to learn Mandarin, as the "mother tongue" of their race, was weighty. A number described failing Mandarin as a subject in school, often needing extra tuition to pass the class. For these individuals, Mandarin had no connection to their home lives and families, and they felt at a disadvantage compared to those who spoke Mandarin in their daily lives. One

108 *Being and belonging*

woman found herself confused by the category of "mother tongue" and its connections to her as a person.

> And then also bilingualism was introduced into the education system,
> so apart from the English language as the administrative language and teaching and all that,
> children were encouraged to take on what you would call their mother tongue.
> And that term in itself confused the heck out of me, because what is my mother tongue? [laughs]
> I mean, I grew up with English at home, so English is my mother tongue.
> But then I, I had grandparents, great-grandparents from Portugal, and from China, so, I was, it was difficult.
> I mean, as a child, to figure out where you actually belong, I mean, what slot?
>
> (Sandra Pereira-Ivansson, SG, 36, female, Hakka and Peranakan Chinese/Chinese and Portuguese)

She ended up deliberately distancing herself from Mandarin as a language, and the culture that she saw accompanying it. As a young child, she felt that her identity was not in any way connected with this language, and so she emphasized the role of English in her life. Her narrative carefully worked around ideas of reinforcement, as she took on ideas of language and cultural alignment within a racial framework, asking "what slot?". Interestingly, she reflected the state discourse regarding language and heritage, questioning for herself what her *true* "mother tongue" would be.

In addition to language, food was commonly discussed as a way to connect to (or disconnect from) heritage. Participants in both countries described the mix of food, reflecting a mix of cultures, that they ate growing up. For most people, diversity of food was unremarkable, and many enjoyed talking at length about their childhood favourites and their connections between family and food. Singaporean participants spoke with particular gusto, reflecting a common Singaporean enthusiasm for different cuisines. In both contexts, food was seen as a tangible link to culture, both in positive and negative ways. For some, fondness for Chinese food was the strongest link to that side of their heritage. Food also served as a point of connection, allowing for a sharing of culture and communication across generations, even when there were linguistic barriers.

Food emphasized both feelings of belonging and exclusion. One woman in New Zealand felt that Chinese food was quite foreign to her, mirroring her feelings about her heritage.

> I usually eat Western food.
> Um . . . I started branching out recently when I met my, my last boyfriend, my boyfriend that I'm with at the moment, the Taiwanese Chinese guy.

Um . . . 'cause he was like "oh well, we should open you up a little bit more, you know, if you're, if you're struggling so much with being, you know, half Asian, maybe if we, if you were more open to things of Chinese culture and things, why don't we just, you know, why don't you try eating this sort of thing, and use chopsticks, and do this, and dadada, I'll teach you some Mandarin" 'cause he can speak Mandarin.

And, um . . . so, I, recently, I've started eating a lot more Chinese food, but . . . if I had a choice over eating like, going to Chinese restaurant, or having like Italian, I'd choose Italian [laughs].

Yeah, so . . . yeah. I don't . . . we don't . . . even when my dad cooks, he won't cook Chinese food.

Hmmm . . . the closest we get is like stir-fried vegetables.

Like my dad will be more likely to cook like, an Indian curry for dinner, even though he's Chinese. Than to cook like, something Chinese, I don't know [laughs].

(Jenny Griffiths, NZ, 25, female,
Pakeha New Zealander/Chinese New Zealander)

Jenny's story again highlighted her sense of disconnection from her heritage, as her feelings of belonging were not always recognized by others. Her boyfriend had taken it upon himself to better acquaint her with a culture that he saw as hers, yet she did not identify in the same way. Chinese food was exotic and unusual for her and served as a marker of her unease with the complexity of her ancestry, nationality and cultural affiliations.

Food and stories about food often addressed gender roles and highlighted connections between family and gendered cultural identity (Ali 2003:112). The majority of Singaporean participants spoke of their mothers or maids preparing food when they were children. Some mentioned that their mothers cooked both Asian and Western food, and for them, this mixture was normal. Others described how they had a mix of foods, particularly because of the preferences of one parent: the father, for instance, preferring to eat only Western food, as was the case for Hannah and Alastair. This illustrates the intersections between familial gender roles, culture, and food as a cultural practice. For these families, compromises and flexible interpretations of culture and heritage were expressed by traditions surrounding food.

In New Zealand, participants also spoke of their mothers as the primary cooks in the family, although for some families, food preparation was equally shared between parents. Food was closely linked to appreciation of culture, and often had associations with extended family and family traditions: many spoke of Chinese grandmothers and the importance of food as a way of bringing family together. For Alexis and her family, food was a way of emphasizing integration, with "typical Kiwi" food being the norm. Others were conscious of the different foods they ate at home when they were children. However, this generally shifted towards a fondness for a diversity of foods as they grew older, with home food seen as comfort food.

In both New Zealand and Singapore, rice was important in participants' stories. Many people agreed with Ang, that ". . . rice arguably sets Asians apart from Westerners" (2007:177):

> The thing is, I think if you ask me whether I'm a bread or rice person, I'm rice, lah.
> Not bread, ah. [laughs]
>
> (Terence Peaks, SG, 26, male, Filipino Chinese/Anglo Australian)

> In terms of other stuff, like eating rice. Our friends always laughed at us, but we . . . that's all we ate was rice and meat dishes and stuff.
> Um, and I just remember, I actually did a Facebook posting not long ago saying "oh, you know you're Chinese when you sort of carry a sack of rice through town and think nothing of it". You know . . .
> But yeah . . . and my friends thought that was quite funny.
>
> (Nathan Fleming, NZ, 39, male, American Chinese/Pakeha New Zealander)

Both narrative fragments used rice as a way to distinguish Chinese identity from European practices. This bread (or potatoes)/rice and Western/Asian dichotomy was echoed in many other stories. Rice was seen as a marker of difference in New Zealand, of sameness in Singapore, and in both cases was a way for participants to practically show their connections to their heritage. Stories around rice allowed participants to emphasize their links to their Asian heritage, particularly in the New Zealand context where differences and diversities in "Asian" culture are often overlooked. For many, including Nathan and Paul, rice was comfort food, and an assertion of their family backgrounds. For others, such as Jenny, not eating rice highlighted their feelings of distance from their heritage, and their connections with experiences growing up. Eating rice was then seen as a way of being Chinese, a practical demonstration of difference or a point of commonality.

Public and private identities: exclusion and reinforcement

Ancestry was then interpreted in different ways for participants, encompassing aspects of Chineseness, understandings of being European, and negotiations between the two. Individuals narrated a sense of identity for themselves, but inevitably, these nuanced understandings were both created and constrained by the reactions of and interactions with others. Racial and ethnic identity is widely understood as a dialectical process: constructed from within and from without (Lee 2008:23). A number of previous studies on both ethnic/racial and "mixed" identity have found that external perceptions and denials of identity have a particularly powerful effect on an individual's view of themselves (see, for example, Butler-Sweet 2011; Cheryan and Monin 2005;

Oikawa and Yoshida 2007). For participants in both countries, a key theme in their stories was that of external acceptance and belonging. Set apart from how they personally identified themselves, seen in narratives of accommodation and transcendence particularly, individuals spoke of how others reinforced or denied their feelings of belonging. In Singapore, Richard described how his feelings of being Chinese changed over time, as his peers denied his identity as authentically Chinese.

> 'Cause back then you get all the questions, so you start . . . and you're hanging with all these Chinese kids.
> And so you start wondering, you start thinking to yourself that you are one of them, you are Chinese yourself.
> And then, yeah.
> They, they constantly remind you that you're not.
> So . . . yeah. And over the years you kind of accept that.
> (Richard Ong, SG, 22, male, Singaporean Chinese/Anglo Australian)

His narrative described an interaction between internal and external perceptions of his identity, as the questioning of others leads him to question himself. His personal negotiations of belonging became less about accommodation, and more about acceptance: reinforcing the reality of social divisions. Another woman portrayed belonging as an either/or, based on external perceptions.

> I think it's like acceptance by other people around you,
> and like them agreeing that you belong.
> Um, so like, yeah.
> If no one doubts your belonging then I think that's where you belong.
> (Amber Smith, SG, 19, female, Singaporean Chinese/Anglo Australian)

For Amber, unless everyone agreed that she belonged, she felt like an outsider: a purely external definition of belonging. Her story illustrated a black and white narrative of reinforcement through acceptance or rejection. This led to powerful feelings of alienation for her, from both the national and ethnic groups in which she felt she could have belonged.

Participants reported similar sentiments in New Zealand, as feelings of ethnic identity were not always reinforced by others within that ethnic group. Melanie highlighted the importance of phenotype as an ethnic marker of belonging, as her appearance led others to believe that she was not Chinese, despite her strong feelings of Chineseness. Paul expressed close personal connections to both sides of his heritage but had found that neither side accepted him as "truly belonging". He worked to accommodate internal and external differences, as he allowed for dissonance. For him, the public and private versions of his identity could remain distinct, as his identifications were influenced by, but not determined by, the perceptions of others.

112 *Being and belonging*

Interestingly, Andrew in Singapore discussed the relationship between external perceptions and his reactions to these perceptions.

> Maybe I'm being too hard on myself?
> Maybe, you'll find that in the scheme of things,
> people don't care too much.
> Maybe first and second, they'll say
> "Who's this bald-headed fellow who looks quite white? Is he one of us?"
> But maybe they'll move along.
> Maybe, this chip on my shoulder I talked about, maybe I'm playing it up.
> Maybe it's simply not there.
> This, this, this, this subjectivity of it all is quite delusionary, you know?
> Maybe it is.
> Maybe if I were to ignore a lot more, maybe it wouldn't, maybe it would go away. I think it's . . . maybe, by being conscious about,
> at some subconscious level, I'm playing up that difference.
> You know, in terms of my disposition, my body language, I come off as being unfriendly.
> Maybe if I just tried to blend in, whatever that means, maybe it would be a lot better.
> So I think perhaps it is.
> Perhaps it is the whole thing that goes with you.
> Push hard on the world, and the world pushes hard on you. If you push gently, it will push gently back.
> Maybe if I'm more gentle about it, maybe people will be gentler with me.
> But maybe it's something that I'm creating out of my own perception. Of the world. Yeah.
> But I have to resolve this. Because I . . . she and I find that, yeah. It's just very tiring.
> It shouldn't be tiring, it shouldn't be tiring from the very society you come from.
>
> (Andrew Wang-Jones, SG, 36, male, English and German/Eurasian)

For him, national identity was closely tied to racial identification, reflecting the structures and history of Singapore. He highlighted the difficult to conceptualize relationship between agency and structure, between personal feelings and social reactions, questioning his role in how others saw him. His narrative was very self-aware, illustrating both subversion in this awareness and a reinforcing desire for simplicity of belonging. He appeared uncertain in his questioning, repeating "maybe" and "perhaps", as he sought a better understanding of his own uncertain positioning. This narrative presented him as excluded and weary of asserting his identity and sense of belonging to Singapore. His personal sense of being Singaporean, and necessarily a legitimately racialized Singaporean, was constantly denied. As a result, he questioned whether he could work to change the perceptions of others, or whether he should temper his own expectations, in order to feel that he belonged.

A similar dissonance was echoed when participants talked about their families and friends, and the similarities and differences with how strangers would see them. In participating in this research, one woman in New Zealand found that her husband's and friends' perceptions of her Chinese identity were different to her own.

> Well, it's funny you ask that, because when I was doing the questionnaire online, my husband was standing there like shouting out answers for me, 'cause I was reading them out, and he was trying to answer for me [laughs].
> And his answers were completely different to mine.
> It did make me think, huh actually . . . yeah.
> 'Cause, one of them, was about, you know, what percentage are you Kiwi versus Chinese or something like that culturally, and he was like "100% Kiwi!" and I was thinking "no, it's more like 75%", I would say.
> And I think . . . and I asked a few other people after this experience with him, like, what do you see, like how do you see me? And they were all like "yeah, no I don't see any Chinese at all, nothing." [laughs]
> And no, I still feel like I've a sense of Chinese to me.
>
> (Alexis Conrad, NZ, 33, female, Chinese New Zealander/New Zealand European)

For Alexis, Kiwi and Chinese were necessarily distinct, and she found ways to identify with both. She reflected the ways in which ethnicity can be private and symbolic (and potentially imperceptible), subverting wider narratives of belonging by allowing herself a different way of being Chinese.

The social reality of mixed identities often came to the fore when discussing physical appearance and external reactions to phenotype. Mixedness can be marked on the body as a form of difference, and this difference is interpreted in highly gendered ways (Alcoff 2006; Perkins 2005), highlighting the ways in which *race is gendered and gender is racialized* (Omi and Winant 1994:68). As a vivid example of the intersections of race and gender, "mixed race" as a category, ancestry, identity and racial project describes key issues of racial inheritance and gendered power dynamics. This is notably illustrated in popular understandings of "mixed race" as either marginal or exotic, and in individual experiences of the meanings and hierarchies of gender and race: women as (re)producers of race and the nation, placing female sexuality and gender roles at the centre of how racial identity is understood (Yuval-Davis 1997). The interpretations and reactions of others towards physical appearance can have a strong impact on how individuals see themselves. Of course, interpretations of phenotype are relative for the self and for others, and while phenotype is important, previous research on mixedness has come to no firm conclusions about the power of appearance in shaping identity (Khanna 2004, 2012; Song 2010a).

114 *Being and belonging*

In this case, participants often spoke of being judged and categorized on the basis of their physical appearance, and how they *thought* that others saw them. Individuals found such external judgment destabilizing, as it frequently contradicted how they saw themselves. They described being constantly "raced": having their identities simplified on the basis of their physical features (see Perkins 2007). These assumptions about identity often went hand in hand with positive and negative stereotypes about mixedness and minority groups.

One man in Singapore felt that his ambiguous appearance would allow him a certain amount of leeway, but not as much as he had imagined when he was younger.

> I thought when I was growing up, that I was very chameleon – that I could stand in a Chinese you know, like . . .
> Stand around Chinese and look like Chinese.
> Stand around English, look like English, you know.
> But, no, I think they see the difference clearer than I do.
> I . . . I do have a bit of a . . .
> I think all the Eurasians have a bit of a cosmopolitan face, you know, and so they can pass off a little bit but the people within themselves will know that you're not.
> You're different definitely.
> You have got distinct features that make you look different from the crowd.
> Yeah, you can't hide! You can't merge.
>
> (David Faulkner, SG, 64, male, Singaporean Chinese/White British)

For David, he could superficially "pass" as English or Chinese, but "authentic" Chinese or English people (defining himself as inauthentic as a result) would know that he was not genuine[2]. In this book, a small number of individuals described how their physical appearance and cultural aptitude enabled them to "pass" – to appear to be a member of a singular racialized group, without being marked as different. This was more common in New Zealand, as individuals were able to identify with the majority group.

> But in terms of being Chinese, nah, no one really probably knew.
> 'Cause I was, well my sister did her own thing, and it was a big school, so no one would have linked us.
> And in terms of the way, I don't know, I didn't really,
> I don't think I exhibited outwardly Chinese traits if there are any.
> So no one would have known.
>
> (Nathan Fleming, NZ, 39, male, American Chinese/Pakeha New Zealander)

Nathan's narrative highlighted how his feelings of identity and others' perceptions aligned neatly, as he distanced himself from "Chinese" traits. Other individuals described how this was a result of both appearance and of cultural upbringing, and how, unless told otherwise, others would assume commonality rather than difference. Rose Stein's mother told her that she was glad that she looked predominantly European, as her life would be easier in New Zealand, reflecting dominant social narratives of inclusion and belonging.

In Singapore, ambiguous appearance was often related to stereotypes around Eurasian identity and "mixed race", for both men and women. Several individuals commented on these stereotypes, and how these did not match the reality of their lives, as they drew on historical prejudices around European and Asian identities. Safiyah Matthews mentioned that others had thought that as a Eurasian, she would be arrogant and promiscuous. She linked this stereotyping to the reliance on race as a categorizing principle in Singapore, a sentiment echoed by Andrew's story:

> The old expression for Eurasians used to be "Happy Charlie". I don't know where that comes from, but they'd say the "Happy Charlie", the Eurasians are . . . the British colonizers would call them party-goers, bossing people round, holding high positions. Really just the leisure class they used to be.
> And we still have that today.
> I always get that from . . . I got that from a taxi driver, he just said, "You look like a player to me."
> I said, "Excuse me, you don't know me. How can you say I'm a player? What do you mean by a player?"
> "You know, all Eurasians, always chasing women, chasing skirts . . ."
>
> (Andrew Wang-Jones, SG, 36, male, English and German/Eurasian)

For Andrew, stereotypes were at odds with wider discourses of multiracial harmony in Singaporean society. His "mixed race" identity placed him outside of singular racial categories, but nevertheless, subjected him to racialized assumptions about his character and morality. He found the Eurasian stereotypes particularly tiresome, wishing to decouple ascribed notions of group identity from individual characteristics and experiences.

In New Zealand, appearance was an important part of women's stories. However, there was less of a tendency to fall back on stereotypes of "mixed race", and more of a focus on features that identified someone as a minority. Almost half of the women described looking Chinese or Asian, and how that point of difference made them stand out growing up. Several of the women talked about the concept of "normal":

> I wished that I was normal. All the time.
> And I wished that my name wasn't Alexis, I wished I was called Jessica, or . . . Elizabeth, or something normal.
> I just wanted to be normal. Yeah.

116 *Being and belonging*

> But now, I'm so glad that I'm different, you know.
> It goes, I'm glad that it goes the other way when you get older.
> (Alexis Conrad, NZ, 33, female,
> Chinese New Zealander/New Zealand European)

Her narrative described normal as white New Zealander, positioning physical and symbolic markers of Asian identity as abnormal and undesirable for her in her youth. For Alexis, Jenny, Rose and Li Lin, feelings of belonging and normality were intricately tied in with appearance and other markers which set them apart from the majority group. For some, these feelings passed as they grew older, and difference became a point of interest, rather than of exclusion. For three women, their heritage and difference continued to cause them discomfort, as in the following fragment:

> Sometimes I think I still get, like pangs of "oh I just wish that I was just like . . . I wish I was just a white person", like I wish . . .
> which sucks, and nobody should ever think that.
> But, um . . . sometimes stuff happens, and you're like, "I wish . . ."
> Life would probably just be easier if I was just a standard, blond-haired, white person [laughs].
> But yeah, I guess you have to have those times, everyone does.
> (Li Lin Zhen, NZ, 22, female,
> Pakeha New Zealander/Fijian Chinese)

Her story highlighted this same understanding of normality, reinforcing wider narratives of race and belonging in New Zealand. For these women, the dissonance between external interpretations of appearance and their own feelings of belonging left them feeling isolated and disconnected. Jenny used very visual words in her story, highlighting how her visibility affected her feelings of identity. She described how she would *look* at herself, without *seeing* her physical characteristics, and *view* herself as "just a Kiwi".

> I think like other people see me as, like some people think I'm full Asian, and so they'd think . . .
> they'd see me and think, even if they talk to me, they still may think . . . like although I have a totally Kiwi accent, and everything, they'd still think that I . . .
> they'd have these misconceptions and expectations that I . . . am like . . . fully immersed in an Asian culture.
> Whereas, I see myself as like a . . . without looking at me, if I saw myself [laughs],
> you can't really do that, but I um, would just, I would view myself as . . . like a, just a Kiwi.
> 'Cause I'm fully Westernized, like I don't, I don't do anything Asian at all.

I don't even really like Asian food [laughs].

(Jenny Griffiths, NZ, 25, female,
Pakeha New Zealander/Chinese New Zealander)

One woman, Anne, in Singapore had a similar experience of wanting to change herself, but in her case, exclusion from the Singaporean Chinese community led her to disconnect from feelings of Chineseness. As someone with a larger build and ambiguous features, she described how she was ostracized as a child, both by her peers and institutionally, through the school system which labeled her as overweight and abnormal.

> You know, when I was here in school, I had to join like the trim and fit club.
> And, um, you know they were always, "oh you're fat, you're fat, you're fat" and when I was a kid, I wasn't fat. You know, and I was a very active child. And, but I have very big bones.
> And, they don't get that here. You know, and . . . and, I know that now, but I'm 27 years old.
> You know, and, I hated that as well.
> You know, because it just made me feel like I wasn't pretty, and I wasn't attractive, and you know, I mean, I didn't wear skirts for years, you know.
> And, I remember when I was like, when I . . . I only started wearing skirts actually, because one of my friends in England was like "why don't you wear any skirts?" and I was like " I don't like them."
> And he was like, "but why? You've got really nice legs" and I was like "no I don't, shut up, you don't know anything."
> And, you know, but . . . so when I came back I was like . . . is that going to happen again? Am I going to get to that point when I'm like "oh, you know . . ." do I feel comfortable with myself? Is it okay that I look different from everybody else?
> And um, and I had, it has gotten to the point where I'm like "you know what, fuck you" like, I don't care what you think.
> But then that has never allowed me to feel like I belong here.

(Anne McNeil, SG, 27, female,
Singaporean Chinese/English)

Again, phenotype was important, as she felt that her gender, race and physical appearance made her an outsider in Singaporean society. She felt more connected to her Chinese heritage as she grew older, as she was better able to make a distinction between private and public identifications. Her feelings of connectedness to her British heritage remained strong, as she perceived that community to have accepted her without question. She further described how her beautiful, ambiguously raced younger sister was bullied at the girls' school she attended. Based on her appearance, other students spread rumours about her promiscuity, reflecting a stereotype of Eurasians as untrustworthy and "players". Another woman experienced, and perpetuated, the same stereotyping, but in reverse. She described how Eurasian girls were frequently beautiful, and often worked as models, as she had done. She described the appeal of the mixed "look" as more relatable to both sides, but interestingly also indicates it is "more classy", perhaps reflecting lingering historical preferences in Singapore.

> It seems like, um, they [mixed models] seem to be in demand.
> The pan-Asian look. In Singapore.
> Because it's better than having ah, someone completely white.
> Um . . . to do an ad, that you know, the locals, the Asians, cannot really relate to the face. So as long as there is kind of an Asian look, it looks more classy and also I can relate to the face.
>
> (Hannah Alley, SG, 33, female, Singaporean Chinese/Welsh)

Appearance was not only important for women, and men described a distinct set of experiences related to being mixed, particularly in New Zealand. Several men discussed the disparity in expectations for mixed men and women in New Zealand society. They indicated that cultural preferences were for larger, European-looking men, meaning that men who exhibited Asian physical traits were not seen as manly or as attractive to the opposite sex. For women, as in Singapore, ambiguous and Asian features were stereotyped as feminine and attractive, meaning that mixed women could be accepted more easily (a theory which was not necessarily borne out by the experiences of the women above). As one man said:

> Oh . . . I personally was happy, and I don't know if anyone else would admit this but, I'm happy looking European in this society.
> I would struggle to get dates with chicks, ah, the ones I wanted to go out with, if I looked full Chinese.
> Whereas if you're a Chinese girl in New Zealand, that's acceptable.
> And you can date just about anyone, and a lot of guys would go for that Chinese look. Whereas a lot of girls would not, definitely not.
> Like I know my brother struggles when it comes to, you know, dating women and stuff. And I'd say part of it is because he's inherited a lot more of the Chinese gene.
> He's a lot shorter than I am, probably about 2 inches shorter, and looks full-on Chinese. So, yeah, I suspect that, you know, it's not favoured in this society.
> Whereas in New Zealand, the girls'll go for ah, physically bigger guys, stay away from gingers, and you know . . . a half like me is probably okay, even though I'm on the slight build I can, you know.
> But yeah, it's, I think being European looking is definitely, for this area anyway, an advantage.
>
> (Nathan Fleming, NZ, 39, male, American Chinese/Pakeha New Zealander)

He honestly expressed his relief that he looked more physically European, as compared to his brother who looked "full-on Chinese". He was straightforward in his assessment of preference in New Zealand society, identifying primarily as a European New Zealander. For him, relationships with and attractiveness to women in society played an important part in his identity as a man, and his mixed heritage did not prove more important than a social reinforcement of his masculinity.

A second man, Joel Andrews, narrated an interesting experience at university, where his heritage, gender and appearance intersected in an unexpected way. He felt that he did not appear particularly Asian or relate to his Chinese heritage in a meaningful way, and was content that people treated him as such. However, when he started drinking alcohol in large quantities, he found that his face turned very red: a quality which is associated with individuals of Asian descent in New Zealand.

> Like when we were, went down to Otago [university] and everyone, you know you start drinking and whatever [laughs].
> And . . . I don't know if you know, but a lot of Asian people when they drink get really flushed, and your face goes red.
> And, um, like I'd already known about this, I guess I started drinking in school, and I knew this happened.
> But it's a distinctly kind of Asian thing.
> It's one thing that you know, this bright red flag is your face, and it's like kind of waving and saying like "look at me, I'm drunk!".
> Um, and that was kind of an interesting thing for me to kind of like deal with.
> 'Cause, you know, for a start it's kind of embarrassing, but like, by that time, I was kind of, you know I wasn't so embarrassed about my identity.
> So, I'd kind of like, you know, I'd make fun of it by then, by that time, yeah.
> But that's, I mean . . . for me, because I'm not visually Chinese that was an interesting thing for me, because like the visual aspect is like really present.
> You know it's almost like I put on this mask that was, you know, a Chinese person mask or something.
>
> (Joel Andrews, NZ, 24, male, Chinese New Zealander/Pakeha New Zealander)

Joel described feeling as though he had put on a "Chinese person mask", as his red face signaled to others a heritage which was not immediately obvious otherwise. As he felt that his background did not significantly influence how others treated him generally, this experience brought different feelings about his identity to the fore. Turning red drew out how powerful physical markers of difference can be, placing a mask on his features which revealed as much about his heritage as it concealed about who he thought he was.

Difference was not always perceived negatively, and reflecting a historical legacy of exoticization, some participants described being seen as exciting and exotic. Seeing "mixed race" as embodied fluidity must also bear in mind the racialized and gendered processes and structures in which this mixedness is lived (Mahtani 2005:78). "Mixed race" does not necessarily overturn conceptions of race, nor is a mixed identity always a stand against racism or racialization, drawing as it does on historically determined racial categories. Such exoticism is closely related to marginalization, echoing sentiments of inherent difference, but from a different perspective. In New Zealand, exoticism was both around being Asian, and different, and being mixed as secondary. Participants were not always comfortable with such sentiments, feeling that it emphasized their ethnic backgrounds unnecessarily. One woman described feeling flattered, but distanced from the celebratory discussions of something that she could not control.

> You know, a lot of people think of it as quite a privilege.
> And they think it's, um, you know, really exotic and desirable, or whatever you want to call it. And I never thought that. Even in my teens.
> But I guess now, when I come to an age where [pause] um, I am aware that people see them like that,
> and I feel flattered, but it feels awkward to me.
>
> (Melanie Townsend, NZ, 30, female, Taiwan Chinese/Pakeha New Zealander)

In Singapore, exoticism tended to be more marked around mixedness, as an unusual (and potentially transgressive) racial background. One woman highlighted the changes in public opinion towards mixed heritage in Singapore.

> Um, we went through a phase . . . so, growing up it started off as it wasn't cool to be mixed. It was not the done thing.
> Then, you know, we went through, I think the 2000s, the year 2000, there was a phase of Eurasian children are always prettier, than others, and the boys are always more handsome, and it's suddenly great.
> And then I think now in 2010, it, I think more and more people are just getting, it's kind of more of a more common thing. And, it's no longer big like "oh my gosh!", it's just "alright, you're Eurasian."
>
> (Katrina Henry, SG, 27, female, Singaporean Chinese/English)

Katrina described wider narratives as going through different stages, moving from exclusion, towards exoticism, and now, in her opinion, to a place where mixed heritage is not seen as particularly exciting. This chronology reflected her national context, with attitudes shifting as Eurasian identity was promoted more publicly, and as mixedness was symbolically acknowledged by the state. This view of change represented one perspective towards "mixed race" and racialized acceptance, echoed by a number of participants in both countries. Thus, they described increasing levels of intermarriage, and growing numbers of young people of mixed heritage, as personal experience and social change intertwined.

Interestingly, while participants understood the flexibility of phenotype in their own families, and the power of external labelling in everyday life, several people in either country described how mixedness could be recognized through physical characteristics. James from Singapore described having "this sort of innate sense of being able to tell whether or not people have a similar background", while Philippa from New Zealand felt that "you can always tell if you are half Chinese half European, or even if someone's a quarter. I don't know why, you can just tell". For both, they described a combination of physical, cultural and attitudinal characteristics, as well as a more abstract form of connection or commonality that helped to identify others of a similar background. Therefore, wider narratives of phenotype and racial characteristics influenced participants, despite their own experiences of fluidity and ambiguity. Whilst being very aware of the external gaze of others, individuals were not exempt from similar curiosities and impulses to categorize.

Conclusion

Reflections of a colonial past shaped contextual narratives at the meso level in both Singapore and New Zealand. In Singapore, within the legacy of classificatory structures, participants showed how their identities were influenced by family and location, as inflected by historical notions of culture, worth and diversity. Identifying as European in particular was strongly affected by the colonial legacy of hierarchy. Participants often felt that in the Singaporean context, having European heritage both excluded and set them apart from the rest of the population, frequently with tangible material consequences related to socioeconomic positioning and opportunities. Intersections between gendered and racialized identities were also noticeable in participants' stories of their parents. More participants had Chinese mothers than European mothers, and some described what they saw as a pattern in contemporary Singapore, stemming from past beliefs about acceptable boundary crossing, where Chinese women were freer to marry European men than the other way around.

The colonial past was also evident in New Zealand, illustrating both the dominant position of the European/Pakeha group and the long history of marginalization and exclusion of the Chinese. Historical threads of racism were present in many participants' stories, as belonging in New Zealand continued to be symbolically bounded along racial lines, reflecting an intertwining of transcendence and accommodation. Rather than focusing on intermixing, transgressions were more present through difference, making Chinese identity a form of transgression from the norm in itself.

Of course, narratives were not solely inflected by British colonial beliefs. The interplay between dominant and minority identities reflected both colonial and post-colonial processes, as well as links to other national and cultural bases for belonging. The strength of Chinese identity in the stories of Singaporean participants highlighted how Chineseness was an important marker and identification in everyday life, encompassing practices, traditions, symbolic beliefs and, in some cases, imagined links to place. This was also reflected in parental stories, particularly concerning the strong opposition of many Chinese families to intermarriage and similar narratives of reinforcing exclusion. Chineseness in New Zealand was more frequently represented as symbolic, rather than practical, and was often held up as a point of difference in participants' stories of belonging to the nation.

In both countries, Chineseness was seen as a more coherent form of identity, whether it was presented as the dominant culture (masking innumerable variations and understandings), or as a minority culture which was marked by difference. This reflected the position of European identity in both contexts, understood as somehow less "ethnic" and less cohesive, determined more by power and positioning than by a recognizable set of cultural traits. Reflecting how whiteness can be unnoticeably racialized in both majority and minority contexts, Chinese identity was the focus of most participants' stories, when they described the ways in which they were both Chinese and not Chinese.

When elaborating on the ways in which they felt Chinese and/or European, the vast majority of participants in both countries described the ways in which they personally identified with both in stories of accommodation: an interesting contrast to North American studies, where singular racial identities were more common. Chineseness was key in each context, and practical and symbolic assertions of being Chinese served to illustrate this dual belonging. Stories of belonging tended to be more practical in the case of Singapore, and more symbolic in New Zealand, but far from entirely voluntary or costless in either (see Waters 1990). In Singapore, Chinese identity was often seen as fragmented and diverse, along lines of generation, ancestral origin, language and immigration status. Language was a key marker of authentic Chinese identity, as well as associations with food. In New Zealand, divisions were also important, particularly when looking at new immigrants versus Chinese New Zealanders, but many people also described a broader, abstract sense of general Chineseness or Asianness with which they occasionally identified in everyday life. Language, as a practical marker, was less present for New Zealand participants, whereas symbolic attachments to food and celebrations were more common.

The ways in which participants felt Chinese were often set against how they felt they were not Chinese, particularly in Singapore, where this set them apart from the majority population. However, in both countries, Chinese identity was not often equated with feelings of connection to China or to an ancestral homeland, reflecting a lack of fit with theories of diaspora and highlighting how Chineseness developed and changed for participants and their families. Being European or identifying with European ancestry was less associated with practical traits and traditions in either country. In Singapore, European identity was often made manifest through socioeconomic differences, seen in choice of schools, housing and leisure activities. In New Zealand, European identity was frequently unnoticed and seen as "just being Kiwi", not as a particular set of racialized or ethnic traits and markers.

Phenotype was an important marker in determining external perceptions in both countries, seen in stories of exclusion in the face of accommodation. In New Zealand, phenotype marked individuals as different from the majority, and a number of women spoke of feeling excluded and classified as part of a minority group as a result of gendered interpretations of this difference. Men also experienced public/private disconnections, highlighting assumptions about whiteness, masculinity and normality in New Zealand society. In Singapore, phenotype equally highlighted difference, but more in terms of being mixed, as part of being a minority. Perceptions of difference and exclusion brought to the fore historical stereotypes of mixedness and Eurasians, which many participants felt in their everyday lives.

Being marked as different meant that participants in both contexts spoke of being seen as exotic, but in different ways. In New Zealand, exoticism was primarily through not being European, while in Singapore, the exoticism stemmed from mixedness. Interestingly, although participants often encountered a dissonance between external perceptions and their own feelings of identity, this flexibility was not always applied to others. Even if, in their experience, phenotype did not easily align with identity, some described a narrative of reinforcement where an ambiguity in appearance was an indicator of mixedness, a marker of racialized mixing. Personal narratives were thus shaped by a broad range of meso-level factors, and were not always easy to position within wider narratives of belonging. For all participants, context and history constrained and delimited the stories that could be told.

Notes

1 These references refer to the US context. Interestingly, in the New Zealand context, Kukutai has found that ethnic identity transmission is related less to the mother or father, but more to the head of household, which is itself a gendered role (Kukutai 2007).
2 This concept of "passing" is frequently discussed in the North American context, drawing on a long history of black/white relations. See Khanna and Johnson 2010; Smith 1994; Williams 1997.

5 Roots, routes and coming home

Stories of mixedness, difference and hybrid identities push at ideas of bounded nations, cultures and racial groups. They highlight the intricacies of everyday negotiations of identity, in contrast to simplistic theoretical and historical understandings of race and belonging (Mahtani 2002b). As individual stories in this book show, identities and narratives are fluid at micro, meso and macro levels. This chapter draws out mixedness at the micro, personal level, focusing on the fluidity and boundary crossing narrated by individuals of mixed descent.

Such fluidity can pass over socially established borders between groups. Participants described these negotiations using narratives of demonstrable and symbolic locations for identity and belonging. Rather than seeing themselves as culturally homeless or rootless (or even marginal), identities were often described as evolving. Individuals positioned themselves as moving through different categories and collectives, belonging and rooting themselves in multiple places.

As an important starting point, the theme of belonging and not belonging came up frequently. In describing feelings of location and identification, individuals spoke of belonging in multiple places and of belonging nowhere at all. A feeling of belonging nowhere was mentioned with particular emphasis in Singapore, when describing the position of Eurasians or those who did not fit easily into the CMIO categories.

> Yes, I've always, um, you know, I've always sort of
> felt a notion of being
> ah, the other.
> Sort of being an outsider, um,
> and I think, and I think that sort of started when I first moved to Australia.
> Um, and everywhere else I go, I've always sort of been an outsider.
> Um, and I think that has somewhat,
> you know, um, created in me, or the image that I have of myself, um,
> an image of someone who is, who will always be, um, you know,
> a little left of whatever the status quo is.
> You know, something other to what of the whatever the status quo is.
> And I think it's made me more, how do you say, um,
> I don't know, more,
> more fluid, in that respect.

You know, as if identity is sort of more fluid, you know.
And I think it's made me, um, want to gravitate towards being,
being other than,
than the other way which would be to fall hard into the community, you know.
Sort of similar to what we were talking about at the beginning of the conversation, you know,
when I said I've never really
had a greater identity of being a part of, you know, the Singaporean nation.
Or being a part of a group of, you know,
a group of Australians, or part of a neighbourhood.
You know, you know how some people grow up in communities, like suburbs or I don't know, and they feel like they're part of that, like "Oh, I'm part of you know, greater Harlem" or something like that.
Never had that, um, and ah,
and I think, and I don't think I ever will.
You know, because I think it's true, I think my propensity is to sort of fight that.
Sort of resist that.
Um, resist being sort of put into a box, and fitting somewhere.
Because I like the idea that you know, I can sort of go anywhere, and just be a part of it, and then move on.

(James Field, SG, 25, male, Singaporean Chinese/Anglo Australian)

James, who earlier described not belonging in any community, here placed his feelings of dislocation in context. His narrative was strongly transcendent, holding himself apart from common categories of belonging. He talked of how being treated as an outsider led to his perception of himself as outside of social categorizations of belonging. Belonging nowhere became an important part of who he was, as he subverted social norms to assert his individuality and avoid being "put into a box".

Belonging was also frequently described as situational, and influenced by external perceptions. Many participants mentioned that they were not seen as Chinese enough or European enough to be considered authentic, either in Singapore or New Zealand, or the range of countries from which their parents had come. Some participants in Singapore extended this sense of dislocation, describing how they felt that their difference was their most identifying feature, wherever they found themselves. Jeanne's narrative centred around difference, and ways of accommodating that difference. Her feelings of belonging shifted and changed, depending on where she was and how other people treated her. For her, and several others, the Chinese and European aspects of their identities were emphasized at different times in different contexts, and not always in ways that participants felt matched their personal feelings of belonging.

At 30 years old, when I'm in France, I feel Asian,
but when I'm in Singapore, I feel French.

So, I don't really feel always French, or always Singaporean.
>
> (Jeanne Goh, SG, 30, female,
> French/Singaporean Chinese)

Individuals negotiated these shifts for themselves, accommodating difference within a wider framework of belonging. Interestingly, feelings of identification and connection to Singapore and New Zealand changed when other differences became more pronounced. Alison described feeling a closer bond to each country once she no longer lived there. For her and others, by removing themselves from the national context, they were able to focus on their feelings of belonging and commonality, without being reminded of external perceptions of their difference.

> It's always been an issue for me, about how I moved to Singapore,
> and how I fit in there or don't fit in there.
> Most of the time I didn't feel like I fit in there.
> Until I moved to Holland, and then I feel like I fit in, in Singapore.
>
> (Alison Lijuan, SG, 27, female, Russian Chinese
> and Japanese/Hong Kong Chinese)

Feelings of belonging were sometimes also linked to diasporic identifications, but in unusual ways. A few individuals spoke of the importance of a defined geographic place of origin in which to belong. David, Anne and Amber in Singapore and Jenny in New Zealand talked about "belonging" as intrinsically linked to a place, an ancestral or symbolic homeland that would give a sense of rootedness to a mixed identity.

> Because, and when you think very carefully, once in a while you sit down and you think about it, the Indians have somewhere to go.
> The Chinese have somewhere to go.
> The Malays have somewhere to go.
> Where do Eurasians go to?
> There's no Eurasia to go to. There's not any place that you can go to.
> It's just like you . . . you have to find a . . . you have to lean one way or the other and make a decision, you know.
>
> (David Faulkner, SG, 64, male,
> Singaporean Chinese/White British)

> I don't feel like I really belong anywhere.
> And . . . yeah, so I mean I can't . . . I can't say you know, where feels like home.
> And you know, ideally, I always joke about this . . . but I'm actually a hundred percent serious.
> If there was like a little island in between both Singapore and England, which had, you know, which had everything I loved about both of these

places put into one place . . . with my friends and my family, that would be perfect.

You know, because I'd be in between the two countries and cultures that I do love.

You know, but . . . each place just kind of makes me go . . . that's not . . . there's something about that that's not quite right.

There's something about this that's not quite right.

And . . . there's no . . . *home* home.

You know, the idea of home, to a lot of other people is not the same, you know for me. Or doesn't fit in to my . . . I guess, I can't . . .

I can't make, I can't say what is home, because . . . I don't feel like I have one.

You know, that has everything.

You know what I mean? That's so sad! [laughs]

(Anne McNeil, SG, 27, female, Singaporean Chinese/British)

These participants spoke of an imaginary homeland, a "Eurasia", as a way to illustrate their feelings of not having anywhere to belong. These narratives subverted existing national and racial categories but, at the same time, reinforced notions of belonging as directly linking a homeland and people. "Eurasia" was described as being exactly in-between, bringing aspects of Chinese and European cultures together and providing an imaginary space where mixedness could be commonplace.

These narratives around "Eurasia" were not common overall, but provided powerful images for those who subscribed to them. One woman brought together ideas of belonging everywhere and nowhere, brought about by this lack of homeland.

Definitely something that transcends countries, like I think it's sort of um, a race thing. Um, it's like if you're European and Asian.

Um, and . . . um, there is one sort of thing, and I think that's the cool thing about it, because like,

well sort of the cool thing and the bad thing, because there are Eurasians all over the world, like, it's just . . . there's not really one country that you can find them all in, because really they're just like everywhere.

And I think that's cool because like wherever you go, there's a chance you'll find one and as well . . .

Like with my Eurasian communities, like we'll come together 'cause we're Eurasian, but then we learn stuff, because we're not the same.

Like, the same in our genetics in a way, but the culture that makes up is so different [. . .]

But, I guess the bad thing about it is not being able to find them sometimes, and there's not really anywhere you can go to feel as though you belong.

Like, um, I mean, um, if you're like sort of a Korean-born, I mean Korean or something born and raised in Australia, like even if you're like

128 *Roots, routes and coming home*

    discriminated against your whole life in Australia, you can always go back to Korea.

    Like even though you may not feel as though you belong, like um, other people will probably accept you and like, at least you'll be in a place where like everyone looks like you. I don't know.

    I feel like, I feel like they do have a sort of like backup, that kind of thing.

    But um, I feel like with Eurasian, like, there's nowhere to go really.

    Um, maybe like, you can go to like a place like Singapore, where I guess there's a lot of mixed people, but um, I don't know if it's really the same, um as having sort of your own country or something . . . um.

    But, that's why I feel like building, um, like an online community sort of group. Because, we can go . . . like, for me I feel like that's kind of like my home.

    Like um, because, like you can, no matter where you are, you can always like find each other.

                            (Amber Smith, SG, 19, female, Singaporean Chinese/Anglo Australian)

Amber stressed that racial heritage was inextricably linked to a homeland, and that authentic belonging was not possible for individuals with multiple racial heritages. Race came through strongly in her reinforcing narrative of belonging/not belonging, as she spoke of the importance of locating herself somewhere where people look like her. She mentioned "having your own country", conflating race and nation in a directly racialized conception of belonging, a racial homeland. Not finding such a homeland available to her, she set out to create a symbolic place to belong: an online community, an imaginary Eurasia, populated with Eurasians.

The role of new media, and particularly the Internet, is important when looking at identity negotiations and feelings of belonging. There has been increasing research in this area focusing on immigrant groups, diasporic communities and second-generation immigrants (see Franklin 2003; Parker and Song 2006, 2009; Thompson 2002). Online groups and communities provide much potential for feelings of cohesion and belonging, and even cultural adaptation and change. Such virtual spaces provide opportunities to express cultural complexity in a nonjudgmental environment, creating a small space where individual and group identities can be tested.

Several participants in both countries mentioned that they had browsed or been involved in online groups for individuals of mixed heritage. Interestingly, these individuals were all younger females, and each described a sense of comfort in learning about the experiences of others with a similar background. Amber, who created an online group for Eurasians, did so to delimit a place where Eurasians could "stay together", and to have a distinct place where she (and they) could belong. In her narrative, belonging is inseparable from external acceptance, and she reinforces racialized connections between belonging, place and home. This leaves her adrift, without a homeland "in real life", looking instead to a virtual homeland as she sought to reconcile her private feelings with wider public conceptions of belonging.

But I feel like, rather than trying to find a place, more like I try to create one. Like in the online community.
Um, because I don't think, like I could really find one in real life.
Um, yeah, I don't think I could, like . . . in Australia like . . .
um, I don't know. I like it here, and it's like my home, but I don't know if I sort of belong. Like, um . . .
I don't feel like I don't belong, but I don't know if I do.
Like, but I mean I feel like, um, you have to be embraced by everyone to belong.
And that's like, I guess, maybe I wouldn't be.
So if you did a survey, like maybe there would be people who didn't think I did, so . . . like I wouldn't feel confident saying that I do belong here.

(Amber Smith, SG, 19, female, Singaporean Chinese/Anglo Australian)

Belonging as a process: the dynamics of home and choice

Home is often highlighted as fluid and uncertain for individuals of mixed heritage (see Ifekwunigwe 1999). However, home can be understood and constructed in many different ways: as racialized, gendered, historically contextualized and shaped through experience. The idea of home can connect mixedness on different scales when seen less as fixed and bounded, and more as connecting the personal and the domestic to the social, national and global levels of identification. Home can be seen as a house, as a set of relationships, as a community, a nation or even as dislocated emotions. Each level reflects a link to an individual's sense of self, as positioning oneself in a domestic home is juxtaposed against wider feelings of national belonging and group inclusion. Being at home and feeling at home contrasts with being away, feeling excluded and being displaced, tying conceptions of home closely to feelings of belonging and identity (Blunt 2005; Blunt and Dowling 2006; Mahtani 2002b). Narratives of home bring together the personal, the social and the national, looking at how a sense of self is constructed out of identifications and locations within the family, the society and the nation.

Feelings of belonging and home were not simple for interview participants. Different ideas of belonging and identification brought together aspects of the past, present and future.

What I really describe, I describe more, my . . .
I don't know the word in English.
Like, my . . . [pause] like the phases of . . . the process maybe of where I am, and how I am . . . yeah?
And not so much, I guess, the box.
Maybe more what I did at the beginning, with where I grew up, and then, how that links to the future.

(Celine Chin, SG, 24, female, French/Singaporean Chinese)

Celine's narrative looked at identity from a different angle: rather than the "boxes" of identity categories, she saw her own identity as a process over time. Similarly, other individuals made use of varying connections to national identity, geographic place and symbolic spaces in negotiating a complicated and shifting way to belong. In this way, mixedness was a process for many people, constantly in flux and influenced by internal and external factors, by personal sentiments and social contexts, and by the amorphous concept of home (see Rockquemore et al. 2006; Tyler 2011).

A broader idea of home was particularly important for participants. The links between home and identity are key in qualitative and autobiographical work on "mixed race", reflecting a move away from historical conceptions of "mixed race" as inherently out of place and not at home. Home has been shown to mean different things for those who find it hard to locate themselves within traditional categories and communities (Blunt 2002; Ifekwunigwe 1999; Mahtani 2002b). This study was no exception. Participants often talked about feeling at home or not at home, feeling homeless as both positive and negative, or even how a different type of home could be created and lived within wider structural constraints.

Narrative understandings of home were roughly divided into four broad conceptions, many of which overlapped: home as a singular location, imbued with important memories; home as family, friends and culture; home as a choice, constructed and changing within certain constraints; and home as fluid and multiple. Firstly, for a number of people in both Singapore and New Zealand, home was where they had grown up, reflecting an accommodation of their personal feelings within the wider surroundings.

> Um, well, immediately I would say in Shanghai is my home.
> But meaning in a more sort of spiritual sense or whatever, I guess, I would probably consider Wellington home, maybe forever. Or, I was born in Palmerston North but don't . . .
> I consider Wellington home.
> I mean, um, saying I, I spent most of my formative years there,
> and I you know, my closest friends are still um, from, people I knew from Wellington.
> And I would say that's mostly what shaped me as a person.
> The environment there, or whatever.
>
> (Tai Feng, NZ, 31, male, Irish/Malaysian Chinese)

As in Tai's narrative, even if participants had moved to a different city or country, and felt comfortable there, many described an important connection with the city they had grown up in, and the experiences they had had. Participants in both countries expressed strong feelings of connection to these places as their home countries: subversive narratives of belonging, as they were not necessarily based on an ancestral link, but more related to experiences and comfort levels. For those who had spent significant time in two countries, both countries were described as home. For some currently living elsewhere, they described how they might eventually return home: back to the environment in which they felt the most comfortable.

> It's something that I kind of feel like I feel New Zealand is ... is ...
> Feels like a comfy sofa in the back of my head that I can go and, like, you know it's something that is sort of safe that I could just sort of go back there.
> Like, if anything went really wrong, New Zealand feels safe to me inside.
> But it would be somewhere that I would quite like to be when I'm older.
> (Emmeline Tan, NZ, 32, female, Pakeha New Zealander/Singaporean Chinese)

Other participants described home as less about the location of formative experiences, and more about a set of relationships and personal connections. Home was then determined by proximity to family members and friends, or even colleagues or groups which shared particular interests. This was often the case for those who travelled frequently, or who had family in many locations around the world, such as James in Singapore or Rose in New Zealand.

> Home for me is where my loved ones are, that's where my family is.
> So, 'cause I have family all over the world, like I feel as long as I'm sort of near them, that could be where I'd feel closest to.
> And also even just friends.
> You know, you can, if you have really good friends, you consider them part of your family, and you have your own culture with them.
> So really wherever you belong is where people are.
> 'Cause you live in their memories, and those rituals that you do together.
> So that's ... where I am.
> (Rose Stein, NZ, 22, female, Hong Kong Chinese/Dutch)

Her narrative described home as more symbolic, and less about location. This subverted commonplace understandings of home as fixed, or linking ancestry and place. Family as home was often linked to fond memories and emotional connections, which could sometimes be associated with a particular space. In this sense, home was seen as very intimate and largely organic, something that developed naturally over time. Some participants in New Zealand described different degrees of home, moving outwards from family bonds to a family home, to a city and then a sense of belonging within a country.

Home was also related to traditions and comfort levels, particularly at the level of practice. David in Singapore described how he felt at home in his family, and within wider contexts where he felt comfortable and culturally fluent.

> My family meets on Saturday and we get together.
> So I think family and the bigger area is the relatives, and then I think the environment where you feel comfortable is a lot to do with language.

For example, if I lived in India I would not feel very comfortable.
Or China I wouldn't feel very comfortable because language is different.
You might settle in and speak the language which then you make . . . make yourself feel comfortable. Great. That's okay. Maybe I'm not working hard enough.
So I think I will feel comfortable where language is common.
That means, I will know . . . signs are familiar, or you know what's going on by just a feel what's going on.

(David Faulkner, SG, 64, male,
Singaporean Chinese/White British)

His narrative described a flexible concept of home, but one that is also delimited by the surroundings and cultural practices of the wider context. He saw home and belonging as a language that could be learned, and stressed that perhaps such fluency could be acquired over time, meaning that home could change. Nevertheless, he felt at home where he was at ease, drawing on memories and experiences of places that were familiar to him.

For other people, home was something that they deliberately built. Their narratives focused more on the constructed nature of home, as they described ways in which they created their own homes. For these participants, home was not always something to be taken for granted, or easy to define. They highlighted home as choice, but importantly, choice constrained within circumstance. One woman felt that home could change over time, depending on her choices.

I feel like I belong in Twizel, 'cause I had a very happy childhood there. And I still know a lot of people there.
And my best friend lives up the road, and she's obviously from Twizel, so we have that . . . it's always present in our mind, I guess.
But . . . and I feel like I'm starting to belong here. I've lived here two years. Um . . . so you know we're starting to put down roots.
And we want this to be our, you know our family house, so, um, that's the aim . . .
to belong here.

(Philippa Warner, NZ, 38, female,
Pakeha New Zealander/Chinese New Zealander)

Her narrative highlighted belonging as a goal, something to be built towards, as she started to "put down roots". Although she had a strong connection to her childhood home, she was focused on building a new home in her new city, to provide a sense of belonging for her family. This subverted notions of rootedness through ethnic/racial belonging, as she described being able to root herself, focused on choice and agency.

The constraints around choice were much more pronounced for the Singaporean participants. One man in Singapore was attempting to create a new type of home for himself and his fiancée. He described being constrained by the small-scale home that he was able to control, while feeling dislocated by his exclusion from larger ideas of community or nation. He felt limited by the individual nature of this home, a home not necessarily rooted in a wider collectivity. For him, home was something that he sought to create within the narrow space available, as he couldn't fit his feelings of connection into national conceptions of belonging. The ways in which he felt that he belonged did not align with how he perceived home *should* be: contrasting the reality of his agency with the limitations of structure.

> I don't know where home is.
> I think maybe my case is very specific, I told Jeanne, I said "maybe home is what we make of it".
> And maybe home has been very narrowly defined for us.
> I think home is just, she and I building a home, in any one place in Singapore. But for me, home needs to be more all-encompassing.
> Like home used to be, um, rooted in something much larger. A community I suppose.
> Um, and maybe one nation state, if you want to be academic about it.
> (Andrew Wang-Jones, SG, 36, male, English and German/Eurasian)

Andrew's discomfort with this dissonance was mirrored in the case of William, who felt at home in both Singapore and the United Kingdom, but was being forced to choose between the two citizenships, clashing with his personal feelings of belonging.

The final understandings of home as fluid and multiple often passed over dissonances between external perceptions and internal feelings, describing home as predominantly personal, and carried within oneself. This was most common for participants from New Zealand who had lived in multiple places, although a small number of Singaporean participants also identified with this multiplicity. Some individuals felt that home was everywhere they had lived, as they (literally) made themselves at home.

> Well, I mean, I've basically lived in three different places, and, and I've spent quite a lot of time in each.
> So, um, I would say that I call all three places home.
> (Melanie Townsend, NZ, 30, female, Taiwan Chinese/Pakeha New Zealander)

Melanie saw her home as three places equally, defining what home means for herself, regardless of external perceptions. For her, belonging was a matter of situation, experience and location. Li Lin described how external perceptions wouldn't allow her to belong entirely in either of her parents' ancestral communities:

> And it was strange, 'cause you go, like, in New Zealand, you know, I feel like I belong, but there's always that kind of, you're a little bit different from the norm.

And then you go to China and it's the same thing, because you're not really Chinese to them either, you know, I'm quite Western, and they can see the difference.
So you don't get treated like a, um, like you totally fit in there either. So you don't really have a, anywhere, like, that you're based.
I don't really believe in like people having separate communities that can't integrate or mingle, because there are so many people that don't have like one community, that that's all they've grown up in.
And even though, even though I am quite Western in the way that I grew up and everything, um,
I still feel like I kind of float between cultures, and, I don't think there's anything wrong with that.
Everyone's, I guess, all people are just people.
And we all, we're all the same.
(Li Lin Zhen, NZ, 22, female, Pakeha New Zealander/Fijian Chinese)

Despite being "different from the norm" and not fitting in in an uncomplicated way, her private sense of self enabled her to move between communities and feelings of belonging. While home was flexible and fluid for her, she didn't limit this personal construction to her own experience. She emphasized the fluidity and complexity that she saw in the backgrounds of people around her, regardless of cultural heritage, and pieced together a more complex understanding of belonging as a combination of personal and social qualities.

Furthermore, for others, home was not necessarily limited to particular places, but was connected to the ability to belong anywhere: home could be everywhere. For several Singaporean participants and many New Zealand participants, individuals felt that they could both belong and not belong simultaneously. A number of people mentioned that in fact, they didn't need to belong in a single, bounded place.

I would say planet earth!
I don't have a . . . I don't have a place where I belong and . . . but I don't feel bad about that.
(Emmeline Tan, NZ, 32, female, Pakeha New Zealander/Singaporean Chinese)

Can I say the planet? [laughs]
Yeah, pretty much.
No, um, home . . . home is really where . . .
I can be home anywhere. As long as there is water and green, I can be home, and friends.
And I have a tendency now, I'm seeing, that wherever I go, um, I'm getting in touch with old friends. Instead of just starting from scratch.
And places are feeling like home a lot more quickly.
Um, but I feel at home really, anywhere now.
(Celine Chin, SG, 24, female, French/Singaporean Chinese)

These narrative fragments described multiple and wider homes, determined more by a personal propensity to feel at home rather than a strong link to a singular place. Both women described how they felt at home lightly, or even humourously, almost downplaying the importance of their flexible self-positioning. Home became less about a set external location, and more about a location of self from within, subverting narratives of singularity.

The view from somewhere in-between

Experiences of being mixed were decidedly varied and complex. Participants described feelings of belonging and home as multiple and shifting, often with a degree of flexibility. Labels and categories did not always correspond to lived experience, showing how identifications along racial, religious, ethnic, national and cultural lines were blurred and changing. So what does it mean to be mixed? Previous research, mostly in the United States and the United Kingdom, has reached a variety of conclusions, from assertions that being mixed is too fragmented for easy analysis, to finding a common "multiracial" experience (see, for example, Bernstein and De la Cruz 2009; Brunsma 2006; Jackson 2010; Root 1996).

Participants in this research described a wide range of experiences, framed by wider narratives, as they negotiated what being mixed meant to them. A number of common themes emerged, and these were expressed in different ways across both contexts. Firstly, individuals in both Singapore and New Zealand commonly discussed how being of mixed heritage made them open-minded and flexible as people, uniquely receptive to cultural differences and ambiguities.

> I don't treat anyone differently, just based on culture.
> I grew up just thinking it's normal, no problems,
> and I enjoy Chinese New Year, I enjoy Christmas, I enjoy all those holidays . . .
> I, I, I feel it makes me, I would say, a nicer person, 'cause I am a more open-minded person.
> I don't, I, I, I don't, I don't know how to explain it . . . just like you don't treat anyone differently.
> You respect other people's cultures, and you kind of understand why maybe people do things differently.
> Um, it's quite good, I guess [laughs].
>
> (William Briggs, SG, 21, male, Singaporean Chinese/English)

This often came through in narratives of accommodation, such as this one, which allowed for public and private differences in everyday life. Even William's narrative was very focused on his individuality, repeating "I, I, I" and unconsciously emphasizing the personal nature of this trait.

This open-mindedness was also often reflected in an ease with fluid identities, and a personal acceptance of multiplicity through accommodation. Being mixed was seen as an inherent boundary crossing, making arbitrary identity choices unnecessary.

> I feel like I'm quite like a sort of open-minded, flexible person.
> And I feel like um, I think being like biracial has sort of affected that.
> Like, because I'm sort of, I believe in everything,
> sort of not just black and white, but grey.
> Um, I feel like, I feel like I don't have to choose one or the other, when it comes to things.
>
> (Amber Smith, SG, 19, female, Singaporean Chinese/Anglo Australian)

Over an underlying thread of racialization (biracial as positioned between racial groups), this woman positioned herself as in-between, not forced to make a choice and therefore subversive. This personal location within and between two cultures allowed for a dual insider/outsider perspective on culture and values, also seen in Alexis's narrative.

> I'm grateful, that . . . you know, that I've got this ability to understand, you know, different, different cultures and different sets of right and wrong values.
> Like I don't think unless, unless you've been brought up with different cultures, you don't . . . I don't think you can really understand it, not from the inside.
> You can't really get the grasp of how one side of the family can be saying something that's the complete opposite to the other side.
> But then . . . neither of them are wrong, it's just . . . it's different.
>
> (Alexis Conrad, NZ, 33, female, Chinese New Zealander/New Zealand European)

Others in New Zealand went further, mentioning that this dichotomy made them less likely to see value systems as absolutes, and more willing to try to consider other points of view.

A further characteristic of mixedness related to feelings of difference. This could be both positive and negative, with participants describing feeling excluded and marginalized, or celebrated for their uniqueness and exoticism. This was related to context, as personal narratives developed in different ways against narratives of belonging. A greater number of participants in Singapore described how their mixed heritage made them feel out of place, different in a negative sense, with identities that were difficult to reconcile. For these participants, fluidity was not always welcome, and made them feel alienated from the seemingly simple racialized identities of other Singaporeans.

> I think maybe I . . . for a time . . . it was there, and then it went away, and now I'm back, it's back.
> A chip on my shoulder. Yeah.
> I have a slight chip.
> You understand?

> As long as I have it, I will be on edge, a little bit bitter, maybe sometimes, very, very . . . abrupt with Singaporeans who approach me in an ignorant manner.
> And it's not to do with my daily conduct.
> I don't like myself, I don't like myself being this way. Ah . . . I think I just need to be relaxed about it.
> Maybe . . . just learn to laugh at myself. And laugh at it all, you know?
> I think people don't understand . . . they can't come to terms with this ambiguity.
> And so what, you know? It's okay. I don't know.
> Um . . . yeah. I would like to think that it would be done, his or her self-identity by the time you finish your pubescence or adolescence.
> But I think ah, with some Eurasians, I have friends, who have had this constant identity crisis. It never leaves you.
> It's something that you should, you should know who you are.
> I mean, all of us, I think we all have a multi-faceted identity.
> Different people in different situations, I think we all know that.
> There must be, there's one only master status, master identity. I would like to think that.
> I think I really, with Singaporeans, they probably have that. They seem quite comfortable in themselves, in who they are.
> More or less, they don't have . . . but for me, it's . . . it's still very fluid. Very fluid. I need to . . . I would like that to be sorted out.
>
> (Andrew Wang-Jones, SG, 36, male, English and German/Eurasian)

Difference was a struggle for Andrew, and his narrative portrayed fluidity as something unresolved, in contrast to the "sorted out" and comfortable identities of others. Flexibility and fluidity were negative attributes, and left him feeling uncertain and in crisis, in a context where he saw definite and defined (racial) identities. His narrative reinforced the racialized framework around him, as he sought to resolve his identity, in order to "know who you are".

Some participants in New Zealand also described negative associations with difference, usually related to childhood experiences of exclusion and racism. Interestingly, many stories of adversity and exclusion in this context had definite lessons or conclusions at the end, and were often resolved with personal growth for the participant.

> Well in the end I think it's good for you, that you . . . like it's good, it's an eye opener having two different, like having a mum who's a New Zealander and a dad who's Chinese, 'cause you kind of become aware of two different cultures.
> And . . . that's good.
> Um . . . but it has definitely had some negative influences on me, because there've been times when I've been quite unhappy and I would put it down to being confused about who I was as a person.
> And where I belong.

But then again, you know, what doesn't kill you only makes you stronger. So it helps you to think about things, and like . . . discover who you are. And . . . and, perhaps, like, like my brother said, you do a get a bit of the best of worlds.

Like, you can live in both cultures, and, get to experience it.

But at the same time, it's isolated, 'cause you don't ever really feel you belong in both.

So it's a little . . . it is confusing.

Um . . . but, what would I say? Um . . . [pause]

But it has made me have like a good, hard look at myself, and think about what's important to people. Like what makes you happy. And I think that, like I said before, having a sense of belonging, anywhere in this world, does make a person happy.

Like humans are quite, you know, our nature is that we like to feel we belong. And . . . if you don't, it can make you quite unhappy.

So it's about find . . . I guess it's about finding people and places that do make you feel like you belong.

(Jenny Griffiths, NZ, 25, female, Pakeha New Zealander/Chinese New Zealander)

For Jenny, negative experiences of difference had a significant impact on her life, but also led her to reconceive of what it meant to belong somewhere, and to take her feelings of belonging into her own hands. She searched for "people and places that do make you feel like you belong". As in this narrative of accommodation, many people spoke of becoming stronger for being different, learning to be more accepting and better able to deal with adversity as they accommodated complexity in their own lives.

On the other hand, positive expressions of difference were common in both New Zealand and Singapore. Many participants enjoyed their heritage as a distinguishing characteristic, particularly as they grew older.

Oh, I love it [being from a mixed background].

I love it, yeah.

I kind of like the attention [laughs].

It's like the, at some point, I feel like I'm more unique, like . . . I can't get pigeonholed into a particular group.

And um, I'm my own person, so to speak.

(Safiyah Matthews, SG, 28, female, Singaporean Chinese/New Zealand European)

The value of Safiyah's difference was its ambiguity, as she couldn't be easily categorized as European or Chinese. She focused on a narrative of uniqueness, allowing for shifting identifications as a form of subversion. In this case, difference became an asset, perceived as a way to assert individuality, and create an identity which went against the CMIO framework. Another woman from New

Zealand found that her ambiguity allowed her to reveal aspects of her identity as she chose.

> Um, I think a lot of the time I'm misunderstood.
> But, um, but you know I think I, I've somewhat been misunderstood my whole life.
> You know, to a certain degree, um, because of my background.
> And, that doesn't bother me that much, really.
> So, I think of it more as a secret weapon [laughs].
> You know, for example, people don't think I speak Chinese, but I do.
> And you know, and that's something that I might not let on right away.
> (Melanie Townsend, NZ, 30, female, Taiwan Chinese/Pakeha New Zealander)

She described her identity as her "secret weapon", subverting the expectations of others, and turning misunderstanding into an integral part of her identity. Positive interpretations of difference encompassed both exoticism and ambiguity, and even in some cases, the ability to be Chinese, European, both and neither.

Expressions of mixedness therefore took various forms: often related to, but not always determined by, socially available categories. Participants developed their own personal narratives that included aspects of racial categorization, but frequently combined these aspects in unorthodox ways. Contrary to previous studies of marginality, individuals often viewed being of mixed heritage in a positive light. Most people in both countries professed positive or extremely positive feelings about their heritage. Yet interestingly, more individuals described being neutral or shifting about their feelings in New Zealand, indicating that the greater flexibility in racial classification in New Zealand did not necessarily equate with positive feelings about mixedness.

The wider social context, above and beyond classifications, was key. The context of race in either country provided the background for personal negotiations of identity, and individuals acknowledged that others' perceptions of their identities were largely coloured by wider narratives of race and belonging. In both countries, over half of all participants felt that their heritage was particularly important in how others perceived them, potentially overlooking other aspects of their individuality that they felt were important. However, public and private narratives were not always deliberately aligned. Participants described personal ways of being both Chinese and European, choosing and piecing together aspects of culture and ancestry (see Gans 1979, 2009; Song 2003). Some participants identified most with something in-between: a negotiation between heritages, between past and present, in a process of cultural hybridity.

These negotiations took different forms. First, some participants in both countries spoke of their identities as *a mix of both their ancestries*, with individuals often equating different traits with different parents, in an indirect narrative of reinforcement.

140 *Roots, routes and coming home*

> Yeah . . . in, in my case, if you are talking, um, racial background, there isn't really anyone, other than the fact that I'm probably heavily influenced by my mum's side, the Chinese side.
>
> So, and since I grew up in Singapore system, I probably think more like a Singaporean than say an Australian for example. Yeah.
>
> But I think my dad has some influence on me, in the sense that, um, my peers have said I'm usually more outspoken than, than a typical Asian.
>
> And, um, which can be good and bad, right?
>
> (Alastair Jenkins, SG, 30, male, Singaporean Chinese/Anglo Australian)

As in this case, individuals often drew on wider narratives of racial characteristics when describing themselves, highlighting behaviours that set them apart from the wider context as associated with the "other" parent. Yet, moving away from reinforcement, such a mixed positioning allowed many people to feel that they had strong connections to both sides of their heritage, regardless of how this heritage was practised in their everyday lives.

> But you know if, like I talk to a white person, then I feel like I can connect with them 'cause I'm like half white, and when I talk to an Asian person I can connect with them 'cause I'm half Asian.
>
> And I feel like a sort of affinity to both of them. Um, and well, I feel like an affinity to other people, because they're minorities and so am I.
>
> And it's sort of like I feel like I can connect to everyone.
>
> Um, yeah. So it's like yeah. Connect with like both majorities and minorities as well.
>
> (Amber Smith, SG, 19, female, Singaporean Chinese/Anglo Australian)

This feeling of symbolic inclusion in two groups emphasized an in-between space for Amber and for other participants, as they felt linked to both majority and minority groups. As before, this narrative was both reinforcing and subversive, going against expectations while being underpinned by racialized language.

For others, this in-between positioning was largely positive, although the two sides of heritage were kept largely separated as they described having *the best of both worlds*. This sentiment was more prominent in Singapore, as participants spoke of trying to reconcile two "worlds" which they experienced in very different ways. One woman, Katrina, felt that this was largely due to her parents, who emphasized the benefits of being in-between, while at the same time keeping the two "worlds" separate for her. Another woman, Anne, described how this feeling had developed for her over time, as negative childhood experiences gave way to an appreciation of cultural access and uniqueness.

This concept of two separate worlds coming together was also reflected in narratives of acknowledgement, with individuals in both Singapore and New Zealand

Roots, routes and coming home 141

stressing the importance of coming to terms with ancestry as a way to reconcile a mixed identity.

> It's good sometimes to know that you're different [laughs].
> Yeah. And ah . . . I think . . . even though, like people may think that the Western culture is better, I think it's important to embrace the Eastern side as well. Yeah.
> I think having a balance of both cultures, or like all the cultures in our heritage is important.
> I mean, sooner or later, if you don't do that then you will just be lost, eventually. And no one will know.
> So . . . that would be sad.
> (Skye Sia, SG, 23, female, Eurasian/Singaporean Chinese)

> I think it's good, it'd be good for children to grow up obviously knowing that they're from two different cultures and to acknowledge both sides.
> Because I think perhaps if you try and disown or ignore one culture, it leads to you feeling more lost and kind of . . . confused.
> So . . . yeah I think it is important for people to . . . um, acknowledge both sides.
> Um . . . that can be hard to do obviously, if you live in a Western society, like it's not really that easy.
> And if you don't necessarily have friends of that culture then you may not do anything.
> (Jenny Griffiths, NZ, 25, female, Pakeha New Zealander/Chinese New Zealander)

Although both sides may not be equally important in practical terms, for these women, a symbolic acknowledgement allowed them to locate themselves within their families and wider contexts. In both of these statements, acknowledgement, as form of accommodation, was portrayed as a way to not be lost, to find oneself, and to position an identity within wider frameworks of belonging.

For many, connections to ancestry were complex. Some participants felt that they were *both Chinese and European*, and could not easily separate one from the other. They described how both sides were important, although they didn't necessarily feel a strong sense of belonging to both. Jacob saw himself as inseparably both Chinese and European:

> [A friend] always asks me, "so are you Chinese or are you European?" and I was like "I'm both".
> And . . . I guess I can never really choose one side. I am both, and that's who I am. And I guess, to my benefit or to my detriment, I can choose either one anytime I want [laughs].

Um . . . but yeah. At the end of the day I guess, it depends on what you want to do, and who includes you.
Um . . . yeah, I guess I've no real inclination . . . like I guess I'm made up of half Chinese, half New Zealand European.
I've also grown up in Hong Kong, as well, I've grown up in New Zealand.
So, I don't know . . . pros and cons both ways, yeah.
I just stand in the middle. I'm an "on the fence" kind of guy.

(Jacob Roberts, NZ, 24, male, Malaysian Chinese/Pakeha New Zealander)

Being both in this sense was related more to private feelings than to public inclusion in wider groups. As with Jacob, many participants constructed a personal identity that created something holistic from external narratives of racialized parts.

Participants were also aware of how private narratives could potentially contrast with public discourses of inclusion and belonging. Some individuals reconciled this contradiction through stories that described being *both and neither*, often at the same time. This approach was positive and negative, perceived as a necessary accommodation or an uncomfortable dissonance. A public/private accommodation was most common for the New Zealanders, as for Paul:

It's funny, when I came back from Italy, I thought of myself as quite Italian. And when I came back from China, I thought of myself as quite Chinese.
Yeah, yeah, so I really immersed myself in both when I was there.
Um . . . but you know, interestingly enough, both the Italians and the Chinese never accepted me as either, anyway, so . . .

(Paul Moretti, NZ, 48, male, Chinese/Italian)

His story described feeling connected to both sides, while recognizing that neither side fully accepted him. He allowed for this contradiction, accommodating difference in his day-to-day life. For others, such as Jenny and Andrew, this became more of a public/private dissonance: an inconsistency of identity that was particular to being of mixed heritage. In this case, other forms of identity were often emphasized, such as nationality or occupation, to allow for a narrative of transcendence as belonging.

As personal experiences of mixedness did not fit neatly within wider narratives of belonging in either country, many individuals felt that they were pushing at existing boundaries and struggling to fit themselves into categories which did not allow for flexibility.

I think . . . yeah, like most of my friends they don't think I have, they don't realize how insecure I've been, because of being mixed race.
And . . . some people have quite like a positive reaction when they know that I'm of mixed race, but I still feel negative about it.

But people won't be able to tell that I am, cause I won't, I'm quite good at hiding how I feel about things.

(Jenny Griffiths, NZ, 25, female, Pakeha New Zealander/Chinese New Zealander)

This dissonance meant that participants such as Jenny were very conscious of having a public and a private face, as they had to work to simplify complexity or to mask emotions and identifications. This duality was seen as both positive and negative: a way to project a confident, public image for some, and a façade to hide underlying confusion for others.

The sameness of being different

Negotiations of race and "mixed race" illustrated that although a typical "multi-racial" experience was not evident in either Singapore or New Zealand, being of mixed heritage often made individuals feel different from others. Some even found a kind of commonality in this difference. Difference was most evident in cultural practices, experienced by participants in comparing themselves to their extended families, and to wider Chinese and European communities. As a result, a number of participants described a feeling of recognition in the mixed backgrounds of others, a kind of affinity for mixedness, rather than a cultural commonality from within a single group.

Almost half the participants from Singapore indicated that they felt most comfortable with others of a similar mixed background, emphasizing that this was because of similar experiences of cultural multiplicity and even exclusion. Amber went out of her way to meet and make friends with others of a similar background, even choosing to listen to music by primarily Eurasian artists, feeling that this created a space for her to belong. For others, the institutionalized nature of the Eurasian community in the country provided a place to meet others who felt similarly in-between, a potential meeting point for mixedness within the Singaporean framework. A number of men and women mentioned having one close "mixed" friend, to whom they were able to relate easily.

In the New Zealand context, perhaps because of the geographical distribution, the majority of participants had less contact with people of a similar background, with a small number never having met anyone else of mixed heritage. Most described mainly having friends who came from a single cultural background, and a few mentioned a small number of close friends who came from mixed cultural backgrounds. Mixedness was less commonly seen outside of larger cities, and individuals felt unique because of this. Jenny met someone whose background reflected hers in her early twenties, and found that this allowed her to feel less isolated, finding "someone that was the same".

When I was about . . . about 20, um, my boyfriend at the time, who knew about all my issues that I had with being Eurasian, he knew another Eurasian boy, who's also, who's just a couple of years older than me.

And he introduced me to him.

And we met up and had this big talk about . . . what life was like being a half-caste, growing up in New Zealand and things like that.

And it was funny, because I found that he had exactly the same like perceptions and ideas and negative experiences as I did.

And I was like "oh my gosh, you're like my long lost brother! Why haven't I found you earlier?" So that was really funny.

Um . . . but that was good, it was nice to find someone that was the same.

'Cause, yeah. Yeah, no.

I don't really know many Eurasian people.

At all.

Um . . . and so he was the first one that I've met, that we had a good chat about it, and I felt like "oh my god, I've finally found someone who understands where I'm coming from!"

(Jenny Griffiths, NZ, 25, female, Pakeha New Zealander/Chinese New Zealander)

This notion of sameness in difference was also present in the stories of some participants who related to the multiplicity of their partner's background. This was especially prominent in Singapore, as five individuals mentioned that their partner's mixed heritage provided a key point of connection for them. Anne described how her partner came from a diversity of cultures, making it easier for her to relate to her. Katrina stressed that a mixed or Eurasian identity carried with it certain values, making for a more harmonious partnership. For her, it was important to find someone who understood her cultural complexity as she grew older, someone like her.

Interestingly, while commonalities could be found in mixedness, some individuals went further, and described wider common ground based on character and the potential for common humanity. Such commonality could be found in geographic location, career aspirations, religious beliefs, or even common values. Participants often referred to this type of commonality across difference when referring to the relationship of their parents, as they found common ground on which to meet. From this perspective, race and mixedness were one aspect of a wider spectrum, illustrating one form of difference within a wider human sameness.

Racial categories or experiences of being mixed were then not the only ways in which participants defined themselves. Other social axes of difference such as religion, profession and education were equally important to individual stories, highlighting that although race and heritage were important, for many people they were tangential to how they perceived themselves (see Mahtani 2005; Song and Aspinall 2012). In personal stories, there was a noticeable difference between the two countries in how individuals narrated their identities, often in response to the very broad question: "tell me about yourself". For over half the New Zealanders, other aspects of identity took preference in their stories, frequently nationality, but also religious or professional identities.

Religious identity was an important form of belonging for a number of people in both countries. Half of participants in Singapore described themselves as Christian of some denomination (primarily Roman Catholic)[1], while one third were not religious. For those whose religious identity was strong, religion was a point of commonality and a form of belonging. Religious identity was frequently seen as a matter of choice, much more so than racial identity, and provided a way for participants to feel connected to a wider community. Although most participants followed the religious traditions of their families, a small number had converted to a particular religion themselves; in effect, they had chosen a religious community in which to belong. For one man, Terence, his religious background was a key point of commonality in relating to his fiancée, over and above heritage. For another woman, her religion played an important part in her life and her husband's beliefs, but in a more symbolic way:

> We are all, um, Muslim. And um, I thought my dad left the religion, but apparently he's still, he still considers himself Muslim.
> So for my, um, for my . . . in Muslim terms, they call it Nikah, which is the religious ceremony for the wedding. So, he gave me away. So . . . and it's like, and he has to be Muslim to give me away so, yeah.
> Um . . . he's, he doesn't pray, or . . . yeah. Same as my mum.
> So we are quite liberal in that sense. I think, for me it's like, I guess periods where I'm quite, I'm quite . . . I try to pray and make an effort, but it's up and down. Yeah.
> It's not really . . . yeah. I wouldn't say it's very, ah . . .
> We, we, we want to make it important, but somehow it's just not.
> (Safiyah Matthews, SG, 28, female, Singaporean Chinese/New Zealand European)

Safiyah discussed her religious identity as a symbolic and shifting part of her life, relating to both her background with her parents, and her future with her husband. Her uncertainty highlighted her occasional ambivalence, as she saw religion as something that should be important, but did not always become important in her day-to-day life.

In the New Zealand group, just under half of the participants identified as Christian of some denomination, and half were not religious. Many of those who were not religious described the religious affiliations of their parents, and how these translated to cultural practices and beliefs that had influenced them, despite not identifying with the religion itself. Several of the Christian participants stressed that Christianity was one of the most important aspects of their lives. As Angelina Ng said: "[It is] kind of like the driving force behind everything we kind of do".

Religion was seen as not inherited by blood, but passed on through practice and experience, as in the case of one participant:

I'm a Christian, and that's a big part of my identity.
I didn't really say heaps about that, but my adopted family um, are quite, committed Christians. Um, not really . . .
Well, mum is fairly conservative. Dad not so much. Ah, but from a Baptist background, so not fundamentalist, but fairly, you know . . . born-again Christian, you'd say.
And that's kind of, that's been something I've just carried on in my own life
and it's a big part of who I am.

(Jason De Vries, NZ, 39, male, Pakeha New Zealander/Chinese New Zealander)

Jason described how his beliefs as a Christian were important in defining who he was, and helped him to feel a sense of belonging, providing an overriding form of identity. For another participant, Andrea, her religious identity as Baha'i was very much related to practice, and it shaped much of her life: her activities in her free time, and the friends that she felt closest to. As in Singapore, religion provided a point of commonality that transcended heritage and cultural similarities for some people, negotiating a different form of belonging and group membership.

A small number of people in New Zealand and Singapore, Pamela, Katie and David, defined identity in very individual terms, focused on personality traits, as "just who I am". These individuals felt that they were not defined by external or ancestral parameters, and that this uniqueness of personality was seen by those close to them.

[pause] I'm a 20-year-old female who goes to Otago University [laughs]. No, I don't know . . .
I just never gave much thought into describing myself either,
I'm just like "I'm Pamela, that's it."

(Pamela McLane, NZ, 20, female, Singaporean Chinese/Pakeha, Fijian and Japanese)

Rather than focusing on ethnicity or race, they separated their identities from external categorizations in narratives of transcendence. They stressed that they were simply themselves. This view of identity from the inside out de-emphasized the role of external perceptions and understandings of race, setting their individual stories outside of wider narratives.

This theme of individuality continued in the descriptions of those who emphasized agency as the defining point of their identities. For these participants, it was their choices that defined who they were.

Has my background influenced who I am as a person?
No, I think we've made ourselves into what we want to be.
You know, we're not held back . . .

We're not being rooted into the origins and say, "Oh, no, we can't move away from that."
(David Faulkner, SG, 64, male, Singaporean Chinese/White British)

David's narrative is also transcendent, as he highlighted his choices and who he has made himself, above race or heritage. Having lived through numerous changes in state policy towards race and shifting attitudes towards the Eurasian community, he chose to take responsibility for his identity over and above his origins. In both New Zealand and Singapore, a small number of individual narratives developed in this way. They focused on identity as a choice, emphasizing that although external perceptions could influence the individual, it was ultimately the individual who decides how to respond. These ideas of choice and negotiation reflected the ways social structure and context shaped identity, yet also how agency could be asserted and maintained in different conditions.

Regardless of a public/private identity dissonance, individual identities could not exist completely divorced from context, and other participants described how they created their own symbolic spaces in which to belong. These spaces were often elaborated in more detail when talking about the next generation. Although there was no single definition of what it meant to be mixed, most participants were very definite that they wanted to pass on the importance of a mixed heritage to their children. In both countries, participants wanted to make sure that the next generation was aware of mixedness and the uniqueness of their ancestry.

Many Singaporeans discussed the practical ways in which these heritages could be made real to their children, through food, traditions, language and festivals. Some were concerned that their mixed ancestry meant that the culture they would pass down would be too diluted to be meaningful, while others spoke of making a deliberate attempt to make cultural aspects an important part of everyday life.

> If I, um, you know marry someone from a different background, I would want all three of the backgrounds to be integrated. You know, into my child's existence.
> You know, and um . . . and I think it's really important.
> I think it's really important to know where children, for children to know where they come from.
> And . . . you know, I think that . . . and . . . and I think what I'd like to do, what I'd aim to do is just take the good, not dismiss the bad, but take the good things from each one, and you know, integrate it into our lives.
> And . . . um . . . you know, celebrate Chinese New Year, celebrate Christmas [laughs], celebrate Hari Raya [laughs]. Whatever!
> And I think like . . . yeah, I think I wouldn't want them to miss out on, you know, on that. You know, because I come from two different cultures, then they come from two different cultures plus one, one more, or two or more, you know?

And . . . yeah. I just, I want them to know about where they come from, and you know, and experience like the cultures and that kind of thing, and yeah. I think it would be quite important.

(Anne McNeil, SG, 27, female, Singaporean Chinese/British)

Anne's narrative highlighted this deliberate integration, as she saw herself passing down her own form of appreciation to her children. She described wanting them to know "where they come from", highlighting cultural backgrounds as spaces to belong, rather than necessarily a definite place.

For the New Zealanders, awareness of heritage was also seen as very important. Rather than focusing on the practical aspects of transmitting culture, individuals spoke of the power of symbolic recognition, and how this had often been lacking in their lives as children. One man, Jason, described how his feelings of shame about his heritage dissipated as he learned more about the Chinese side of his family, a "turning point" for him. Emmeline and Alexis felt that a strong sense of being Chinese would have strengthened their identities as children, and Emmeline intended to pass that on to her children in turn.

Um, I would want to tell them all about their background and how . . .
I'd want to make them feel good about their background.
That's something that I'd say that my friends who are full-blooded Chinese have had a really strong sense of their Chineseness and it was . . .
and it's strengthened their identity
and it meant that if anyone was sort of giving them a hard time I think it was going to affect them less because they had such a strong sense of identity.
Whereas I think that I didn't so if somebody started making fun of me because of my heritage it hurt me a lot more because I didn't,
yeah, I didn't have that strong sense of what it was to be mixed race.
Um, so I'd want them to feel really good about it and, you know, teach them that it's a positive thing.

(Emmeline Tan, NZ, 32, female, Pakeha New Zealander/Singaporean Chinese)

This story was important, as Emmeline described two key points as she talked about her future children. First, she highlighted her recognition of culture and mixed race as passed down through symbolic connections to identities. Second, however, she reflected a belief that there is a single way in which to be strongly Chinese, or mixed race, and this was something she lacked growing up. This connection was something that she would seek for her children, to give them a "strong sense of identity".

Paul looked at this generational shift from a different, more ambiguous, point of view. Reflecting a potential shift, he described how his children were able to negotiate a multiplicity of identities, in ways that he was not able to do growing up.

I know my daughter in particular loves the fact that she is part Chinese, part Italian, and on my wife's side, part Scottish, part English and part Maori.

So she revels in the fact that she's got all these different traits in her.
And she goes to a fantastic school, where they celebrate differences.
And so they have international day. So every international day she goes dressed as something different.
So this year she was Italian, and the previous year she was Chinese, the previous year before that she was Maori . . . and everyone's going "how can you have all these different things?"
And she loves the fact, and I think it's great,
and I think it's a real maturity in New Zealand that we can do that kind of stuff.

(Paul Moretti, NZ, 48, male, Chinese/Italian)

His daughter's appreciation of her identity subverted many expectations in the New Zealand context. Illustrating both the choices of the parents and the changing social context in New Zealand, mixed identity became less about heritage for her. It was more about cultural diversity and acceptance: a mindset as well as an awareness of ancestral lines.

Looking at identities over time and generation, some participants described how their attitudes towards their heritage changed over time – as they got older, and as the social attitudes around them shifted. For the oldest participant in Singapore, his memories of negative attitudes towards mixing influenced his feelings of being excluded from wider group identities.

I've been trying to collect memories of why other . . . what other people said to us, that we were like half-breeds, you know, and these words were used, you know.
They were used not in a negative but sort of a like maybe a partial nickname or so.
And you would grow up knowing that you're not like them.
Okay, so that's one. I . . . I think that makes a big difference, it makes you feel assimilated into a group or not.
But I think after you reach maturity it doesn't matter any more . . . doesn't make a difference any more.
You can fight your way in the world, you can . . . you can . . . you have a right to be where you are and that kind of stuff and . . .
and it doesn't . . . you don't go back and say, "I'm not so good," or, you know, you don't . . .
We grew up poor and so that also had some influence, but not in the subject we're talking about now.
I guess everybody grew up poor. [laughs]

(David Faulkner, SG, 64, male, Singaporean Chinese/White British)

As he got older, David found he was more easily able to make a distinction between external attitudes and his personal identity, and to better accommodate the two. His experience had proved to him that identity was more about choices and actions, rather than heritage. He also spoke about being poor in a lighthearted manner, belying the seriousness of the subject, and stressing that other forms of identity, including occupation, socioeconomic status and generation, had influenced him significantly.

For many of the New Zealand participants, age also had an impact on how they felt about their backgrounds. Many people described discomfort, embarrassment or unhappiness when they were younger, generally in reaction to social exclusion and discrimination for being different.

> Yes, I've become more positive.
> Like I'm not . . . it doesn't sit as . . . um . . . it's not as uneasy anymore as it used to be.
> Um . . . um . . . so yeah, I definitely, I've come to a place where I'm more comfortable with it.
> I still have . . . yeah, sometimes I still find it tricky, because I find myself in the middle of like, feeling like . . . yeah . . . I don't belong, or racism . . . I find myself in the middle of that.
> Um . . . but definitely not as confused anymore.
> And I kind of, I guess because I've found like direction in my life,
> like I love my job, it's something that I'm very passionate about.
> You kind of, all those other sort of problems disappear because you feel more content about things.
>
> (Jenny Griffiths, NZ, 25, female, Pakeha New Zealander/Chinese New Zealander)

Some individuals indicated that their feelings had shifted from negative to positive, as they learned to reconcile private and public identities and to negotiate a sense of belonging within social groups and wider structures.

> So when I was growing up I'd often, you know, when people would say to you, "so, you look different, so why are you different?", I would . . .
> I wouldn't say I was ashamed of it,
> but I wouldn't openly talk about the fact that I had a Chinese mother and an Italian father. So, I'd skirt around the topic.
> Whereas now, I'm very open about it. I'm very happy to tell everyone.
> I think it's also a reflection of how New Zealand's changed too.
> Yeah, so New Zealanders are far more open about race and ethnicity.
> So I think it's a good thing.
>
> (Paul Moretti, NZ, 48, male, Chinese/Italian)

Paul's story reflected both a personal and a social change: his changing attitude resulting from personal growth and from the changing social context in New Zealand. Similarly, a number of people in both countries commented on increasing levels of intermarriage and the higher numbers of young people of mixed heritage in schools. For them, this suggested that asserting mixedness would be easier for the next generations. Public/private dissonance would be reduced, and personal negotiations and accommodations would be less difficult, with increasing diversity and higher levels of social comfort around the idea of mixed identities. Rose in New Zealand highlighted the drawing together of threads of time, experience, heritage and belonging.

> I think maybe your roots are inside of you.
> Like... that's where the power comes from, that's where your identity comes from, and your identity is never, it's never fixed.
> Like, there's that study, like there's no cell in your body that's that same after 7 years or something.
> So like whoever you are, or you think you are at this moment in time, it's completely different to where you'll be in the future.
> And so I'm like, well, I agree with that idea.
> Who I am now was not what I was when I was younger.
> You're the sum of all your experiences.
> (Rose Stein, NZ, 22, female, Hong Kong Chinese/Dutch)

Her narrative positioned mixedness as shifting and subversive, redefining the conception of roots as heritage and belonging. In her case, mixed identity was less about confusion and dissonance, and more about fluidity and compromise, as ideas of race, ethnicity, culture and nation combined in a personal narrative of belonging.

Conclusion: where you're from and where you're at

Moving across stories of belonging, generation, growing up and being left out, identity was complex, fluid and changing for all participants. Although such multiplicity is not exclusive to experiences of mixedness, simplistic conceptions of race, ethnicity, nation and belonging often miss the ways in which identity is less easily categorized for individuals of mixed heritage. In both Singapore and New Zealand, individual stories were pieced together within a particular set of circumstances, as personal narratives reflected and absorbed wider narratives of the nation. Contextual differences between countries highlighted key differences in identity construction, illustrating the dissonance and tension between macro categorization of identities and the lived, gendered and racialized experiences of individuals. Echoing previous research and theory in the United States, the United Kingdom and New Zealand, participants spoke of reflexive and shifting identities, and personal conceptions of mixedness that encompassed multiple identities and spaces to belong.

Discussions of belonging and not belonging were key in both places, and interestingly, distinctions were frequently made between public and private forms of belonging in narratives of accommodation and subversion. Wider social acceptance of personal feelings could be seen as optional in validating a private feeling of attachment, particularly so in New Zealand, where private identity was often seen to override public identification. Traditional feelings of belonging, aligning nation, race and family, were commonly discussed in Singapore, but in both countries, such belonging was not always seen as desirable or necessary. Belonging could instead be conceived of as a process, encompassing symbolic and geographical locations and journeys, drawing on experience as much as heritage in order to locate oneself. For participants in both cases, experiences of travel highlighted this, as people told stories of experiencing multiple cultures and locations in their lives. This movement and awareness of other contexts often led individuals to stress the importance of diversity in their feelings of belonging: finding a sense of commonality in difference.

In Singapore, a number of participants spoke of belonging in many places and, simultaneously, nowhere at all. Such conceptions of belonging often had a strong racialized undertone, drawing on discourses of race and nation and narratives of reinforcement, as well as ideas about ancestral homelands and diaspora. Building on this, several participants spoke of a mythical homeland of Eurasia, where Eurasians could belong by aligning race and nation in a similar way. For some, online groups provided a way of creating a virtual Eurasia, to search for commonality in the experiences and heritages of others. For the New Zealanders, the contemporary alignment between race and nation was less pronounced, with many participants focusing instead on an attachment to New Zealand as a physical place, highlighting also the diversity within the country as affecting their feelings of belonging.

In both cases, belonging was related to feelings of being at home or not at home: both on an intimate, personal scale, and in the wider sense of national identity and citizenship. Participants described subversive narratives of belonging, as they spoke of being at home in Singapore and New Zealand, or not at home, and sometimes both at the same time. Feeling homeless was conceived of as both positive and negative in this sense, and a number of individuals redefined their ideas of home. In New Zealand, home was often understood on a very personal level, as connected to a localized space such as a town or a house, and imbued with important memories. In both countries, participants saw home as closely linked to family, friends and cultural connections. Home was also seen as a choice, something to be constructed and changed within wider circumstances: this was mentioned in both countries, but the circumstances were described as more constraining in the Singaporean context. Much like identity, home was also seen to be fluid and multiple, as expressed by a small number of Singaporean participants, but more commonly mentioned in New Zealand.

Being "mixed" related to conceptions of home and belonging in different ways. Similarly, mixedness meant different things to participants in itself. Singaporean participants often fractionalized their heritages along racial lines in narratives of reinforcement, while non-racial identities were more commonly put forward as transcendent narratives in New Zealand. However, in both countries, individuals described how being mixed meant that they felt open-minded, tolerant and flexible when it came to cultural identity and personal traits. A form of difference inherent in being mixed was emphasized in both contexts within stories of accommodation, but as both positive and negative. Feeling negatively different, and out of place, was more pronounced in the Singaporean context, although participants in both places stressed that negative feelings of difference could often be balanced by positive difference and uniqueness. The interviews revealed mostly positive views of heritage and identity in both countries, although interestingly, one quarter of participants in New Zealand had neutral or shifting feelings about their heritage, more than in the Singaporean context. In the context of personal narratives, it appears that while classification shapes and is shaped by wider social narratives, it is individuals' experiences with inclusion and exclusion (and discrimination) that are key. Many more Singaporeans had friends with similar backgrounds, or were familiar with the idea of mixedness as an identity. In New Zealand, mixed heritage was much less talked about, and many participants had very few or no friends with similar experiences.

The intercountry comparison illuminated significant sameness, but a sameness that encompassed much diversity. As shown in the previous chapters, mixedness was often understood to mean experience within narratives of subversion and accommodation, rather than simply an ancestral or biological authenticity. In both countries, narratives of "mixed race" showed individuals as they worked to locate themselves in their families, their communities and their countries: "the process of becoming rather than being: not 'who we are' or 'where we came from', so much as what we might become, how we have been represented and how that bears on how we might represent ourselves" (Hall 1996:4).

Supporting recent research, and countering theories of marginality, personal stories showed how ethnic, racial and cultural identity was not always tied to ancestry or parentage, nor to external validation of such ancestry. Beliefs around mixedness were not fixed, and identities were necessarily lived differently across time and space, reflecting both changing contexts and shifting personal locations (Mahtani 2002b, 2005). Mixed identities were then as much about "routes" as "roots", as participants negotiated their feelings of inclusion, exclusion and belonging through differing understandings of home: "not the so-called return to roots but a coming-to-terms with our 'routes' " (Hall 1996:4).

These personal "routes", individual life experiences, were key in how participants saw who they had come to be. In both countries, many participants were clear that it was the myriad of cultural influences in their lives that had shaped their identities, rather than more abstract notions of biology and lineage. This was reflected in the context where they grew up, as for many people, the emotions associated with a childhood home provided a strong connection for them. The culture(s) of their families also proved important, as the learned family practices and traditions influenced the meanings of these cultural associations. This was important for individuals who were raised by a family from a different cultural background, for those whose family created an intimate and new form of family culture, and for those who found a third culture in their immediate surroundings in which they felt at home. One Singaporean woman, Safiyah, felt most comfortable with Malay culture, as the culture of her family, and one New Zealand woman, Andrea, felt connected to Maori culture, as something that she felt drawn to and embraced by. Life experience proved practically important, even if heritage was symbolically valued.

154 Roots, routes and coming home

The concepts of home and belonging also changed for participants across time and space. Associations and identifications from the past did not necessarily carry over into the present or the future. As people moved geographically, their conceptions of home as a located place and symbolic space changed, and home could be multiple, singular, or not located at all. Such movement often meant that identity was less about the fixed past, and more about the possibilities of the future.

Most importantly, public and private conceptions of identities converged and diverged, shifting across time and contexts. For some, the dissonance between their understandings of multiplicity and fluidity were in stark contrast with wider narratives of singularity and belonging, positioning accommodation within reinforcement. This was particularly present in Singapore, and led some individuals to feel constrained and dispossessed by racial and national categorizations. This struggle also existed for a small number of individuals in New Zealand, as racial narratives underpinned much contemporary discussion on fluid ethnicity and voluntary belonging.

Public and private differences were addressed in different ways. Some fought against the system in subversion; some sought to position themselves within simple categories by emphasizing one aspect of their heritage and reinforced wider narratives; and others attempted to reconcile external and internal understandings to create a wider sense of self through narratives of accommodation. For some, particularly in New Zealand, public and private categorizations and identifications could exist simultaneously, without inherent contradiction, making accommodation less difficult. Such difference was illustrated as participants defined race, ethnicity, culture and nation for themselves. Roots and routes could then be understood as essentially the same, as public and private identities coexisted, developed and changed. Mixedness was expressed through a complex assortment of practices, beliefs, symbolic attachments and stories, told and retold within wider social narratives.

Note

1 This is likely to be related to the interconnections between Eurasian identity and Christianity in Singapore, where the two are administratively, and often socially, intertwined.

6 Conclusion

This book has brought together 40 personal narratives of mixedness in Singapore and New Zealand, juxtaposing individual stories against wider narratives of race, national identity and belonging. The aim was not to provide direct causal links between context and identity, but to explore how differences in context and history provide for different identity options, and how these options are understood and made use of by individuals of mixed descent. The concept and experience of "mixed race" provided a unique lens through which to review and deconstruct existing racial paradigms, illuminating the permeability of racial boundaries and the fluidity of individual identities. By analyzing the interplay between the state, society and the individual, "mixed race" is positioned as a manifestation of social, historical and political changes in Singapore and New Zealand.

As seen through the myriad of stories, the relationship between national narratives of racial formation and personal narratives of mixedness proved complex and intricate. Historical processes of racial formation in both contexts have had powerful impacts on the shape of contemporary population management (see Gullickson and Morning 2010): the colonial legacies of race and racialized hierarchy are strong in both countries, but they have manifested in different ways. The census provided an important way to track these processes over time, illustrating how state constructions of race and ethnicity have shaped institutional classifications, social understandings and personal experiences of race, by simplifying complex reality into singular, countable categories (Aspinall 2012; Song 2012). In Singapore, historical classification paid special attention to boundary crossing and mixedness, echoed in the Eurasian category today. Intermixing and mixed identities were viewed as unacceptable crossings of boundaries, and many participants experienced stereotypes about rootless, immoral and culturally homeless "mixed race" identities. In New Zealand, mixedness was not always recorded and marked in the same way, and in contemporary record keeping, is not viewed as particularly unusual. However, participants did describe experiences of negative attitudes in New Zealand society. Interestingly, these were more *reactions against difference*, rather than *reactions against mixing* as in Singapore.

Individual narratives were complex and varied, with key similarities and differences occurring both across and within the two contexts. Common to both contexts was the idea of change: personally, in individual stories over time, and socially and/or structurally, as race and ethnicity were dealt with differently at different points. On the macro level, national narratives illustrated shifting trajectories, but towards different outcomes. In Singapore, within a strongly racialized framework with significant material consequences, top-down changes sought to symbolically acknowledge mixedness without upsetting the multiracial balance. Tolerance is promoted for different racial groups, and boundary crossing is increasingly in the public eye, yet individuals are still understood as having a primary race. Mixedness remains out of the ordinary, structurally and socially. In New Zealand, state efforts to remove "race" from public discourse have resulted in ethnicity being understood in a more fluid and flexible manner in official and academic circles. Yet, this flexibility has not always translated easily to everyday life. Some change is evident, as many participants described how they had seen changes in their lifetimes, particularly in terms of tolerance for differently racialized New Zealanders. Being mixed as one way of being different is becoming increasingly acceptable for younger generations in New Zealand.

Given the contrasts in racialized structures, one interesting and potentially counterintuitive finding from participants' stories was the way in which flexibility could be found within structure. Although Singapore has much more structured racial categories, individuals in Singapore who defined themselves as Chinese and European were much more flexible in their personal definitions. They exhibited more tolerance for ambiguity and diversity in their definitions of what it meant to be Chinese and/or European: many had other aspects to their ancestries, but nevertheless identified themselves as both Chinese and European in narratives of accommodation. In New Zealand, by way of contrast, participants' backgrounds were more often half-half: one Chinese and one European parent. Subtleties in culture were then elaborated on this basis of heritage. This personal flexibility and redefinition highlights that in some cases, more clearly defined boundaries are those which are more easily blurred. Although categories in Singapore were seen as constraining, they also presented opportunities for personal hybridity and fluidity, accommodation and subversion.

In both countries, Chinese identity was emphasized symbolically and practically: a marker of sameness in Singapore and of difference in New Zealand. In contrast, European identity was seen as less "ethnic". It was often related to socioeconomic status in Singapore, and national identity in New Zealand, stressing the (often unnoticed) dominance of the majority group in one country, and the legacy of racial hierarchy in the other. Mixedness, of course, meant many different things. In Singapore, participants often focused on the mixing of ancestry, and the practical "proof" of belonging in multiple groups, such as linguistic ability. In New Zealand, mixedness was more cultural and often symbolic, a felt form of connection, with less dissonance experienced between state categories and personal identities and accommodations. In both countries, individuals often spoke of personal growth and strength, as they were better able to appreciate and understand differences as they grew older.

In Singapore, a form of commonality was sometimes seen in mixed identities, drawing on the perceived difference of mixedness within a singular racial framework. Mixedness was seen as more unusual in New Zealand, and commonality was then found along other axes of difference. In both countries, individuals spoke of other aspects of identity that were equally, if not more, important: transcending race along religious, occupational, educational, locational and class lines. In Singapore, several of these coincided with racial classifications, including the expected conflation of race and religion, and the class/race distinctions of expat/local identities. For some, commonality was not sought at all, as participants located themselves purely individually, as "just who I am".

At the meso level, mixedness as a conscious group identity was not obviously present: the commonality of mixedness instead being found in difference. In contrast to the "multiracial" movement and advocacy in the United States, "mixed race" as a communal identity took on very different forms in Singapore and New Zealand. In New Zealand, against a background where flexibility is possible and potentially more normalized, there was no evidence of a mixed community, with many individuals knowing very few others with a similar background. In Singapore, the Eurasian community provided an ostensible space for individuals of mixed descent, but in practice, this created a further category into which mixedness did not easily fit. As a result of historical changes, the initially hybrid Eurasian community has become increasingly racialized, serving to crystallize boundaries rather than provide space for flexibility. This essentialization of Eurasian identity has served a practical purpose in positioning the community as a legitimate part of the Singaporean nation but has also created an identity with which few participants identified strongly. Interestingly, particularly for countries considering a "multiracial" category, having such a category in Singapore served to reinforce existing racialized structures, rather than necessarily promoting a sense of community or an acceptance of mixedness.

In both contexts, then, projects of mixedness often remained personal, with individuals asserting their connections to multiple groups rather than the creation of a separate group which could be extended to others. A few stories expressed a desire for this form of mixed community, an imaginary Eurasia, reflecting the power of racial stories of belonging in both countries. Others sought belonging and community along other axes of identity, with mixedness acting as a way to belong between and within multiple groups.

Macro, meso, micro

Addressing the overall connections between micro, meso and macro conceptions of race and mixedness, this research shows how state narratives of racial formation both coincide with and diverge from personal stories of "mixed race". In Singapore, personal narratives were strongly shaped by a racialized background, as individuals located themselves and made sense of their experiences within everyday, pervasive racial structures. However, there was also an important state/individual disconnect, as complex and fluid identities did not fit easily within a more fixed state framework, with far-reaching practical consequences. In New Zealand, personal stories were positioned against a dual narrative of fluidity and racialization, reflected in narratives that embraced ambiguity while still referring back to racialized categories. The disconnect in this context was more between social narratives of race and personal identities: the fluidity of official categorizations and personal experiences not being widely recognized by the majority of the population, which continues to see race and ethnicity as singular and predefined.

This social aspect of identity proved particularly important in both countries, connecting individual identities to the level of the state and determining which identity options were available to individuals of mixed descent. Social understandings of race and belonging provided options for community inclusion and exclusion. The dissonances between public and private forms of identity drew on these social boundaries, as personal feelings of connectedness were reinforced or discouraged through experiences of belonging in or exclusion from ethnic and racial groups. Race was seen by participants as both a way to belong and as a source of division within society, and occasionally within racial groups. In both Singapore and New Zealand, participants experienced exclusion from groups as a result of perceived difference, but while mixedness was the primary source of difference in Singapore, it was Chineseness (whether being too Chinese to be Pakeha, or not Chinese enough to be legitimately Chinese) that was the main point of difference in New Zealand.

Participants then related to their heritage in different ways: through feeling connected to one group more than the other, feeling very connected to both, feeling like they created something else entirely, or even describing a form of identity that transcended the racial identifications of their heritage. These different options were shaped and constrained by both state and social classifications and exclusions, as individuals sought to reconcile their personal stories with wider narratives of belonging. Mixed identity was then *a process of location, negotiation and experience*, a fluid, contextual and shifting way to belong. Identity as a process pushed against simplistic forms of categorization and wider social norms of racial belonging based on ancestry, leading to a public/private dissonance that was common across both contexts. While identity claims were personal to each participant, their choices between narratives of reinforcement, subversion, accommodation or transcendence reflected the wider context in which they found themselves and the resources with which they were able to negotiate.

These negotiations took many different forms, as individuals sought to reconcile public and private narratives or allowed differing narratives to coexist simultaneously. Overall, many participants described a type of third space of identity in their stories: mixedness set them apart from wider social and national narratives, and personal narratives attempted to address this dislocation. Many located their identities racially and along lines of heritage, seeing themselves as a mix of both, with links to both, or with the best of both worlds, implying that there are indeed separate worlds which could be linked in some way. This type of racialized, reinforcing and then mixed narrative was present in both contexts but was more common in Singapore. For others, in both countries, public and private narratives were reconciled through a symbolic acknowledgement and accommodation of mixedness, negotiating public/private identities simultaneously. Private narratives were most commonly seen as distinct from public narratives in New Zealand. Mixedness was a way to both encompass and distance oneself from different aspects of heritage and culture, with a significant emphasis on the individuality of identity.

Reconciling narratives

Returning to the theoretical framework, narrative characterizations highlighted how micro narratives developed within differing macro narratives. Importantly, in a process of narrative analysis, the fragmented themes from personal stories come together within holistic narratives of identity, bringing narratives back together and comparing their positionings across contexts. Thus, the four major narratives of transcendence, reinforcement, accommodation and subversion can be compared across Singapore and New Zealand, exploring how each occurs in different contexts, and potential reasons for this narrative location.

Narratives of extremes: transcendence and reinforcement

Beginning with the two most extreme narrative, types, personal stories can be held up against broader narratives, looking for coherence and discontinuities. Personal narratives of transcendence reject racialization to a large extent, focusing instead on aspects of experience and non-racial identities. Interestingly, for narratives of transcendence to develop, there needs to be an awareness of a racial narrative to transcend in the first place. Seven participants from Singapore and five from New Zealand could be broadly characterized as situating themselves primarily in stories of transcendence. These include Singaporean participants who focused on the transnational and global aspects of identity (James Field, Susann Nasser, Celine Chin), compared to those who stressed the importance of civic identity and citizenship as primary in determining identity (William Briggs, Alastair Jenkins, Terence Peaks, David Faulkner). These participants are primarily male (those who stressed the importance of just being Singaporean were exclusively male), across a range of ages. This emphasis on civic identity and belonging above racial classification is likely related to the impact of national service on the self-perceptions of men in Singapore, as each of the four men served in the armed forces. For the New Zealanders, four of those who focused on transcendence emphasized the importance of being a New Zealander first (Tai Feng, Pamela McLane, Paul Moretti, Nathan Fleming), while one woman saw her religious identity as a way to transcend racial categorizations (Angelina Ng). Again, national identity appealed predominantly to men, perhaps reflecting a gendered propensity towards a simple, overarching form of identity – even without the additional factor of national service. Each of these individuals downplayed the importance of race in their personal conceptions of self, choosing an alternative way to belong. This was sometimes unconscious, but it was more often a deliberate choice, reacting to experiences of exclusion, perceptions of phenotype, or family emphasis on other forms of belonging.

160 Conclusion

Turning to the opposite extreme, some participants reinforced wider narratives of race and belonging in their personal stories. Confirming one initial theoretical hypothesis, those who focused significantly on narratives of reinforcement were all from the Singaporean group. These five participants were all female, and they reinforced wider Singaporean narratives of race in different ways. The most common was to focus on Eurasian identity as racialized: an inherently different racialized group, and a form of categorization which allowed them to slot into the national framework (Sara Madeira, Francine Phillippe, Sandra Pereira-Ivansson, Amber Smith). Reflecting another aspect of being a racialized Singaporean, the final participant sought to locate herself in a single category, preferring a racial simplicity over acknowledgements of mixedness (Alison Lijuan). Interestingly, four out of five came from backgrounds that were particularly complex, with multiple heritages coming together under the broad label of "Eurasian", and perhaps reflecting a need for simplicity, borne of the Singaporean racial context.

Narratives of ambiguity: accommodation and subversion

The next two narrative characterizations described ways of embracing and positioning personal ambiguity against a public framework. Narratives of accommodation allowed for significant public and private dissonance, with personal feelings of belonging not necessarily reconciled with occasionally contradictory national narratives. Participants' stories could most often be characterized as accommodation, as individuals in both countries negotiated their feelings of identity and connections with their heritage while at the same time working within wider social constraints. Six Singaporean participants told stories about how they accommodated personal mixedness within frameworks of racial singularity, with the predominant narrative reflecting an important break between the role of bureaucratic classification and the reality of personal identity. Five out of six participants were female, and in their stories, individual complexity did not need to be acknowledged administratively, as lived identities were significantly more important than racial labels (Richard Ong, Jeanne Goh, Katrina Henry, Safiyah Matthews, Skye Sia, Hannah Alley).

Eleven participant narratives from New Zealand could also be broadly characterized as accommodating public and private dissonances. This was the most common characterization for New Zealand, potentially reflecting the flexibility in public narratives of race and the fact that the gap between public and private understandings was not as marked as in Singapore. Again, more women than men described this kind of negotiation. Most stories highlighted the difference between personal identity and wider categories, and implicitly, the lack of material outcomes of these wider categories in everyday life in New Zealand. Six individuals described their connections to both sides of their heritage, expressed in different ways, and how this multiplicity needed to be acknowledged personally, but not always publicly. For them, boundary crossing was a way of life, and mixedness was an everyday reality: it therefore did not need to be structurally acknowledged to be real (Jason De Vries, Emmeline Tan, Jacob Roberts, Philippa

Warner, Li Lin Zhen, Nadine Moore). Two women focused on accommodation through other forms of identity and complexity. In this way, they could fit themselves within wider frameworks and then complicate these through what they saw as important about themselves (Jasmine Orana, Katie Murray). For three women, however, the dissonance between public and private identities had been a source of discontent. They were aware of the different interpretations of mixedness, and negotiated their everyday lives around these understandings, but this lack of alignment was occasionally a reason for unhappiness. They also sought to complicate wider understandings of race and belonging by drawing on other forms of identity to locate themselves (Jenny Griffiths, Margaret Jenkins, Alexis Conrad).

The final narrative group can be characterized as stories of subversion: striving to bring together public and private understandings of mixedness, and pushing against social narratives of singularity. Two participants in Singapore talked of seeking to break out of a framework which they saw as constraining. Their identities, based around mixedness and multiplicity, did not have adequate space in the Singaporean system of categorization, something which they were openly critical about. Their attempts at subversion were not always satisfactory to them, coming up against an inflexible social framework. As a result, they spoke of belonging nowhere, reconceiving their identities on a solely personal level (Anne McNeil, Andrew Wang-Jones).

Narratives of subversion were more common in New Zealand, with four participants renegotiating wider narratives of ethnic belonging and biculturalism to include their own mixed identities. These individuals told stories of creating something new from the available tools: developing an identity for themselves which placed significant weight on experience over ancestry, or even approaching ethnic belonging as something impossible to categorize and quantify (Melanie Townsend, Rose Stein, Joel Andrews, Andrea Wei). In an interesting difference, these participants described positive experiences from these projects of subversion, reflecting the increased space for negotiation in the New Zealand system of classification.

Between theory and reality, structure and agency

Narrative locations highlighted how different processes of racial formation resulted in different narrative patterns for individuals of mixed descent. Narratives of transcendence were equally present in both countries, illustrating that historical racialization can be rejected in both contexts. Narratives of accommodation were more common in New Zealand, as the dissonance between public and private understandings of mixedness was less stark than in the Singaporean context. Narratives of reinforcement were more frequently seen in Singapore, mirroring the strength of colonial and post-colonial projects of racial formation. Narratives of subversion were present in both countries, but they were more common in New Zealand, where subversion required less conscious effort and was described as having a positive, strengthening impact on personal identity.

These characterizations illuminate more than the personal stories of participants, showing how wider narratives of race and racial categorization serve to shape these very stories. Racial ideologies both shape and are challenged by personal narratives, as traditional racial boundaries are pushed by the everyday racial projects and locations of participants. Mixedness is negotiated between structure and agency, and individuals find ways to assert themselves within wider constraints. The narrative differences above show how structural constraints positioned stories in different ways in Singapore and New Zealand, with racialized constraints coming out strongly in Singapore. This was demonstrated in the strong thread of racial belonging across the stories of many participants, particularly those whose personal projects worked to reinforce dominant narratives. However, the structure/agency relationship was not simple, and participants' stories in both countries highlighted the complex ways in which agency can be played out within, against and in spite of wider structures.

Personal stories both reinforced and subverted national narratives of race, drawing on racialized categories as explanation yet also deliberately distancing private narratives from public narratives of what it means to belong. The four narrative characterizations illustrated the significant diversity of stories within each context, but equally highlighted certain patterns: narratives shaped by positionality rather than created by simple cause and effect. Processes of racial formation in Singapore have provided an environment in which narratives of reinforcement are more common, working within a pervasive racialized framework, but also narratives of transcendence, which reject this framework entirely. Narratives of accommodation, where a dissonance between public and private identities is accepted, were common in both countries but were more frequent in New Zealand, where national narratives are not as far removed from personal narratives of fluidity. This was similarly true for narratives of subversion, as already flexible categories are bent and reshaped by individuals negotiating their own personal form of mixedness.

"Mixed race" and race in New Zealand and Singapore

This book contributes to the growing body of literature which approaches "mixed race" from an ecological perspective, exploring the wider contextual factors influencing identity and acknowledging the shifting and flexible nature of belonging. Participants' stories reinforced that individuals of mixed descent are not inherently caught between two worlds, nor do they always feel conflicting loyalties, as posited by much early literature. Using mixedness as a lens to understand race and racial identity illustrates the constructedness of race as a whole, as there are not distinct "worlds" to be caught between. Yet studying "mixed race" also potentially emphasizes this separation of groups, through suggesting that there are separate races to mix. As in other recent studies, this book has attempted to balance this contradiction, showing how mixedness challenges static conceptions and measurements of race but also invokes historically ingrained racialized categories.

National narratives of race and "mixed race" have developed and changed over time in Singapore and New Zealand, mirroring broader sociohistorical shifts and post-colonial developments, and highlighting the centrality of mixedness to racialized understandings of social and cultural change (Parker and Song 2001:1). In parallel, personal narratives of mixedness and the options available for personal projects of mixedness have changed in either context. Bringing these two levels together illustrates both narrative convergences and divergences, and importantly, the ways in which private narratives can be played out as alternative narratives of belonging. It highlights the importance of the practical consequences of racial categorization in Singapore, but also the power of symbolic acknowledgment of mixed identity as a way to belong, as in New Zealand and the new hyphenated racial labels in Singapore.

The complexity of these juxtaposed, flexible narratives then highlights another view of race and "mixed race": "neither as a signifier of comprehensive identity nor of fundamental difference, but rather as a marker of the infinity of variations we humans hold as common heritage" (Winant 2000b:188). This draws on Gilroy's conception of human sameness, but rather than leaving race behind, allows everyday understandings of race and "mixed race" to be acknowledged as important to individuals while at the same time shifting away from race as classification and hierarchy (Gilroy 2000; Winant 2000a). By bringing together narratives of racial formation at macro and micro levels and providing an alternative perspective of characterizations of "mixed race", this book sought to illustrate how theories of mixed racial formation can potentially explore the possibility of racial *trans*formation (Nguyen 2008:1557).

This book draws out the potential directions such transformation could take. Through comparing processes of racial formation in Singapore and New Zealand, this work has been able to explore systems of racial classification that address "mixed race" in very different ways, and the personal, symbolic and practical outcomes for individuals of mixed descent. At the macro level, racial formation theory has illustrated how classificatory systems have normalized and ingrained concepts of race and ethnicity in either society, and how mixedness does not fit easily into such racialized frameworks. At the micro level, racial classification in Singapore has meant that individuals frequently portray themselves in racialized terms, or deliberately break out of the racial framework altogether. In New Zealand, the broader spectrum of options for identification allows individuals to identify more flexibly, but it still falls short of the fluidity desired by some participants.

Placing this within a wider global context, there is a definite trend of moving to acknowledge "mixed race" within national categorizations of race, seen for example in the American and British census changes. Singapore's symbolic acknowledgment of racial hyphenation is in line with these shifts. On the surface, they appear to make space within racial categories, but as has been shown, they often serve to re-create and reinforce the existing racialized structures, without ever really challenging their underlying assumptions. This highlights the power of symbolic acknowledgement as a way to claim a place within society, yet also the strength of existing classification structures and historical trajectories, which allow for a nominal rather than a practical change.

Classifying and organizing "mixed race" within existing frameworks is then not an easy task. As shown by the New Zealand experiences, a high degree of choice and fluidity may still not be enough to capture how individuals identify themselves or the changing nature of identities. Both Singapore and New Zealand illustrate the complexity in trying to separate concepts of race, ethnicity, phenotype, ancestry, culture and nationality into measurable variables: concepts which are not easily separable theoretically or in everyday life. Free-text ethnic/racial identifications would allow for increased fluidity in measurement, and was an option suggested by a number of participants in both contexts. This would allow for greater personal self-expression and multiplicity, but it would largely negate the organizational system of race and the use to which these census statistics are put (see Aspinall 2012).

However, as the number of individuals who identify with multiple ethnic and racial groups grows in multicultural societies, the current frameworks will become increasingly strained and detached (Song 2012:4). New Zealand allows individuals to select as many ethnic groups as they desire, providing options for further generations of mixed descent, while Singapore has limited the hyphenation to two, meaning that individuals must select two of their "component" races with which to officially identify. While suggesting policy solutions to this dilemma is beyond the scope of this book, it has aimed to shed light on the histories and outcomes of some of the current forms of categorization. "Mixed race" encompasses a diversity of experiences and ancestries, and individuals live out mixedness by combining public and private identities in novel and unexpected ways. This comparison of two under-studied countries extends the breadth of the growing literature on "mixed race", while the exploration of micro narratives of racial formation adds to the depth: reinforcing that individual understandings of mixedness are shaped by a wide variety of factors and experienced in a multitude of different ways.

As with any research, this work has both strengths and weaknesses. From a theoretical point of view, racial formation theory provided a framework which deliberately focused on the centrality of race and racial identity at macro and micro levels. It also connected these levels, illustrating how individual racial projects were shaped by and themselves shaped wider national processes of racial formation. This lens with which "mixed race" was analyzed allowed for an exploration and comparison of conceptions of race, yet also may have focused on race at the expense of other equally important aspects of identity, such as gender, class, ancestry and sexuality. Furthermore, applying a framework primarily developed in the American context of critical race theory demonstrated its applicability across other national contexts but also potentially missed key aspects of Singaporean and New Zealand society and history. Transposing such concepts could potentially be inappropriate for this reason, but it could also strengthen the applicability if done with sensitivity to both the original context of development and the particularities of the new context of application (Warren and Sue 2011:33).

Adding the analytical layer of narrative served to make the research much richer, more grounded, and more appropriate to intimate discussions of identity. Analysis of narratives was not intended to show direct causal relations or concrete, generalizable patterns, but rather the variety of lived experiences of mixedness, and how these could be narrated differently against different narrative backgrounds. Inevitably, such a methodology has its limitations. With a small sample of 20 participants in either context, the research presents only the experiences of these individuals, without suggesting that these are part of a more general narrative of all manifestations of mixed identity in New Zealand and Singapore. The current group was relatively young, and the research would certainly have been different with older participants or participants across a different socioeconomic range.

In addition, this research presents *my* narrative of narratives, and has been influenced by the way in which I chose to tell the story of my research: which stories I saw as important, and which I decided to leave out. The final monograph was unavoidably limited by my own identity and positioning in the research process. Although I strove to be open and reflexive in the research process, my own biases influenced both the power relations within interviews, and the stories which participants decided to share with me. My feelings of identification with many participants potentially had a positive impact on the intimacy of stories which were told, but also made it hard to distance myself from more negative experiences. I had to strive to find a balance between focusing on the personal and the political, without taking myself out of the research entirely, and avoiding abstracted, impersonal thematic analysis. While my biases and history impacted the research process and outcomes, such influence was not inherently negative. Had I taken a less personal approach, or had a different personal history, the research would have been different, not necessarily better or worse.

Bringing all these theoretical and methodological aspects together, a key challenge of the research was to make sense of narratives of racial formation at macro and micro levels, across the past and the present, intertwining private and public conceptions and meanings of identity. Through a focus on narratives, this book combined these aspects to present a narrative of stories. It looked both forward and backward at national and personal levels to provide a sense of temporality, re-storying key themes to tell a broader story against a wider background. I sought to reflexively include myself in the research process, looking inward to the personal reasons for the research, and then again outward to the possible wider social significance. By acknowledging the inherent limitations of the research, and providing a clear and transparent explanation of the research process, I sought methods that were trustworthy (Riessman 2008:189), leading to grounded and reasoned conclusions.

Looking forward

There is much potential for future research, building on this work and on the work of others. Most broadly, while the theoretical deconstruction of race has been powerful and pervasive in academic circles, the everyday power of racial identity has meant that popular understandings of race remain shaped by discourses of colour, biology and blood. This is especially evident in the continued emphasis on racial and ethnic classification, where these categories have come from, and how they are understood by the state, the individual, and minority and majority groups in society. Future research will need to address these increasing disconnects, particularly as the connections between race and ancestry are being emphasized by projects of affirmative action in many countries, or even business ventures which purportedly link DNA to racial ancestry: finding out where you're *really* from (Omi 2010).

There is equally much work to be done on "new" identities, as diversity within and between populations increases. Again, connecting theory to reality, conceptions of "new ethnicities" and hybridities, and the relationship between race, ethnicity, culture and national identity could all be explored in greater depth. It is particularly important to see the temporal aspects of such complex identities. They are not merely connected to past ancestral affiliations and present experiences of belonging, but also to future cultural formations, frequently encompassing multiple cultural and national allegiances and crossing multiple borders practically and symbolically (Ang 2011; Parker and Song 2009:584).

Most specifically, there are many aspects of "mixed race" and mixedness that are still to be explored in a coherent manner. Further cross-country comparisons could illuminate more clearly the relationships between classification and identity options for mixedness, as well as how such classification is or is not reflected in everyday life experiences. Expanding definitions of mixedness to look at mixed cultural identity would be an interesting step, stepping further away from race as biology and looking more directly at how individuals live their lives. Experiences of racism, discrimination and family relationships could equally provide fruitful topics for research, while studies of generational change would highlight how "being mixed" becomes more or less important as the diversity of mixing increases. A continued focus on mixedness suggests the possibility of seeing the world otherwise: ". . . as well as the many points of similarity, there are also critical points of deep and significant difference which constitute 'what we really are'; or rather – since history has intervened – 'what we have become' " (Hall 1990:225). While "mixed race" currently provides a novel and unusual set of experiences to investigate, it is equally important to see the commonalities and differences across all experiences of ethnic and racial identity: mixed, unmixed, both or neither.

Final thoughts

Singapore and New Zealand provided key examples of how mixed identities are narrated within different structural contexts, and the consequences for the (dis-)continuities between state and individual narratives of race. Individual stories juxtaposed against national narratives illustrated the power of history and the strength of established racialized structures, as well as the flexibility and fluidity of personal stories and identity negotiations. Narratives of mixed Chinese/European identities illustrated experiences of both dislocation and belonging, as mixedness developed at the intersection of internal and external perceptions of identity. Personal stories were told against backgrounds of fluidity and racialization, reflected in narratives that embraced ambiguity while still referring to racialized categories.

All participants drew on a variety of experiences, stories and traits when describing what being mixed meant to them, illustrating the inherent intersectionality of identity. Aspects of race, ethnicity, ancestry, nationality, gender, occupation, education and history emerged in personal stories, reinforcing the complex, fluid, and often situational nature of any identity. Historical context proved important, and dissonances between public narratives and private mixedness had powerful impacts on personal identities, expressed in narratives of reinforcement, subversion, accommodation and transcendence. External impositions and expectations of identity were key in both contexts; shaping, but not necessarily determining, the identity options available to individuals of mixed descent. Expressions of mixedness were complicated and potentially unthinking, bringing together different personal and social narratives to fashion a unique sense of belonging based on multiple experiences and cultures. In living a mixed identity, participants sought, and sometimes found, a form of personal fluidity within an inflexible framework.

Bibliography

Ahmed, Sara. 2000. *Strange Encounters: Embodied Others in Post-Coloniality*. London: Routledge.
Alba, Richard. 1990. *Ethnic Identity: The Transformation of White America*. New Haven: Yale University Press.
Alcoff, Linda Martin. 2006. *Visible Identities: Race, Gender and the Self*. Oxford: Oxford University Press.
Ali, Suki. 2003. *Mixed-Race, Post-Race: Gender, New Ethnicities and Cultural Practices*. New York: Berg.
Allan, Jo-Anne. 2001. "Review of the Measurement of Ethnicity: Classification and Issues." Wellington: Statistics New Zealand.
Anderson, Benedict. 1991. *Imagined Communities: Reflections on the Origin and Spread of Nationalism*, rev. ed. London: Verso.
Ang, Ien. 1999. "On Not Speaking Chinese: Postmodern Ethnicity and the Politics of Diaspora." In *Feminism and Cultural Studies*, Morag Shiach (ed.). 540–564. Oxford: Oxford University Press.
Ang, Ien. 2001. *On Not Speaking Chinese: Living Between Asia and the West*. London: Routledge.
Ang, Ien. 2007. "Between Asia and the West." In *Visibly Different: Face, Place and Race in Australia*. 175–180. Bern: Peter Lang.
Ang, Ien. 2011. "Ethnicities and Our Precarious Future." *Ethnicities*. 11(1):27–31.
Appadurai, Arjun. 1993. "Number in the Colonial Imagination." In *Orientalism and the Postcolonial Predicament*, Peter van der Veer and Carol A. Breckenridge (eds.). 314–339. Philadelphia: University of Pennsylvania Press.
Appiah, K. Anthony. 2009. "Racial Identity and Racial Identification." In *Theories of Race and Racism: A Reader*, 2nd ed., Les Back and John Solomos (eds.). 669–677. New York: Routledge.
Arumainathan, P. 1973. "Report on the Census of Population 1970 Singapore." Singapore: Department of Statistics.
Asia New Zealand Foundation. 2012. "New Zealanders' Perceptions of Asia and Asian Peoples in 2011." Wellington: Asia New Zealand Foundation.
Aspinall, Peter. 2003. "The Conceptualisation and Categorisation of Mixed Race/Ethnicity in Britain and North America: Identity Options and the Role of the State." *International Journal of Intercultural Relations*. 27:269–296.
Aspinall, Peter. 2009. " 'Mixed Race', 'Mixed Origins' or What?: Generic Terminology for the Multiple Racial/Ethnic Group Population." *Anthropology Today*. 25(2):3–8.

Bibliography

Aspinall, Peter. 2012. "Answer Formats in British Census and Survey Ethnicity Questions: Does Open Response Better Capture 'Superdiversity'?" *Sociology*. Online before print: 2 February 2012:1–11.

Barber, Keith. 2008. " 'Indigenous Rights' or 'Racial Privileges': The Rhetoric of 'Race' in New Zealand Politics." *The Asia Pacific Journal of Anthropology*. 9(2):141–156.

Barr, Michael D., and Zlatko Skrbis. 2008. *Constructing Singapore: Elitism, Ethnicity and the Nation-Building Project*. Copenhagen: NIAS Press.

Bedford, Richard, and Elsie Ho. 2008. "Asians in New Zealand: Implications of a Changing Demography." Wellington: Asia NZ Foundation.

Belich, J. 2009. *Replenishing the Earth: The Settler Revolution and the Rise of the Anglo-World, 1783–1939*. Oxford: Oxford University Press.

Bell, Avril. 1996. " 'We're Just New Zealanders': Pakeha Identity Politics." In *Nga Patai: Racism and Ethnic Relations in New Zealand*, Paul Spoonley, David Pearson and Cluny Macpherson (eds.). 144–158. Palmerston North: Dunmore Press.

Beng, Tan Chee. 1993. *Chinese Peranakan Heritage in Malaysia and Singapore*. Kuala Lumpur: Fajar Bakti.

Benjamin, Geoffrey. 1976. "The Cultural Logic of Singapore's 'Multiracialism.' " In *Singapore: Society in Transition*, Riaz Hassan (ed.). 115–133. Kuala Lumpur: Oxford University Press.

Bernstein, Mary, and Marcie De la Cruz. 2009. "'What Are You?': Explaining Identity as a Goal of the Multiracial Hapa Movement." *Social Problems*. 56(4):722–745.

Bettez, Silvia Cristina. 2011. *But Don't Call Me White: Mixed Race Women Exposing Nuances of Privilege and Oppression Politics*. Rotterdam: Sense Publishers.

Binning, Kevin R., Miguel U. Unzueta, Yuen J. Huo and Ludwin E. Molina. 2009. "The Interpretation of Multiracial Status and Its Relation to Social Engagement and Psychological Well-Being." *Journal of Social Issues*. 65(1):35–49.

Blunt, Alison. 2002. " 'Land of our Mothers': Home, Identity, and Nationality for Anglo-Indians in British India, 1919–1947." *History Workshop Journal*. 54:49–72.

Blunt, Alison. 2005. *Domicile and Diaspora: Anglo-Indian Women and the Spatial Politics of Home*. Malden, MA: Blackwell Publishing.

Blunt, Alison, and Robyn Dowling. 2006. *Home*. New York: Routledge.

Bonilla-Silva, Eduardo. 2000. " 'This Is a White Country': The Racial Ideology of the Western Nations of the World-System." *Sociological Inquiry*. 70(2):188–214.

Braga-Blake, Myrna. 1992. "Eurasians in Singapore: An Overview." In *Singapore Eurasians: Memories and Hopes*, Myrna Braga-Blake (ed.). 11–23. Singapore: Times Editions.

Brown, Paul, and Alistair Gray. 2009. "Inter-Ethnic Mobility between the 2001 and 2006 Censuses: The Statistical Impact of the 'New Zealander' Response." Wellington: Statistics New Zealand.

Brunsma, David L. (ed.). 2006. *Mixed Messages: Multiracial Identities in the "Color-Blind" Era*. Boulder, CO: Lynne Rienner.

Butler-Sweet, Colleen. 2011. " 'Race Isn't What Defines Me': Exploring Identity Choices in Transracial, Biracial, and Monoracial Families." *Social Identities*. 17(6):747–769.

Callister, P. 2003. "The Allocation of Ethnicity to Children in New Zealand: Some Descriptive Data from the 2001 Census." Paper presented at the Population Association of New Zealand Conference: Christchurch, New Zealand. 3–4 July 2003.

Callister, P. 2004a. "Ethnicity Measures, Intermarriage and Social Policy." *Social Policy Journal of New Zealand*. 23:109–140.

Callister, P. 2004b. "Seeking an Ethnic Identity: Is 'New Zealander' a Valid Ethnic Group?". Wellington: Working Paper, Callister & Associates.

Callister, P., and R. Didham. 2009. "Who Are We? The Human Genome Project, Race and Ethnicity." *Social Policy Journal of New Zealand*. 36:63–76.

Callister, P., R. Didham and A. Kivi. 2009. "Who Are We? The Conceptualisation and Expression of Ethnicity." In *Official Statistics Research Series*, Vol. 4. Wellington: Statistics New Zealand.

Callister, P., R. Didham and D. Potter. 2006. "Measuring Ethnicity in New Zealand: Developing Tools for Social Analysis." Paper presented at Population Association of America Annual Meeting: Los Angeles, California. 30 March – 1 April 2006.

Callister, Paul, R. Didham and D. Potter. 2007. "Ethnic Intermarriage in New Zealand." *Official Statistics Research Series, Statistics New Zealand*. 1. www.stats.govt.nz/~/media/Statistics/browse-categories/population/census-counts/review-measurement-ethnicity/ethnic-intermarriage-in-nz.pdf.

Callister, Paul, and Tahu Kukutai. 2009. "A 'Main' Ethnic Group? Ethnic Self-Prioritization among New Zealand Youth." *Social Policy Journal of New Zealand*. 36:16–31.

Chang, Rachel. 2009. "Ignoring Racial Differences 'Won't Make Them Go Away'." *The Straits Times*. 6 March 2010.

Chase, Susan. 1995. "Taking Narrative Seriously: Consequences for Method and Theory in Interview Studies." In *Interpreting Experience: The Narrative Study of Lives*, Ruthellen Josselson and Amia Lieblich (eds.). 1–26. London: Sage Publications.

Cheryan, Sapna, and Benoît Monin. 2005. " 'Where Are You Really From?': Asian Americans and Identity Denial." *Journal of Personality and Social Psychology*. 89(5): 717–730.

Childs, Erica Chito. 2002. "Families on the Color-Line: Patrolling Borders and Crossing Boundaries." *Race & Society*. 5:139–161.

Choo, Christine, Antoinette Carrier, Clarissa Choo and Simon Choo. 2007. "Being Eurasian." In *Visibly Different: Face, Place and Race in Australia*. 103–125. Bern: Peter Lang.

Chow, Rey. 1998. "On Chineseness as a Theoretical Problem." *boundary 2*. 25(3):1–24.

Chua, Beng Huat. 1995a. *Communitarian Ideology and Democracy in Singapore*. London: Routledge.

Chua, Beng Huat. 1995b. *Culture, Multiracialism and National Identity in Singapore, Working Paper No.125*. Singapore: Department of Sociology, National University of Singapore.

Chua, Beng Huat. 1998. "Racial-Singaporeans: Absence after the Hyphen." In *Southeast Asian Identities: Culture and the Politics of Representation in Indonesia, Malaysia, Singapore, and Thailand*, Joel S. Kahn (ed.). 28–50. Singapore: Institute of Southeast Asian Studies.

Chua, Beng Huat. 2003. "Multiculturalism in Singapore: An Instrument of Social Control." *Race and Class*. 44(3):58–77.

Chua, Beng Huat. 2005. "The Cost of Membership in Ascribed Community." In *Multiculturalism in Asia*, Will Kymlicka and Baogang He (eds.). 170–195. Oxford: Oxford University Press.

Chua, Beng Huat, and Eddie C. Y. Kuo. 1990. *The Making of a New Nation: Cultural Construction and National Identity in Singapore, Working Paper No. 104*. Singapore: Department of Sociology, National University of Singapore.

Chua, Beng Huat, and Ananda Rajah. 1997. *Hybridity, Ethnicity and Food in Singapore, Working Paper No. 133*. Singapore: Department of Sociology, National University of Singapore.

Collins, Simon. 2010. "One Nation with Many Nationalities." *New Zealand Herald*. 26 November 2010. www.nzherald.co.nz/nz/news/article.cfm?c_id=1&objectid=10690160. Date accessed: 14 February 2012.

Bibliography

Collins, Simon. 2011. "When Saying 'I Do' Opens a Door to Another Culture." *New Zealand Herald*. 14 April 2011. www.nzherald.co.nz/china-and-us/news/article.cfm?c_id=1503058&objectid=10719090. Date accessed: 14 April 2011.

Cormack, D. 2010. "The Practice and Politics of Counting: Ethnicity Data in Official Statistics in Aotearoa/New Zealand." Wellington: Te Ropu Rangahau Hauora a Eru Pomare.

DaCosta, Kimberly McClain. 2003. "Multiracial Identity: From Personal Problem to Public Issue." In *New Faces in a Changing America: Multiracial Identity in the 21st Century*, Loretta Winters and Herman DeBose (eds.). 68–84. Thousand Oaks, CA: Sage Publications.

DaCosta, Kimberly McClain. 2007. *Making Multiracials: State, Family and Market in the Redrawing of the Color Line*. Stanford, CA: Stanford University Press.

Department of Internal Affairs. 2009. "Chinese Poll Tax Heritage Trust." www.dia.govt.nz/diawebsite.nsf/wpg_URL/Services-Trust-&-Fellowship-Grants-Chinese-Poll-Tax-Heritage-Trust?OpenDocument. Date accessed: 25 May 2010.

Dickens, Lyn. 2010. "Being a Eurasian Australian." *Yemaya: Sydney University Law Society 2010*. 2010:34–36.

Didham, R. 2009. "Maori and Chinese: Encounters and Intersections." In *The Dragon and the Taniwha: Maori and Chinese in New Zealand*, Manying Ip (ed.). 120–147. Auckland: Auckland University Press.

Didham, Robert, and Paul Callister. 2012. "The Effect of Ethnic Prioritisation on Ethnic Health Analysis: A Research Note." *The New Zealand Medical Journal*. 125(1359): 58–66.

Dikotter, Frank. 1996. "Culture, 'Race' and Nation: The Formation of National Identity in Twentieth Century China." *Journal of International Affairs*. 49(2):590–605.

Dikotter, Frank. 1997. "Racial Discourse in China: Continuities and Permutations." In *The Construction of Racial Identities in China and Japan*, Frank Dikotter (ed.). 12–33. Honolulu: University of Hawai'i Press.

Edwards, Rosalind, Suki Ali, Chamion Caballero and Miri Song (eds.). 2012. *International Perspectives on Racial and Ethnic Mixedness and Mixing*. London: Routledge.

Ee, Wen Wei Jamie. 2010. "Mixed-Race, but No Mixed Feelings: Six Citizens of Mixed Parentage Share Their Singapore Dream." *The Straits Times*. 8 August 2010. Retrieved from LexisNexis Academic. Date accessed: 6 September 2010.

Eurasian Association. 2010. "Eurasians in Singapore: What Is Our Future?" *The New Eurasian*. April–June 2010:7–11.

Ferber, Abby L. 2000. "A Commentary on Aguirre: Taking Narrative Seriously." *Sociological Perspectives*. 43(2):341–349.

Fong, Ng Bickleen. 1959. *The Chinese in New Zealand: A Study in Assimilation*. Hong Kong: Hong Kong University Press.

Franklin, M. 2003. "I Define My Own Identity: Pacific Articulations of 'Race' and 'Culture' on the Internet." *Ethnicities*. 3(4):465–490.

Fraser, James, and Edward Kick. 2000. "The Interpretive Repertoires of Whites on Race-Targeted Policies: Claims Making of Reverse Discrimination." *Sociological Perspectives*. 43(1):13–28.

Freeman, Victoria. 2005. "Attitudes Toward 'Miscegenation' in Canada, the United States, New Zealand and Australia, 1860–1914." *Native Studies Review*. 16(1):41–69.

Gans, Herbert J. 1979. "Symbolic Ethnicity: The Future of Ethnic Groups and Cultures in America." *Ethnic and Racial Studies*. 2(1):1–20.

Gans, Herbert J. 2009. "Reflections on Symbolic Ethnicity: A Response to Y. Anagnostou." *Ethnicities*. 9:123–130.

Gibson, Helen Margaret. 2006. "The Invisible Whiteness of Being: The Place of Whiteness in Women's Discourses in Aotearoa/New Zealand and Some Implications for Antiracist Education." Thesis for Doctor of Philosophy in Education. Christchurch: University of Canterbury.

Gilbertson, Amanda. 2007. "Symbolic Ethnicity and the Dilemmas of Difference: Talking Indianness with New Zealand-Born Gujaratis." Thesis for Master of Arts in Anthropology. Wellington: Victoria University.

Gilroy, Paul. 2000. *Against Race: Imagining Political Culture beyond the Color Line*. Cambridge, MA: Belknap Press of Harvard University Press.

Goh, Daniel P. S. 2007. "States of Ethnography: Colonialism, Resistance, and Cultural Transcription in Malaya and the Philippines, 1890s–1930s." *Comparative Studies in Society and History*. 49(1):109–142.

Goh, Daniel P. S. 2008a. "From Colonial Pluralism to Postcolonial Multiculturalism: Race, State Formation and the Question of Cultural Diversity in Malaysia and Singapore." *Sociology Compass*. 2(1):232–252.

Goh, Daniel P. S. 2008b. "Protecting Chek Jawa: The Politics of Conservation and Memory at the Edge of a Nation." In *Biodiversity and Human Livelihoods in Protected Areas: Case Studies from the Malay Archipelago*, Navjot S. Sodhi, Greg Acciaioli, Maribeth Erb and Alan Khee-Jin Tan (eds.). 311–329. Cambridge: Cambridge University Press.

Goh, Daniel P. S., and Philip Holden. 2009. "Introduction: Postcoloniality, Race and Multiculturalism." In *Race and Multiculturalism in Malaysia and Singapore*, Daniel P. S. Goh, Matilda Gabrielpillai, Philip Holden and Gaik Cheng Khoo (eds.). 1–16. London: Routledge.

Goldberg, David Theo. 1997. *Racial Subjects: Writing on Race in America*. New York: Routledge.

Gray, Claire, Nabila Jaber and Jim Anglem. 2013. "Pakeha Identity and Whiteness: What Does It Mean to Be White?" *Sites: A Journal of Social Anthropology and Cultural Studies*. 10(2):82–106.

Grbic, Douglas. 2010. "Social and Cultural Meanings of Tolerance: Immigration, Incorporation and Identity in Aotearoa, New Zealand." *Journal of Ethnic and Migration Studies*. 36(1):125–148.

Grimshaw, Patricia. 2002. "Interracial Marriages and Colonial Regimes in Victoria and Aotearoa/New Zealand." *Frontiers: A Journal of Women Studies*. 23(2):12–28.

Gullickson, Aaron, and Ann Morning. 2010. "Choosing Race: Multiracial Ancestry and Identification." *Social Science Research*. 40(2):498–512.

Gunew, Sneja. 2004. *Haunted Nations: The Colonial Dimensions of Multiculturalisms*. London: Routledge.

Hall, Stuart. 1990. "Cultural Identity and Diaspora." In *Identity: Community, Culture, Difference*, Jonathan Rutherford (ed.). 222–237. London: Lawrence & Wishart.

Hall, Stuart. 1996. "Who Needs Identity?" In *Questions of Cultural Identity*, Stuart Hall and Paul du Gay (eds.). London: Sage.

Harris, David R. 2001. "Does It Matter How We Measure? Racial Classification and the Characteristics of Multiracial Youth." Ann Arbor: Department of Sociology and Institute for Social Research, University of Michigan.

Harris, David R., and Jeremiah Joseph Sim. 2002. "Who Is Multiracial? Assessing the Complexity of Lived Race." *American Sociological Review*. 67(4):614–627.

Hassan, Riaz, and Geoffrey Benjamin. 1973. "Ethnic Outmarriage Rates in Singapore: The Influence of Traditional Socio-Cultural Organization." *Journal of Marriage and Family*. 35(4):731–738.

Hassan, Riaz, and Geoffrey Benjamin. 1976. "Ethnic Outmarriage and Socio-Cultural Organization." In *Singapore: Society in Transition*, Riaz Hassan (ed.). 205–217. Kuala Lumpur: Oxford University Press.

Henson, Bertha. 2010. "Blurring of Racial Lines Bodes Well." *The Straits Times*. 14 January 2010. Factiva. Date accessed: 14 January 2010.

Hill, Michael, and Kwen Fee Lian. 1995. *The Politics of Nation Building and Citizenship in Singapore*. London: Routledge.

Hirschman, Charles. 1986. "The Making of Race in Colonial Malaya: Political Economy and Racial Ideology." *Sociological Forum*. 1(2):330–361.

Holden, Philip. 2009. "A Literary History of Race: Reading Singapore Literature in English in an Historical Frame." In *Race and Multiculturalism in Malaysia and Singapore*, Daniel P.S. Goh, Matilda Gabrielpillai, Philip Holden and Gaik Cheng Khoo (eds.). 19–35. London: Routledge.

Howard, S., and R. Didham. 2007. "Ethnic Intermarriage and Ethnic Transference amongst the Maori Population: Implications for the Measurement and Definition of Ethnicity." In *Official Statistics Research Series*. Wellington: Statistics New Zealand.

Human Rights Commission. 2009. "Tui Tui Tuituia: Race Relations in 2009." Wellington: Human Rights Commission/Te Kahui Tika Tangata.

Ifekwunigwe, Jayne O. 1999. *Scattered Belongings: Cultural Paradoxes of 'Race', Nation and Gender*. London: Routledge.

Ifekwunigwe, Jayne O. 2001. "Re-Membering 'Race': On Gender, 'Mixed Race' and Family in the English-African Diaspora." In *Rethinking 'Mixed Race'*, David Parker and Miri Song (eds.). 42–64. London: Pluto Press.

Ifekwunigwe, Jayne O. (ed.). 2004. *'Mixed Race' Studies: A Reader*. London: Routledge.

Immigration and Checkpoints Authority. 2010. "Greater Flexibility with Implementation of Double-Barrelled Race Option from 1 January 2011." www.ica.gov.sg/news_details.aspx?nid=12443. Date accessed: 30 December 2010.

Ip, David. 2011. "Simultaneity and Liminality: Identity Anxieties of 1.5 Generation Chinese Migrants in Australia." In *Transmigration and the New Chinese: Theories and Practices from the New Zealand Experiences*, Manying Ip (ed.). 163–182. Hong Kong: Hong Kong University Press.

Ip, Manying. 2003a. "Chinese Immigrants and Transnationals in New Zealand: A Fortress Opened." In *The Chinese Diaspora: Space, Place, Mobility and Identity*, Laurence J.C. Ma and Carolyn Cartier (eds.). 339–358. Lanham, MD: Rowman & Littlefield Publishers, Inc.

Ip, Manying. 2003b. "Maori-Chinese Encounters: Indigine-Immigrant Interaction in New Zealand." *Asian Studies Review*. 27(2):227–252.

Ip, Manying. 2008. *Being Maori-Chinese: Mixed Identities*. Auckland: Auckland University Press.

Ip, Manying (ed.). 2009. *The Dragon and the Taniwha: Maori and Chinese in New Zealand*. Auckland: Auckland University Press.

Ip, Manying (ed.). 2011. *Transmigration and the New Chinese: Theories and Practices from the New Zealand Experience*. Hong Kong: Hong Kong University Press.

Jackson, Kelly F. 2010. "Living the Multiracial Experience : Shifting Racial Expressions, Resisting Race, and Seeking Community." *Qualitative Social Work*. 11(1):42–60.

Jackson, Moana. 2003. "The Part-Maori Syndrome." *Mana*. 52(June–July):62.

Jayawardena, Kumari. 2007. *Erasure of the Euro-Asian: Recovering Early Radicalism and Feminism in South Asia*. Colombo: Social Scientists' Association.

Jimenez, Tomas R. 2004. "Negotiating Ethnic Boundaries: Multiethnic Mexican Americans and Ethnic Identity in the United States." *Ethnicities*. 4(1):75–97.

Katz, Ilan. 2012. "Mixed Race across Time and Place: Contrasting Australia with the UK." In *International Perspectives on Racial and Ethnic Mixedness and Mixing*, Rosalind Edwards, Suki Ali, Chamion Caballero and Miri Song (eds.). 23–35. London: Routledge.

Keddell, Emily. 2006. "Pavlova and Pineapple Pie: Selected Identity Influences on Samoan-Pakeha People in Aotearoa/New Zealand." *Kotuitui: New Zealand Journal of Social Sciences Online*. 1:45–63.

Kertzer, David I., and Dominique Arel. 2002. "Censuses, Identity Formation and the Struggle for Political Power." In *Census and Identity: The Politics of Race, Ethnicity, and Language in National Censuses*, David I. Kertzer and Dominique Arel (eds.). 1–42. Cambridge: Cambridge University Press.

Khanna, Nikki. 2004. "The Role of Reflected Appraisals in Racial Identity: The Case of Multiracial Asians." *Social Psychology Quarterly*. 67(2):115–131.

Khanna, Nikki. 2010. " 'If You're Half Black You're Just Black': Reflected Appraisals and the Persistence of the One-Drop Rule." *The Sociological Quarterly*. 51:96–121.

Khanna, Nikki. 2012. "Multiracial Americans: Racial Identity Choices and Implications for the Collection of Race Data." *Sociology Compass*. 6(4):316–331.

Khanna, Nikki, and Cathryn Johnson. 2010. "Passing as Black: Racial Identity Work among Biracial Americans." *Social Psychology Quarterly*. 73(4):380–397.

Khawaja, Mansoor, Bill Boddington and Robert Didham. 2007. "Growing Ethnic Diversity in New Zealand and Its Implications for Measuring Differentials in Fertility and Mortality." Wellington: Statistics New Zealand.

Kilson, Marion. 2001. *Claiming Place: Biracial Young Adults of the Post-Civil Rights Era*. Westport: Bergin & Garvey.

Kok, Lester. 2010a. "Chinese or Indian? What About Chinese-Indian?" *The Straits Times*. 3 January 2010. Factiva. Date accessed: 12 January 2010.

Kok, Lester. 2010b. "Complications of a Complex Racial Identity." *The Straits Times*. 4 January 2010. Factiva. Date accessed: 12 January 2010.

Kong, Lily, and Brenda Yeoh. 2003. "Nation, Ethnicity, and Identity: Singapore and the Dynamics and Discourses of Chinese Migration." In *The Chinese Diaspora: Space, Place, Mobility and Identity*, Laurence J.C. Ma and Carolyn Cartier (eds.). 193–219. Lanham, MD: Rowman & Littlefield Publishers, Inc.

Kukutai, Tahu. 2007. "White Mothers, Brown Children: Ethnic Identification of Maori-European Children in New Zealand." *Journal of Marriage and Family*. 69:1150–1161.

Kukutai, Tahu. 2008. "Ethnic Self-Prioritisation of Dual and Multi-Ethnic Youth in New Zealand." Wellington: Statistics New Zealand.

Kukutai, Tahu, and R. Didham. 2009. "In Search of Ethnic New Zealanders: National Naming in the 2006 Census." *Social Policy Journal of New Zealand*. 36:46–62.

Kuo, Eddie C.Y., and Riaz Hassan. 1979. "Ethnic Intermarriage in a Multiethnic Society." In *The Contemporary Family in Singapore*, Eddie C.Y. Kuo and Aline K. Wong (eds.). 168–188. Singapore: Singapore University Press.

Kymlicka, Will. 2003. "Multicultural States and Intercultural Citizens." *Theory and Research in Education*. 1(2):147–169.

LaFromboise, Teresa, Hardin L.K. Coleman and Jennifer Gerton. 1993. "Psychological Impact of Biculturalism: Evidence and Theory." *Psychological Bulletin*. 114(3):395–412.

Lai, Ah Eng. 1995. *Meanings of Multiethnicity: A Case-Study of Ethnicity and Ethnic Relations in Singapore*. Kuala Lumpur: Oxford University Press.

Larner, Wendy, and Paul Spoonley. 1995. "Post-Colonial Politics in Aotearoa/New Zealand." In *Unsettling Settler Societies: Articulations of Gender, Race, Ethnicity and Class*, Daiva Stasiulis and Nira Yuval-Davis (eds.). 39–64. London: Sage.

Bibliography

Lee, Hui Chieh. 2010. "Valuable Lesson in Racial Harmony." *AsiaOne*. 18 January 2010. http://news.asiaone.com/News/AsiaOne%2BNews/Singapore/Story/A1Story20100118-192497.html. Date accessed: 18 January 2010.

Lee, Jennifer. 2008. "A Post-Racial America? Multiracial Identification and the Color Line in the 21st Century." *Nanzan Review of American Studies*. 30:13–31.

LeFlore-Muñoz, Candice J. 2010. "I've Got a Story to Tell: Critical Race Theory, Whiteness and Narrative Constructions of Racial and Ethnic Census Categories." Thesis for Doctor of Philosophy in Communication Studies. Bowling Green, OH: Bowling Green State University.

Leow, Bee Geok. 2000. "Census of Population 2000: Demographic Characteristics." Singapore: Singapore Department of Statistics.

Li, Phoebe Hairong. 2009. "A Virtual Chinatown: The Diasporic Mediasphere of Chinese Migrants in New Zealand." Thesis for Doctor of Philosophy in Chinese Studies. Auckland: University of Auckland.

Liu, James H., Mark Stewart Wilson, John McClure and Te Ripowai Higgins. 1999. "Social Identity and the Perception of History: Cultural Representations of Aotearoa/New Zealand." *European Journal of Social Psychology*. 29:1021–1047.

Loh, Kah Seng. 2009a. "Conflict and Change at the Margins: Emergency Kampong Clearance and the Making of Modern Singapore." *Asian Studies Review*. 33(2):139–159.

Loh, Kah Seng. 2009b. "History, Memory, and Identity in Modern Singapore: Testimonies from the Urban Margins." *The Oral History Review*. 36(1):1–24.

Mahtani, Minelle. 2002a. "Tricking the Border Guards: Performing Race." *Environment and Planning D: Society and Space*. 20:425–440.

Mahtani, Minelle. 2002b. "What's in a Name? Exploring the Employment of 'Mixed Race' as an Identification." *Ethnicities*. 2(4):469–490.

Mahtani, Minelle. 2005. "Mixed Metaphors: Positioning 'Mixed Race' Identity." In *Situating "Race" and Racisms in Time, Space, and Theory*, Jo-Anne Lee and John Lutz (eds.). 77–93. Montreal: McGill-Queen's University Press.

Mahtani, Minelle. 2012. "Not the Same Difference: Notes on Mixed-Race Methodologies." In *International Perspectives on Racial and Ethnic Mixedness and Mixing*, Rosalind Edwards, Suki Ali, Chamion Caballero and Miri Song (eds.). 156–168. London: Routledge.

Mallard, T. 2004. "First Results of Review of Targeted Programmes." www.beehive.govt.nz/node/21856. Date accessed: 6 June 2011.

Maré, Gerhard. 2001. "Race Counts in Contemporary South Africa: 'An Illusion of Ordinariness.'" *Transformation*. 47:75–93.

Matthews, Julie. 2002. "Deconstructing the Visual: The Diasporic Hybridity of Asian and Eurasian Female Images." *Intersections: Gender, History and Culture in the Asian Context*. 8:1–16. http://intersections.anu.edu.au/issue8/matthews.html. Date accessed: 25 April 2011.

Meredith, Paul. 2000. "A Half-Caste on the Half-Caste in the Cultural Politics of New Zealand." In *Maori und Gesellschaft*, Eli Maor (ed.). Berlin: Mana Verlag.

Mok, Tze Ming. 2004. "Race You There." *Landfall*. 208:18–26.

Moore, R. Quinn. 2000. "Multiracialism and Meritocracy: Singapore's Approach to Race and Inequality." *Review of Social Economy*. LVIII(3):339–360.

Morning, Ann. 2002. "New Faces, Old Faces: Counting the Multiracial Population Past and Present." In *New Faces in a Changing America: Multiracial Identity in the 21st Century*, Herman DeBose and Loretta Winters (eds.). 41–67. Thousand Oaks, CA: Sage.

Morning, Ann. 2008. "Ethnic Classification in Global Perspective: A Cross-National Survey of the 2000 Census Round." *Population Research Policy Review*. 27:239–272.

Morning, Ann. 2011. *The Nature of Race: How Scientists Think and Teach about Human Difference*. Berkeley: University of California Press.
Motoyoshi, Michelle M. 1990. "The Experience of Mixed-Race People: Some Thoughts and Theories." *The Journal of Ethnic Studies*. 18:77–94.
Murad, Nora Lester. 2005. "The Politics of Mothering in a 'Mixed' Family: An Autoethnographic Exploration." *Identities: Global Studies in Culture and Power*. 12:479–503.
Murphy, Nigel. 2003. "Joe Lun v. Attorney General: The Politics of Exclusion." In *Unfolding History, Evolving Identity: The Chinese in New Zealand*, Manying Ip (ed.). 48–67. Auckland: Auckland University Press.
Murphy, Nigel. 2005. "Poll Tax & Other Anti-Chinese Legislation." Paper presented at Crouching Tiger, Hidden Banana: Auckland University of Technology, Auckland. 3–5 June 2005.
Nakashima, Cynthia L. 1992. "An Invisible Monster: The Creation and Denial of Mixed-Race People in America." In *Racially Mixed People in America*, Maria P. P. Root (ed.). 162–178. Newbury Park, CA: Sage Publications.
Nash, Philip Tajitsu. 2004. "Will the Census Go Multiracial?" In *"Mixed Race" Studies: A Reader*, Jayne O. Ifekwunigwe (ed.). 214–218. London: Routledge.
Neo, Chai Chin. 2010. "Putting a Race to a Name: Mixed-Race Children to Have 'Double-Barrelled' IC Race." *Today Online*. 13 January 2010.
Ng, James. 1993. *Windows on a Chinese Past: How the Cantonese Goldseekers and Their Heirs Settled in New Zealand*, Vol. 1. Dunedin: Otago Heritage Books.
Ng, James. 2001. "Chinese Settlement in NZ, Past and Present." *Chinese in New Zealand, Amity Centre Publishing Project*. www.stevenyoung.co.nz/The-Chinese-in-New-Zealand/History-of-Chinese-in-NewZealand/Chinese-settlement-in-NZ-past-and-present.html. Date accessed: 9 April 2010.
Ng, James. 2003. "The Sojourner Experience: The Cantonese Goldseekers in New Zealand, 1865–1901." In *Unfolding History, Evolving Identity: The Chinese in New Zealand*, Manying Ip (ed.). 5–30. Auckland: Auckland University Press.
Nguyen, Viet Thanh. 2008. "At Home with Race." *PMLA*. 123(5):1557–1564.
Nobles, Melissa. 2000. *Shades of Citizenship: Race and the Census in Modern Politics*. Stanford, CA: Stanford University Press.
Oikawa, Sara, and Tomoko Yoshida. 2007. "An Identity Based on Being Different: A Focus on Biethnic Individuals in Japan." *International Journal of Intercultural Relations*. 31:633–653.
Omi, Michael. 1997. "Racial Identity and the State: The Dilemmas of Classification." *Law & Inequality*. 15(7):7–23.
Omi, Michael. 2010. " 'Slippin' Into Darkness': The (Re)Biologization of Race." *Journal of Asian American Studies*. 13(3):343–358.
Omi, Michael, and Howard Winant. 1986. *Racial Formation in the United States: From the 1960s to the 1980s*. New York: Routledge & Kegan Paul.
Omi, Michael, and Howard Winant. 1994. *Racial Formation in the United States: From the 1960s to the 1990s*, 2nd ed. New York: Routledge.
Omi, Michael, and Howard Winant. 2008. "Once More, with Feeling: Reflections on Racial Formation." *PMLA*. 123(5):1565–1572.
Orange, Claudia. 1997. *The Treaty of Waitangi*. Wellington: Bridget Williams Books Ltd.
Ortmann, Stephan. 2009. "Singapore: The Politics of Inventing National Identity." *Journal of Current Southeast Asian Affairs*. 28(4):23–46.
Palat, Ravi Arvind. 1996. "Curries, Chopsticks and Kiwis." In *Nga Patai: Racism and Ethnic Relations in New Zealand*, Paul Spoonley, David Pearson and Cluny Macpherson (eds.). 35–54. Palmerston North: Dunmore Press.

Bibliography

Paragg, Jillian. 2011. "Ambivalence, Negotiation and the Everyday Gaze: Exploring Mixed Race Identity." *Journal of Religion and Culture: Conference Proceedings. 16th GRSA Interdisciplinary Conference*. February 2011:143–154.

Park, Robert E. 1928. "Human Migration and the Marginal Man." *The American Journal of Sociology*. 33(6):881–893.

Park, Robert E. 1931. "Mentality of Racial Hybrids." *The American Journal of Sociology*. 36(4):534–551.

Parker, David, and Miri Song. 2001. "Introduction: Rethinking 'Mixed Race.'" In *Rethinking "Mixed Race"*, David Parker and Miri Song (eds.). 1–22. London: Pluto Press.

Parker, David, and Miri Song. 2006. "New Ethnicities Online: Reflexive Racialisation and the Internet." *The Sociological Review*. 54(3):575–594.

Parker, David, and Miri Song. 2009. "New Ethnicities and the Internet." *Cultural Studies*. 23(4):583–604.

Pearson, David. 2001. *The Politics of Ethnicity in Settler Societies: States of Unease*. Houndmills, UK: Palgrave.

Pearson, David, and Patrick Ongley. 1997. "Multiculturalism and Biculturalism: The Recent New Zealand Experience in Comparative Perspective." *Journal of Intercultural Studies*. 17:5–28.

Pereira, Alexius. 1997. "The Revitalization of Eurasian Identity in Singapore." *Southeast Asian Journal of Social Science*. 25(2):7–24.

Pereira, Alexius. 2006. "No Longer 'Other': The Emergence of the Eurasian Community in Singapore." In *Race, Ethnicity and the State in Malaysia and Singapore*, Kwen Fee Lian (ed.). 5–32. Leiden: Brill.

Perkins, Maureen. 2005. "Thoroughly Modern Mulatta: Rethinking 'Old World' Stereotypes in a 'New World' Setting." *Biography*. 28(1):104–116.

Perkins, Maureen. 2007. "Visibly Different: Face, Place and Race in Australia." In *Visibly Different: Face, Place and Race in Australia*, Maureen Perkins (ed.). 9–29. Bern: Peter Lang.

Phinney, J. 2000. "Identity Formation across Cultures: The Interaction of Personal, Societal, and Historical Change." *Human Development*. 43:27–31.

Poon, Angelia. 2009. "Pick and Mix for the Global City: Race and Cosmopolitanism in Singapore." In *Race and Multiculturalism in Malaysia and Singapore*, Daniel P.S. Goh, Matilda Gabrielpillai, Philip Holden and Gaik Cheng Khoo (eds.). 70–85. London: Routledge.

Popatial, Asha. 2010. "Double-Barrelled Listing Won't Have Big Impact on Ethnic Policies: PM Lee." *Channel News Asia*. 15 January 2010. www.channelnewsasia.com/stories/singaporelocalnews/view/1030929/1/.html. Date accessed: 22 January 2010.

Portes, Alejandro, and Min Zhou. 1993. "The New Second Generation: Segmented Assimilation and Its Variants." *Annals of the American Academy of Political and Social Science*. 530:74–96.

Poston, W.S. Carlos. 1990. "The Biracial Identity Development Model: A Needed Addition." *Journal of Counseling and Development*. 69:152–155.

Prentice, Chris, and Vijay Devadas. 2008. "Postcolonial Studies and the Cultural Politics of Everyday Life." *SITES: New Series*. 5(1):1–19.

PuruShotam, Nirmala. 1998. "Disciplining Difference: Race in Singapore." In *Southeast Asian Identities: Culture and the Politics of Representation in Indonesia, Malaysia, Singapore, and Thailand*, Joel S. Kahn (ed.). 51–93. Singapore: Institute of Southeast Asian Studies.

Qian, Zhenchao. 2004. "Options: Racial/Ethnic Identification of Children of Intermarried Couples." *Social Science Quarterly*. 85(3):746–766.

Rahim, Lily Zubaidah. 1998. *The Singapore Dilemma: The Political and Educational Marginality of the Malay Community*. Oxford: Oxford University Press.
Rahim, Lily Zubaidah. 2009. *Singapore in the Malay World: Building and Breaching Regional Bridges*. New York: Routledge.
Richards, Lynn. 2005. *Handling Qualitative Data: A Practical Guide*. London: Sage Publications.
Riessman, Catherine Kohler. 1993. *Narrative Analysis*. London: Sage Publications.
Riessman, Catherine Kohler. 2008. *Narrative Methods for the Human Sciences*. Los Angeles: Sage Publications.
Rocha, Z. 2010. "Mixed Messages, Mixed Memories, Mixed Ethnicity: Mnemonic Heritage and Constructing Identity through Mixed Parentage." *New Zealand Sociology*. 25(1):75–99.
Rocha, Z. 2012a. "Identity, Dislocation and Belonging: Chinese/European Narratives of 'Mixed' Identity in Aotearoa/New Zealand." *Identities: Global Studies in Culture and Power*. 19(6):673–690.
Rocha, Z. 2012b. "(Mixed) Racial Formation in Aotearoa/New Zealand: Framing Biculturalism and 'Mixed Race' through Categorization." *Kotuitui: New Zealand Journal of Social Sciences*. 7(1):1–13.
Rocha Z. 2012c. "Multiplicity within Singularity: Racial Categorization and Recognizing 'Mixed Race' in Singapore." *Journal of Current Southeast Asian Affairs*. 30(3): 95–131.
Rocha, Z. 2014. "Stretching out the Categories: Chinese/European Narratives of Mixedness, Belonging and Home in Singapore." *Ethnicities*. 14(2):279–302.
Rockquemore, Kerry Ann. 1998. "Between Black and White: Exploring the 'Biracial' Experience." *Race & Society*. 1(2):197–212.
Rockquemore, Kerry Ann, and David L. Brunsma. 2008. *Beyond Black: Biracial Identity in America*, 2nd ed. Lanham, MD: Rowman and Littlefield.
Rockquemore, Kerry Ann, David L. Brunsma and Daniel J. Delgado. 2009. "Racing to Theory or Retheorizing Race? Understanding the Struggle to Build a Multiracial Identity Theory." *Journal of Social Issues*. 65(1):13–34.
Rockquemore, Kerry Ann, Tracey Laszloffy and Julia Noveske. 2006. "It All Starts at Home: Racial Socialization in Multiracial Families." In *Mixed Messages: Multiracial Identities in the "Color-Blind" Era*, David L. Brunsma (ed.). 203–216. Boulder, CO: Lynne Rienner.
Root, Maria P. P. 1992. "Within, Between and Beyond Race." In *Racially Mixed People in America*, Maria P. P. Root (ed.). 3–11. Newbury Park, CA: Sage Publications.
Root, Maria P. P. (ed.). 1996. *The Multiracial Experience: Racial Borders as the New Frontier*. London: Sage.
Root, Maria P. P. 1998. "Reconstructing Race, Rethinking Ethnicity." In *Comprehensive Clinical Psychology*, M. Hersen and A. Bellack (eds.). 141–160. London: Elsevier Science.
Root, Maria P. P. 1999. "Resolving 'Other' Status: Identity Development of Biracial Individuals." In *American Families: A Multicultural Reader*. 439–454. New York: Routledge.
Salesa, Damon Ieremia. 2011. *Racial Crossings: Race, Intermarriage, and the Victorian British Empire*. Oxford: Oxford University Press.
Sawicka, Theresa, Kirsty Barr, Duane Grace, Louise Grenside, Jonathan Thomson and Gwyn Williams. 2003. "Forming a Cultural Identity: What Does It Mean to Be Ethnic?" *Youth and Family Project, Victoria University*.

Bibliography

Sedgwick, Charles P. 1998. "The Chinese in New Zealand: Persistence, Change and Innovation." In *The Overseas Chinese: Ethnicity in National Context*, Francis L. K. Hsu and Hendrick Serrie (eds.). 115–142. Lanham, MD: University Press of America, Inc.

Shih, Margaret, and Diana T. Sanchez. 2005. "Perspectives and Research on the Positive and Negative Implications of Having Multiple Racial Identities." *Psychological Bulletin*. 131(4):569–591.

Shih, Margaret, and Diana T. Sanchez. 2009. "When Race Becomes Even More Complex: Toward Understanding the Landscape of Multiracial Identity and Experiences." *Journal of Social Issues*. 65(1):1–11.

Siddique, Sharon. 1989. "Singaporean Identity." In *Management of Success: The Moulding of Modern Singapore*, Kernial Singh Sandhu and Paul Wheatley (eds.). 563–577. Singapore: Institute of Southeast Asian Studies.

Siddique, Sharon. 1990. "The Phenomenology of Ethnicity: A Singapore Case Study." *Sojourn*. 5(1):35–62.

Silva, Graziella Moraes D., and Elisa P. Reis. 2011. "The Multiple Dimensions of Racial Mixture in Rio de Janeiro, Brazil: From Whitening to Brazilian Negritude." *Ethnic and Racial Studies*. iFirst Article:1–18.

Sim, Melissa. 2013. "Excuse Me, Are You Singaporean?" *The Straits Times* (Singapore). 2 April 2013.

Sing, Seet Chia, and Wong Wei Lin. 2009. "Singapore's Census of Population 2010." *Statistics Singapore Newsletter*. September 2009:23–27.

Singapore Department of Statistics. 2008. "Statistics on Marriages and Divorces, 2008." Singapore: Singapore Department of Statistics.

Singapore Department of Statistics. 2010a. "Census of the Population 2010: Statistical Release 1 (Demographic Characteristics, Education, Language and Religion)." Singapore: Singapore Department of Statistics.

Singapore Department of Statistics. 2010b. "Yearbook of Statistics Singapore." Singapore: Singapore Department of Statistics.

Smith, Valerie. 1994. "Reading the Intersection of Race and Gender in Narratives of Passing." *Diacritics*. 24(2/3):43–57.

Snipp, C. Matthew. 2003. "Racial Measurement in the American Census: Past Practices and Implications for the Future." *Annual Review of Sociology*. 29:563–588.

Somers, Margaret R. 1994. "The Narrative Constitution of Identity: A Relational and Network Approach." *Theory and Society*. 23:605–649.

Song, Miri. 2003. *Choosing Ethnic Identity*. Cambridge: Polity Press.

Song, Miri. 2010a. "Does 'Race' Matter? A Study of 'Mixed Race' Siblings' Identifications." *The Sociological Review*. 58(2):265–285.

Song, Miri. 2010b. "Is There 'a' Mixed Race Group in Britain? The Diversity of Multiracial Identification and Experience." *Critical Social Policy*. 30(3):337–358.

Song, Miri. 2012. "Making Sense of 'Mixture': States and the Classification of 'Mixed' People." *Ethnic and Racial Studies*. iFirst Article:1–9.

Song, Miri, and Peter Aspinall. 2012. "Is Racial Mismatch a Problem for Young 'Mixed Race' People in Britain? The Findings of Qualitative Research." *Ethnicities*. Online before print:1–24.

Spencer, Jon Michael. 1997. *The New Colored People*. New York: New York University Press.

Spoonley, Paul. 1993. *Racism and Ethnicity*, 2nd ed. Oxford: Oxford University Press.

Spoonley, Paul. 2004. "Defining Identity and Creating Citizens: The Media and Immigrants in New Zealand." Paper presented at a seminar at the National Library, Ottawa. http://

canada.metropolis.net/events/metropolis_presents/media_diversity/Spoonley%20(Eng).pdf. Date accessed: 13 April 2010.
Spoonley, Paul. 2005. "Global Bananas, Transnational Tigers: The Century of China and the Chinese." Paper presented at Crouching Tiger, Hidden Banana: Auckland University of Technology, Auckland. 3–5 June 2005.
Spoonley, Paul, and Andrew Trlin. 2004. "Immigration, Immigrants and the Media." Palmerston North: New Settlers Programme, Massey University.
Statistics New Zealand. 2004. "Report of the Review of the Measurement of Ethnicity." Wellington: Statistics New Zealand.
Statistics New Zealand. 2005. "Statistical Standard for Ethnicity 2005." Wellington: Statistics New Zealand.
Statistics New Zealand. 2009a. "Final Report of a Review of the Official Ethnicity Statistical Standard." Wellington: Statistics New Zealand.
Statistics New Zealand. 2009b. "Classifications and Related Statistical Standards: Ethnicity." www.stats.govt.nz/methods/classifications-and-standards/classification-related-stats-standards/ethnicity.aspx. Date accessed: 30 April 2015.
Statistics New Zealand. 2014. "2013 Census QuickStats about Culture and Identity." www.stats.govt.nz/Census/2013-census/profile-and-summary-reports/quickstats-culture-identity/ethnic-groups-NZ.aspx. Date accessed: 3 March 2015.
Stephan, Cookie White, and Walter G. Stephan. 1989. "After Intermarriage: Ethnic Identity among Mixed-Heritage Japanese Americans and Hispanics." *Journal of Marriage and the Family*. 51(2):507–519.
Stokes-Rees, Emily. 2007. " 'We Need Something of Our Own': Representing Ethnicity, Diversity and 'National Heritage' in Singapore." Paper presented at National Museums in a Global World: Department of Culture Studies and Oriental Languages, University of Oslo, Norway. 19–21 November 2007.
Stonequist, Everett V. 1935. "The Problem of the Marginal Man." *The American Journal of Sociology*. 41(1):1–12.
Stonequist, Everett V. 1937. *The Marginal Man*. New York: Russell & Russell.
Storrs, Debbie. 1999. "Whiteness as Stigma: Essentialist Identity Work by Mixed-Race Women." *Symbolic Interaction*. 22(3):187–212.
Stratton, Jon, and Vijay Devadas. 2010. "Identities in the Contact Zone." *Borderlands*. 9(1):1–7.
Tan, Amanda. 2012. "Singapore: It's Dual-Race for 1 in 6 Babies of Mixed Parentage." *Straits Times Indonesia*. 11 January 2012. Factiva. Date accessed: 1 February 2012.
Tan, Eugene K. B. 2004. " 'We, the Citizens of Singapore . . . ': Multiethnicity, Its Evolution and Its Aberrations." In *Beyond Rituals and Riots: Ethnic Pluralism and Social Cohesion in Singapore*, Lai Ah Eng (ed.). 65–96. Singapore: Eastern Universities Press.
Telles, Edward E., and Nelson Lim. 1998. "Does It Matter Who Answers the Race Question? Racial Classification and Income Inequality in Brazil." *Demography*. 35(4):465–474.
Teng, Emma J. 2010. "Naming the Subject: Recovering 'Euro-Asian' History." *Journal of Women's History*. 22(4):257–262.
Thomas, David R., and Linda Waimarie Nikora. 1997. "Maori, Pakeha and New Zealander: Ethnic and National Identity among New Zealand Students." *Journal of Intercultural Studies*. 17:29–40.
Thompson, K. 2002. "Border Crossings and Diasporic Identities: Media Use and Leisure Practices of an Ethnic Minority." *Qualitative Sociology*. 25(3):409–418.
Tizard, Barbara, and Ann Phoenix. 2002. *Black, White or Mixed Race? Race and Racism in the Lives of Young People of Mixed Parentage*, rev. ed. London: Routledge.

Tremewan, Christopher. 1994. *The Political Economy of Social Control in Singapore*. New York: St Martin's Press.
Tupuola, Anne-Marie. 2004. "Pasifika Edgewalkers: Complicating the Achieved Identity Status in Youth Research." *Journal of Intercultural Studies*. 25(1):87–100.
Tyler, Katharine. 2005. "The Genealogical Imagination: The Inheritance of Interracial Identities." *The Sociological Review*. 53(3):476–494.
Tyler, Katharine. 2011. "New Ethnicities and Old Classities: Respectability and Diaspora." *Social Identities*. 17(4):523–542.
UMR Research Limited. 2009. "Public Attitudes and Understandings of Ethnic Identity." Wellington: UMR Research Limited.
Vasil, Raj. 1995. *Asianising Singapore: The PAP's Management of Ethnicity*. Singapore: Heinemann Asia.
Velayutham, Selvaraj. 2007. *Responding to Globalization: Nation, Culture and Identity in Singapore*. Singapore: Institute of Southeast Asian Studies.
Voci, Paola, and Jacqueline Leckie. 2011. "Beyond Nations and Ethnicities: Localizing Asia in New Zealand." In *Localizing Asia in Aotearoa*, Paola Voci and Jacqueline Leckie (eds.). 7–23. Wellington: Dunmore Publishing.
Wallace, Kendra R. 2004. "Situating Multiethnic Identity: Contributions of Discourse Theory to the Study of Mixed Heritage Students." *Journal of Language, Identity and Education*. 3(3):195–213.
Wanhalla, Angela. 2009. *In/visible Sight: The Mixed-Descent Families of Southern New Zealand*. Wellington: Bridget Williams Books.
Ward, Colleen. 2006. "Acculturation, Identity and Adaptation in Dual Heritage Adolescents." *International Journal of Intercultural Relations*. 30:243–259.
Warren, Jonathan, and Christina A. Sue. 2011. "Comparative Racisms: What Anti-Racists Can Learn from Latin America." *Ethnicities*. 11(1):32–58.
Waters, Mary. 1989. "The Everyday Use of Surname to Determine Ethnic Ancestry." *Qualitative Sociology*. 12(3):303–324.
Waters, Mary. 1990. *Ethnic Options: Choosing Identities in America*. Berkeley: University of California Press.
Wee, Lionel. 2002. "When English Is Not a Mother Tongue: Linguistic Ownership and the Eurasian Community in Singapore." *Journal of Multilingual and Multicultural Development*. 23(4):282–295.
Wetherell, Margaret, and Jonathan Potter. 1992. *Mapping the Language of Racism: Discourse and the Legitimation of Exploitation*. New York: Harvester Wheatsheaf.
Williams, Teresa Kay. 1997. "Race-ing and Being Raced: The Critical Interrogation of 'Passing.'" *Amerasia Journal*. 23(1):61–65.
Wilson, Anne. 1987. *Mixed Race Children: A Study of Identity*. London: Allen & Unwin.
Winant, Howard. 2000a. "Race and Race Theory." *Annual Review of Sociology*. 26:169–185.
Winant, Howard. 2000b. "The Theoretical Status of the Concept of Race." In *Theories of Race and Racism: A Reader*, Les Back and John Solomos (eds.). 181–190. New York: Routledge.
Wong, Gilbert. 2003. "Is Saying Sorry Enough?" In *Unfolding History, Evolving Identity: The Chinese in New Zealand*, Manying Ip (ed.). 258–279. Auckland: Auckland University Press.
Xie, Yu, and Kimberly Goyette. 1997. "The Racial Identification of Biracial Children with One Asian Parent: Evidence from the 1990 Census." *Social Forces*. 76(2):547–570.

Yee, Beven. 2003. "Coping with Insecurity: Everyday Experiences of Chinese New Zealanders." In *Unfolding History, Evolving Identity: The Chinese in New Zealand*, Manying Ip (ed.). 215–235. Auckland: Auckland University Press.
Yong, Jeremy Au. 2010. "Ethnic Self-Help Groups Don't Expect Significant Impact." *The Straits Times*. 14 January 2010. Factiva. Date accessed: 14 January 2010.
Young, Robert J.C. 1995. *Colonial Desire: Hybridity in Theory, Culture, and Race*. London: Routledge.
Yuval-Davis, Nira. 1997. *Gender & Nation*. London: Sage Publications.
Zimmern, Kirsteen. 2010. *The Eurasian Face*. Hong Kong: Blacksmith Books.

Index

adoption 79, 83–4
amalgamation of populations 17, 21
ancestry 4, 110, 165–6; belonging and 7, 83, 97–8; complexity of 35, 59, 109; interpretation of 34, 40, 42–3; 73, 122, 153; mixed 50–2, 139, 141, 147; race and 62
Ang, I. 9, 36, 110, 166
Asian values 28, 30
Aspinall, P. 5, 11, 155, 164
assimilation 17, 20, 22
authenticity 19, 72, 97, 153

being both and neither 71, 111, 139, 142–3
being Chinese 37, 97, 98–9, 100–4, 110–11, 113–14, 156; *see also* Chineseness
being Chinese and European 135–7, 139, 141–2; *see also* mixedness
being European 103–4, 118, 122–3
being "raced" 3, 31, 114
belonging 78, 125, 129, 157–8; in a community 67, 79, 87; in different ways 12; in multiple places 11, 87–8, 125–6, 133–5, 151–2; to the nation 46, 63–78, 85–6, 111, 122, 125–6, 159–60; nowhere 124–5, 137–8; online 128–9
Benjamin, G. 16, 18, 22
best of both worlds 5, 138, 140–1, 158
biculturalism 16, 25–6, 32–3, 36–7; and multiplicity 28, 32, 36, 42, 58
bilingual 104–8; education system 23, 29
biological difference 3–4, 6, 33, 40
biracial identity 6, 136
blood: and belonging 17–9, 33, 61–2; and descent 4, 40, 42–3, 69–70, 88; mixed 5, 39; relatives 83–4
boundary crossing 24, 80–1, 94, 121, 135–6, 155–6, 160

bounded identities 10, 12, 42–3, 57, 121
Brazil, census classification in 7

Callister, P. 7, 20, 27–8, 34–5, 37, 41, 44
categorization 11–13, 49, 60–1, 154, 158–9; constraints of 61, 66; different forms of 7–8; *see also* classification
Caucasian 49, 60, 63, 85; *see also* European
census classification 7, 10–11, 155; colonial history of 11; future of 163–4; in New Zealand 17–18, 20, 27–8, 34–5, 57; in Singapore 19, 22–3, 31, 40–1, 49–50; *see also* classification and identity
census question on race/ethnicity: in New Zealand 27, 57; in Singapore 22, 31, 49
characterization of narratives 2, 12–13, 159–63
Chase, S. 14
Chinese, Malay, Indian, Other *see* CMIO
Chineseness 37, 97–9, 111, 122, 148, 158; as descent/ancestry 80, 98
Chua, B. H. 7, 21–3, 28–30, 32, 37, 43
citizenship 63–8, 71–2, 133, 152; exclusion from 65, 67, 91; *see also* national identity
civic identity *see* national identity
civil rights movement 6
class 54, 104, 157; *see also* socioeconomic status
classification: and identity 7–12, 46, 49–52, 61, 64, 73, 77–8, 166; of "mixed race" 7–8, 11; narratives of 2–3; 10–12, 76–8, 153, 158, purpose of 11, 15, 40; racialized nature of 12, 16, 50, 76–7
CMIO 3, 7, 31, 38
colonialism 16, 43, 103, 155; history of 11; in New Zealand 17–18, 57; in Singapore 18–19, 21, 57

Index

diaspora 97, 122, 152
discrimination: anti-Asian 26, 81; anti-immigration 26; institutional in New Zealand 16–18, 20; protection against 20; racial 36, 90–3
dislocation/location 11, 50, 66, 78, 84–6, 95–6, 131–5; and physical location 86–7
dissonance: between classification and reality 8, 11, 29, 42, 59; and identity 3, 7–8, 59, 142–3, 154, 158–62; public/private 11–13, 37, 61, 71–3, 77–8, 111–13, 151, 154; *see also* public/private identities
diversity 16, 19, 21–3, 36–9, 86–9, 152; and location 90–1; narratives of 3
divorce 79, 82
double-barrelled race 38–40; 56; *see also* hyphenated identities
dual citizenship 65, 71–2

ecological approach 5–7, 9, 162
English as mother tongue 29, 104, 106–8; *see also* mother tongue
equivalent approach 5–6
essentialization of race 11, 21–2, 31–2, 43
ethnic group 22, 27, 31, 33–4
ethnicity 4, 34; conflation with race 4, 27, 33, 69; as cultural affiliation 42; measurement of 7, 11, 27–8, 33–6, 40–1, 44, 164; shift towards 20, 27, 44
ethnic prioritization 27–8, 34, 44
Eurasia 126–8, 152, 157
Eurasian: classification of 19, 23, 25, 49, 52, 61, 77; divisions within community 54–5; historical 19, 51, 53–5, 115, 118; identity 52, 56–7, 157; "new" 38–9, 53; marginalization of 25, 30, 158
Eurasian Association 19, 30, 38–9, 53–6
European identity 122, 156
exclusion 62, 68–9, 77, 90–1, 110–12, 122–3, 158–9; historical 18–19, 36
exoticism 113, 120–3, 136, 139
expat identity 85–6, 157
external perceptions 53, 78, 86, 98–9, 110–13, 125–6, 133, 146–7

family: influence 79, 97–8, 103–4, 146; opposition 80–2; stories 79–84, 109–10; values 20
flexible identities 71–3, 132–6, 156, 162–3
fluidity of identity 6–8, 12–13, 120–1, 124–5, 129–30, 151–2

food: and belonging 98–100, 108–10, 122, 147; and difference 95, 116–7; and gender 109; and hybridity 32
fractional measurements 20, 27–8, 33, 152

Gans, H. 46, 139
gender and "mixed race" 5–6, 17, 24, 37, 69, 82, 109, 113, 120–3; and discrimination 92–3
generational change 20, 36, 41, 64, 77–8, 128, 147, 149–50, 156
geographical location 63, 85, 88, 154
Goh, D. 18–19, 42
group identity 3–4, 79, 115, 157

half-caste 17, 41, 81
half-identities *see* hyphenated identities
Hall, S. 3, 10, 13, 153, 166
heritage *see* ancestry
hierarchies of race 4, 7–8; in New Zealand 17, 20, 70; in Singapore 23, 30, 37, 44, 83–4
home: as a process 87, 129–30, 139, 152; as a location 130–1, 152; as constructed 132–3; as fluid 129, 133–5; as relationships 131–2; feeling at home 64–5, 86–9, 124–7, 129–35, 152–3
homelessness 128, 137–8, 152
hybridity 11, 24–5, 32, 36, 37–8, 41–3, 139
hyphenated identities 37, 39–41

identification: external 8, 53, 61, 77–8, 111–12; internal 13, 78, 111, 154
identity: choice of 2, 12–13, 65–6, 129–30, 145–7; as experience 153; narrating 2–3, 9–14
identity cards 22, 49–51, 53, 60, 74
identity denial 56, 65, 110–11
immigration and identity 99–100
immigration policy in New Zealand 18, 20, 25–6
in-between identities 5, 8, 11, 28, 67, 96, 136, 139; and Eurasians 19, 85
intermarriage 17, 20, 24, 30, 37, 43–4, 88, 104; and gender 24–5, 37; and religion 24; opposition to 80–1
interracial relationships *see* intermarriage
intersectionality 9, 166
Ip, M. 18, 20, 32, 37, 42, 78

"Kiwi" identity 71–3, 97–9, 122; *see also* New Zealander
Kukutai, T. 18, 27–8, 34–5, 45, 123

labels 96–7, 121
language: ability 81, 97–8, 104–6; across generations 105–6; as a barrier 103, 105–8; commonality of 32, 81; complexity of 59
Lee Kuan Yew 21, 24
life stories 13–14; *see also* narrative analysis
limitations of research 59–60, 164–5
linking micro and macro 12, 79
local identity 84–90; *see also* dislocation/location
losing face 80

macro: categorizations 8, 11, 76; narratives 10–11, 76, 78, 156
Mahtani, M. 5, 13, 15, 120, 124, 144, 153
majority group identity 21, 35–6, 46, 114–15
Maori identity 17–18, 20, 25–6, 32–7, 58; resurgence of 19
marginality 5–6, 12, 139, 153
meritocracy in Singapore 21, 30, 39, 44
meso narratives 10–11, 4, 121, 157; around race and national identity 18
micro narratives 10, 11–12, 124
military service *see* national service
minority group identity 6–7, 25, 58, 77, 97–8, 103, 115, 140
mismatch between theory and reality 5, 7–8, 9, 10–12, 42
"mixed blood" 5, 12
mixed ethnic identity 2–3, 4, 7
"mixed ethnicity" 7
mixed identity *see* mixedness
mixed marriage *see* intermarriage
mixedness 9–10, 12–13, 121–3, 139, 143–4, 155–7; and ancestry 139–40; and being both 104, 141–2, 151; and being open-minded 135–6; as commonality 143–4; as difference 88, 136–7, 139, 152–3
"mixed race" 4–8, 162–6; categorization as 7; and difference 5, 143–4, 138–9; definitions of 4–6, 11–12; ; research on 5–6; *see also* mixedness
model minorities 20
models of identity development 6, 12
mother tongue 104–6; policies 23, 44, 29–30, 107–8; *see also* language
multiculturalism 16, 21, 25–6, 43, 164; and everyday life 32, 43
multiple ethnic groups: selection of 7, 27–8, 41, 50, 57, 156, 164

multiracial framework in Singapore 3, 16, 19, 21–5, 28–32, 37–41; 42–3; and "mixed race" 24–5; and public institutions 31
multiracial identity 6, 135, 157
multiracial movement in the United States 7–8, 15

narrative analysis 2, 9–10, 12–14, 159–61, 164–5
narrative inquiry *see* narrative analysis
narratives: of accommodation 12, 78, 87, 122, 138, 160–1; as contradictory 13, 46, 79; of "mixed race" 10–14, 162–3; of racial formation 9–10, 11–14, 163–4; of reinforcement 12, 50–1, 62, 83, 152, 159–60; of subversion 13, 50, 67, 75, 160–1; of transcendence 13, 63–6, 69, 73, 77, 125, 146–7, 159–60
national identity 30, 35, 37–9, 63–9, 71–3, 77–8, 152, 159; and race 18, 35, 68–9
national service 64–6, 85, 159
nation-building 2; in New Zealand 17–18, 25; in Singapore 21–4
New Zealand Chinese: as the racial "other" 18, 36; discrimination against 18, 20, 26, 36, 91–3; identity 37, 99–102
New Zealand European 35, 58
New Zealander: identity 35–6, 69–73, 77–8; ordinary 21
Nobles, M. 11
not being Chinese 101–4
not belonging 51–2, 76–7, 90, 96–7, 124–5; *see also* belonging

Omi and Winant 4, 8–9, 113; *see also* Racial Formation theory
"other" 22–3, 25, 38, 51, 57, 77, 140

Pakeha: definition of 16, 43; identity 32–3, 35–6, 103
parental influence 79–80, 98–9, 103–4, 140; and gender 82 , 109, 121
Parker D. and Song M. 4–5, 128, 162
passing 114, 123
passing on heritage 147–9
pathologies of race 5–6, 10
patrilineal classification 19, 21, 23–5, 31, 40, 50, 82; and language 29
People's Action Party 21, 30
Peranakan identity 25, 44
Pereira, A. 19, 25, 29–30, 39
phenotype *see* physical appearance

Index

physical appearance 33, 74, 91–3, 111, 113–19, 123; and being normal 115–16; and gender 93, 117–19; and skin colour 54–5, 62, 67; and stereotypes 115
politicized identities 3, 6, 26, 55, 62–3, 77
poll-tax 18, 36
post-colonial 11, 16, 21, 32, 35, 43
prejudice *see* discrimination
primary race 38–9, 156
problem approach 5–6
public housing 23, 28, 38; quotas and 28; resettlement into 23
public/private identities 7–8, 10, 46, 151–2; aligning 12–13; and language 107; mismatch between 12–13, 100–1, 142–3; in New Zealand 78; reconciling 140–51; in Singapore 60–1, 73, 77–8, 110–13, 139–43, 154, 158–61; *see also* dissonance and identity
purity; racial 4–5, 18–19

questioning identity *see* "where are you from?"
questioning race 45, 58, 61, 67

race 3; classification of 7–8, 11, 16–19; in everyday life 46; ideology/history of 3–4, 155; as visible 62, 116–7
race relations 33, 44
racial categories in Singapore 16, 21–3
Racial Formation theory 2, 8–9, 163–4
racial harmony 37, 43
racialization: and immigration 26, 36; and the census 11, 19, 23
racial mixing 4, 15; in New Zealand 17–18, 41–2; in Singapore 17, 24; *see also* intermarriage
racial projects 8–12, 19, 43
racial theory 4, 17–18
racism 19–20, 58, 90–6, 121, 137–8; *see also* discrimination
recognition 8; and acknowledgement 41–3; symbolic 7–8, 38–9, 42–3, 141, 148
religious identity 145–6
rice 110; *see also* food
Riessman, C. 14, 165; *see also* narrative analysis
Rockquemore, K. A. 4–5, 7–8, 130
Root, M. 5–6, 135

second-generation immigrants 20, 26, 77, 99–100
Second World War 19, 26
self-help groups 28–30, 38; and "others" 29
settler colonialism 16, 43
Siddique, S. 21–2, 31, 64
Singapore: establishment of 18; independence 19, 21
Singaporean: identity 21, 30–2, 37, 41, 63–9; as racialized 16, 43, 56, 68, 73, 76–7; Chinese 102
Singlish 32, 59, 105
situational identity 7, 28, 34, 125
social construction: of identity 14; of race 2, 4, 8, 110
socioeconomic status 7, 18, 23–4, 33, 103–4, 121–2
Somers, M. 2; *see also* characterization of narratives
Song, M. 5–6, 9, 76, 113, 139, 155, 164
South Africa, census categories in 7
"Speak Mandarin" campaign 29–30, 105–7
Spoonley, P. 17, 20, 25, 37
stereotypes 12, 100, 114–15
Stonequist, E. *see* marginality
stories *see* narratives
structure and agency: relationship between 2, 8–9, 161–2; narrative as linking 10, 14, 162
subversion of racial categories 31, 41, 43
survivalist statehood 3, 21
symbolic ethnicity 56, 99, 113, 139, 154
symbolic recognition *see* recognition as symbolic

terminology 5, 14, 54
travel 87–90, 131

United Kingdom: census categories in 7; terminology in 5
United States: census categories in 8; terminology in 5

variant approach 5–6
virtual communities 128–9, 152; *see also* belonging online
voluntary ethnicity 34, 76

Waters, M. 46, 79, 82, 122
"where are you from?" 73–6
whiteness 45, 58, 77, 103, 122; *see also* Pakeha; European
White New Zealand policy 20